The Complete Poetry of James Hearst

THE COMPLETE POETRY OF

JAMES HEARST

Edited by Scott Cawelti

Foreword by Nancy Price

UNIVERSITY OF IOWA PRESS Ψ IOWA CITY

University of Iowa Press, Iowa City 52242
Printed in the United States of America

Design by Sara T. Sauers

http://www.uiowa.edu/~uipress

The publication of this book was generously supported by
the University of Iowa Foundation, the College of Humanities
and Fine Arts at the University of Northern Iowa, Dr. and Mrs.
James McCutcheon, Norman Swanson, and the family of Dr.
Robert J. Ward.

Permission to print James Hearst's poetry has been granted by
the University of Northern Iowa Foundation, which owns the
copyrights to Hearst's work.

Art on page iii by Gary Kelley

Printed on acid-free paper

Library of Congress
Cataloging-in-Publication Data
Hearst, James, 1900–1983.
[Poems]
The complete poetry of James Hearst /
edited by Scott Cawelti; foreword by Nancy Price.
    p.   cm.
Includes index.
ISBN 0-87745-756-5 (cloth), ISBN 0-87745-757-3 (pbk.)
I. Cawelti, G. Scott.   II. Title.
PS3515.E146 A17   2001
811'.52—dc21   00-066997

01 02 03 04 05 C 5 4 3 2 1
01 02 03 04 05 P 5 4 3 2 1

CONTENTS

~~ *Everything was just barely enough.*

⌇ *What really counted was the work I could do.*

﹃ *I learned resistance from a heart*
of oak that lay charred in the grate,
it was in the fire from the very start
and still is solid.

↝ *His road is hard who bears within himself seeds of the sun,*
who sees how patient earth cracks and strains to bring a flower
to bloom . . .

↝ *I stand my ground and warm the air*
with a man's presence . . .

☙ *I bring you a gift of apples now*
mellowed past spring's desire . . .

� . . . *a vision turns stones of fact to miraculous bread.*

ᴐ . . . *bury the work in its old clothes,*
let's go inside to learn how fire lives
on top of ashes and watch shadows of light
leap to the windows.

A cow is a completely automatic milk manufacturing machine. It is encased in untanned leather and mounted on four vertical movable supports, one on each corner.

∾ *Don't bring any more naked questions*
for me to clothe with answers.
Styles change too fast to keep up with
and I'm going out of business.

ᔓ Anger and hate find new voices
each generation for blasphemies
not dreamed of under the big trees.

⤳ *No one who lives here*
knows how to tell the stranger
what it's like, the land I mean . . .

~ *And I see, with limited view,*
how a man on his threshold
feels betrayed by mischief
in his calendar.

*⌇ In the attic of my mind
sits a trunk packed with the
clothes of old ideas . . .*

ᔾ *Time cuts down the years*
and lays them in swaths
like the grass of a new-mown field.

ᗌ This is my time today
and I better make the most of it,
there may not be many more.

꙰ All my friends and relatives
are welcome to wish me a
Happy Passing and I will
respond to their salute with
my hope to "See you all later."

An Introduction to James Hearst

NANCY PRICE

On Memorial Day 1919 James Schell Hearst was a slight, dark-haired, hard-muscled farmer's son who rode horseback to college classes from his family's Iowa farm. He was eighteen. The world war was over, and so were his months of service.

Hearst wrote that he was "light of foot and fancy-free" that Memorial Day, joining his fraternity brothers for a swim. But Hearst did not know that the Cedar River below the dock had filled in during the winter: it was only two and a half feet deep. His friends yelled a warning—too late—Jim sprang from the dock in a high jackknife dive.

"My head struck the bottom of the river like an explosion," Jim wrote. "I was upside down in a dark cell of water."

He had fractured his spine.

In the hospital his Aunt Mamie whispered to him, "It will be all right, James, if you don't get well?"

"Not by a damn sight," James said.

James Hearst called that year "my nineteenth year where footsteps end." No consideration of his life can avoid the consequences of that year. Neither could Jim.

He needed courage. He had it.

He needed people. He had his parents, his sister, and two younger brothers. He had four doctor-uncles. He had the friends his family had made after sixty years in Black Hawk County. They surrounded him.

He needed the skill of medical people. Somehow his family paid for it.

He needed a wife. He found his first wife, Carmelita, only to lose her to cancer. He found a second, Meryl. Both his wives were professional women with careers of their own: strong women.

For a while Jim could walk a little and drive the tractor on the family farm, but slowly he came to his wheelchair days. One year a good friend gave him classes to teach at the college in town, though Jim had no college degree. He wrote. Hundreds of his poems were published, and they appeared again in more than a dozen of his books. The college in Cedar Falls became the University of Northern Iowa, and he taught there for thirty-four years; he taught in Mexico and Aspen, Colorado. He was honored in many ways during his eighty-two years.

And yet he was, for most of those years, a man in a wheelchair. I met him when he was forty and I was fifteen. Even then I sensed that what had happened to him defined him, confined him, set him apart in a palpable loneliness. One of his finest poems, "Seventy Times Seven," expresses it:

> Let rain discover
> Some other door
> I shall not uncover
> Mine anymore.
>
> The pale voices quicken
> On the dark pane
> Gather and thicken
> In low refrain.
>
> Bird and bee are lying
> Under their leaf
> My heart is crying
> Its ancient grief.
>
> Where under heaven
> Can it be done—
> Seventy times seven
> Is only one.

James Hearst's poetry is full of that solitary "one." Other people do appear in his poems; there are love poems, town poems, and the larger world is there, now and then. But the voice of a farmer—an "I" who looks hard and long at everything the small world of a farm can hold—is the voice I remember in his work. Robert Frost was his friend. Often, like Frost's "Oven Bird," Hearst the farmer, surrounded by chance, time, and the malevolence of nature, seems to be asking "what to make of a diminished thing."

If you had joined one of his classes in his house on Clay Street, you would have seen a man in his wheelchair in his living room. He sat alone under a lamp, following his notes, his best finger scratching the pages to turn them. The students, quiet and respectful, were pleased to be in a professor's home.

Later they sat in rows in the half-basement lower level of his new house on Seerley Boulevard (now the Hearst Center for the Arts). Jim rode his wheelchair downstairs on a lift platform on rails. The room, big and cool, had windows on the backyard. The Hearsts gave me a summer there: long hours of solitude to write poems and a novel while the Hearsts were in Aspen.

The Hearsts often entertained. As he grew more bent, Jim looked up at people and things under his long eyelashes, his elbows propped on the slippery metal arms of his wheelchair and his best hand under his chin. He wheeled himself from group to group, but if he were left for a moment alone, he could seem more lonely than the loneliest person there.

James Hearst triumphed, I think. He won, not only because of his books, his honors, his professorship—even his marriages and his friends. It seems to me that he stood up, broken or not, to his worst marauders, the invaders that could not be fought with tears or the kindness of others:

The Hunter

You cannot kill the white-tailed deer
With tears in autumn when the mellow wind
Fingers the apples and pulls down the grapes
One by one from the cluster, blows the frost
On breathy mornings into a comet's shape.

You cannot kill the white-tailed deer
With kindness no matter how your hounds
Worry them with affection, you will find
Trails through the empty woodlands like the bare
Patterns of their hoofprints in your mind.

You must be ruthless, hunter, and stalk them down
From behind the trees, in covert, blind and mire,
And slaughter them one by one as the hunter's moon
Bloodies its face with clouds of drifting fire.

Editor's Preface

When Professor Robert Ward, my teacher, then colleague and friend at the University of Northern Iowa, asked me into his office in March 1999, I knew he wasn't looking for light conversation. He closed the door, motioned me to sit, then walked behind his desk and looked at me straight. "The doctor says I don't have long to go. A cancer has spread to my stomach, and I'm probably going to have to go to the hospital soon. I won't come out."

"I'm so sorry. Are you in pain?"

"No, not really much. But I'd like you to do something with all this Hearst material. It really needs to be saved and published in one place."

I agreed. I had always admired James Hearst and his poetry and knew that most of his poetry collections had been out of print and unavailable for some time. I also knew Bob had worked with Hearst's poetry for years, dating and ordering the poems and prose as a Hearst bibliographer and scholar.

"I'm flattered, Bob, and I'll do what I can." His office had become a veritable shrine of Hearst material, including photos, quotes, and two four-drawer filing cabinets preserving manuscripts, typescripts, and Hearst's published volumes. (Incidentally, all of this material is available for inspection at the University of Northern Iowa's Rod Library archives.) Hearst had been Bob Ward's mentor and friend for decades, and Ward penned this tribute after Hearst's death in 1983:

A Farmer of Poems: In Memory of James Hearst

He was simply another Iowa
farm boy when he was crippled diving
into the Cedar River. But then
for more than sixty years he stood taller

in his wheelchair and reached higher than most
men could stretching on their tiptoes.
In poems that sang of a land so black and rich
that it made the farmers drunk with promises,
he told us that before we searched the skies
for stars we should plow the fields of our world
where we would find more than enough hard stones.

And his flat Midwestern voice never lied
to us about this land between the Appalachian
and the Rocky Mountains. For he told us
that along with the glory of creating
the farmer too often earned a bowed head,
a harsh life and a back-breaking mortgage
that never let him say, "The farm is mine."

But his honesty also made him show us
the joy of watching a hummingbird feed,
the pleasure of hearing a meadowlark's
song, the glow from a beloved's small gift
of flowering forsythia, and the peace
of bringing some order into your world.

His seeds were the hard facts of this earth
planted and cultivated until they bloomed
into a ripe crop of rich metaphors
and symbols that he harvested for truths.

Robert Ward died on April 8, 1999. His lifelong wish was to pub-
lish all of Jim Hearst's poetry (nearly seven hundred poems) in one
volume. Thanks to the efforts of a variety of people who have sup-
ported and contributed to this project, his wish has come true.

Let me first acknowledge those who worked on this collection
from the beginning: Vince Gotera, associate professor of English at
the University of Northern Iowa and editor of the *North American
Review*, a magazine for which Hearst was a contributing editor;

Mary Huber, director of the James and Meryl Hearst Center for the Arts, Cedar Falls, Iowa; Barbara Lounsberry, professor of English at the University of Northern Iowa and nonfiction editor of the *North American Review*; and Thomas Thompson, emeritus professor of philosophy at the University of Northern Iowa. A special thanks to Trevor Jackson, who worked with Bob Ward on Hearst's bibliographical material as an undergraduate English major at the University of Northern Iowa and who continued to work with this project as a labor of love. Trevor rescued several previously uncollected Hearst poems from certain oblivion, as well as successfully undertook indexing and reordering—no small feat with a collection this large. Without the tireless work and steady support of these people, this volume would not exist.

Also thanks to the State Historical Society of Iowa, which supported a grant for the staff, interns, and volunteers of the James and Meryl Hearst Center for the Arts to collect, collate, and store on computer disks the majority of Hearst's published poems in 1994–95. In addition, thanks to Gerry Peterson, special collections librarian at the University of Northern Iowa, who answered many questions on the Hearst material now archived in the University Library. Also, the University of Northern Iowa Foundation, which owns all rights to Hearst's work, gave permission for Hearst's poems to be published by the University of Iowa Press. Finally, the Cedar Falls Art and Culture Board acted as fiscal agent for the project, and generous support was given by the University of Northern Iowa's College of Humanities and Fine Arts and its dean, James Lubker; Norman Swanson; Dr. and Mrs. James McCutcheon; and the family of Robert Ward.

For more than five and a half decades—from 1924 until the months before his death in 1982—James Hearst wrote and published poems and never stopped polishing them. He wrote variants of well over a hundred of his poems, changing words, phrases, punctuation, spacing, and adding or deleting sections, and in some cases rewriting the whole poem but keeping the same title. (See "After Cornhusking," the 1943 and 1951 versions.)

Hearst's poem "Protest" as first published in 1926 concludes with this:

The beauty of the color is
Not the thing which I protest,
    Gold is good when green is done—
But I cannot bear to think
    How the time has gone.

In 1951, he published the same poem but changed the ending:

The beauty of the color is
Not the thing which I protest,
    Gold is good when green is done—
But a summer in the sheaves
    Marks a season gone.

Most readers would agree, I think, that the newer version is superior because it avoids the near-cliché of outright lamenting the passage of time, revealing instead that same thought with an arresting image.

In deciding which of multiple variations to publish, I have usually selected the most recent version on the theory that Hearst's latest revision represents his last "statement" of the poem and is therefore probably the version he would have preferred to see published in a complete collection. When a poem was reprinted with few or no changes in later editions (or the changes were trivial, such as capitalizing the first words of the first stanza—most likely a publisher's convention), I have placed the poem under the first year published. In a very few cases, I did choose an earlier variant because it clearly seemed superior as poetry, with helpful advice from Vince Gotera, Thomas Thompson, and Barbara Lounsberry.

Occasionally readers will note odd or archaic spellings in Hearst's poems. Unless a word is misspelled, I have left such words as Hearst wrote them. For example, in "Fall Plowing," Hearst spelled "sumac" as "sumach," but that is considered an alternative spelling, so I did not change it. Nor did I change "lambswool" as a poetic variation of "lamb's wool" from his oft-reprinted "Snake in the Strawberries." I have followed Hearst's capitalization and titles as well. This preserves the flavor and the music of Hearst's poetic sensibility, and most readers, I am sure, will find them more charming than distracting.

For reader convenience, the poems are ordered chronologically by year and alphabetically within each year. All of the poems except the previously unpublished poems at the end were published in a large variety of magazines, journals, and poetry collections, including *Poetry*, *Commonweal*, *Ladies' Home Journal*, the *North American Review*, *Harper's Bazaar*, *Saturday Evening Post*, the *Christian Science Monitor*, and the *New York Times*. Scholars interested in pursuing sources may visit the archives at the University of Northern Iowa's Rod Library.

Finally, in reading Hearst's entire work, I found that his poems at times shifted dramatically in mood and tone and sometimes radically from poem to poem within the same year. However, patterns of thought and approach did seem to emerge, from his journeyman poems to his early maturity to his full flowering. These patterns I have tried to capture in headings garnered from his poetry and his 1981 autobiography, *My Shadow Below Me*.

James Hearst wrote in "Statement,"

> It doesn't matter what the critics say,
> I write what interests me in my own way.
> I know they have to fill up the reviews
> With what is called the literary news.
> But you and I have our own thoughts to please
> And as my poems go by I hope you seize
> On one or two that make you nod your head
> As if you liked them. Poet Yeats once said
> Of poetry and the critics' wailing wall,
> "It's not a matter of literature at all."

I can assure readers—there are many more than one or two poems here to please even the most hard-eyed literary critics: powerful, memorable, extraordinarily well crafted poems to treasure, to cite and recite, and to celebrate.

A journeyman takes what the journey will bring.
   ↣ Part of an Eternal Dialogue

The Isle of the Setting Sun

Sailorman, Sailorman, by the dark water,
  Why have you come to this gull-haunted strand,
To watch the long waves rolling in from the sunset
  And spreading the colors they bring on the sand?

Sailorman, Sailorman, in the green twilight,
  Tell me your tale while the black night air
Shades out the glory the sun trailed behind him
  And impudent stars tease the moon from her lair.

   This is the tale he told to me
   There by the flame-touched sea.

"We sailed from here for Java coast with cotton goods and rum,
  Sailing, sailing, on a western sea,
To get a load of tea and spice and nigger slaves and gum,
  Sailing, sailing, in a rush of sky and sea.

"For thirteen days we raced the waves—the wind was fresh and strong
  Singing, singing, to a windy monody,
Till we ran against the setting sun, a land of flame and song,
  Shining, blinding, so bright we could not see.

"The air was filled with madrigals, the sea burned all around,
  Flaming, flaming, a colored melody.
And on an isle of green and gold our ship was run a-ground,
  Sinking, sinking, in the western sea.

"We landed on the island like the Spanish men of old,
  Splashing, dashing, the waves danced merrily.
We found a white-tiled city whose streets were blue and gold,

Where only Beauty's word was law and wine and music flow,
      And languorous and slow,
      Seductive maidens go
With weaving hips and clinging lips and pulsing voices low,
      Wondering, fearing, they met us curiously.

"What drowsy joys we saw and felt, what melodies we heard,
      Laughing, playing, an hour's minstrelsy.
And a dream that I had always known came swiftly as a bird,
      Sobbing, throbbing, love's own harmony.

"But with the passing of an hour the island's life is done,
      —For it has existence only at the setting of the sun—
      Melting, fading, in the moaning sea.
And anything exotic there is changed to effervescent air and
   iridescent foam,
      Roaming, roaming, for an eternity.

"And so my love, to save my life, commanded me to go,
      Weeping, weeping, she wept so piteously.
With trembling lips and troubled face she led me to a secret place,
      Where hidden in a glow
      Of rainbow colors bright,
Within a dazzling coral cave a ship lay staunch and tight,
Which had a shadow for a sail, its hull was tinted light!

"Into the east with breaking heart I journeyed sad and mute,
      Sailing, sailing, on a moonlit sea.
And the wind that sweetly filled the sail was the wailing of a flute,
      Rising, falling, thin and silvery.

"The phantom ship dissolved in foam, the way to me is lost,
      Rolling, blowing, a waste of wind and sea.
But I know she stands each night out where the sun-tipped waves
   are tossed,
      Calling, calling, across the western sea."

The Painter

Our local painter always seemed afraid
  To go above a certain space in height.
And so our domes and steeples would have stayed
  Unpainted, but each year there would alight

From off some train he'd ridden on the sly,
  A painter tramp who limped and acted queer.
And when he'd slung his ropes against the sky,
  Like some lost voice among the spires, we'd hear

Him singing as he daubed his colors on.
  So thin and clear we caught his every word.
He sang: I am a lark that greets the dawn
  For, captive though it is, my soul's a bird.

But they who dealt with things, the trading men,
  Bound by the narrow paths of their conceit,
Gibed to hear this wandering harlequin
  Revealing thoughts their minds could never meet.

But one day on a high, unfriendly cope
  He dared the wind . . . and with a vicious laugh,
It whirled his sling and tugged a vital rope.
  The main knot slipped, the song was cut in half.

Who mocked at him contented go their way —
  Prisoners that blindly love their bars —
Firm roots embrace a mangled cage of clay,
  A silver bird sings high among the stars.

Voices

The restless sea is calling, and I would be away
To where the surf pounds up the beach to thunder in my ears,
To where the salt wind tastes like wine and sailing vessels gay
Go out to strange sea-guarded ports and drift home gray with
    years.
From books and shells and scraps of tales these thoughts have
    come to me,
For I was born far inland, who long to go to sea.

The midland has its voices, but they call to me in vain.
I care not for the whispering road nor drumming city street.
My heartbeats do not quicken to the thrush's joyous strain,
Nor to the sighing music of the wind upon the wheat.
The bees drone their contented song—but what is this to me?
For I was born far inland and long to hear the sea.

The sky is like the sea today and clouds like galleons ride—
I found a tiny river just beginning near the spring,
That called for me to follow and it would be my guide;
A boisterous echo in its tone, that yet was whispering,
Gave me hint of ocean surge, and soon I know that we
Shall leave this inland country and make our way to sea.

NINETEEN TWENTY-FIVE

Part of an Eternal Dialogue

Youth:
What do I hear on my window rapping
Cutting my rest like an edge of pain?

Age:
Only the ghost of a dead bough tapping
or the icy knuckles of long cold rain.

Youth:
Nay, it is something that urges me forward,
a surging that throbs through my veins like fire.

Age:
It is only a lone wave rolling shoreward
Spread on the sand in its last desire.

Youth:
I must be off for the sea and the mountain
are deep and high and life is short.

Age:
Life will leave you an empty fountain
Or a battered ship that never made port.

Youth:
Yet I will go though it lift me or break me,
A journeyman takes what the journey will bring.
Too soon must I sit by the fireside to slake me
A thirst not appeased by remembering.

NINETEEN TWENTY-SIX

Around the Bend

Around the bend the water stills,
And deeper, darker, grows until
      It forms a pool, within whose breast
      Lie mighty bass that fiercely test
Their strength against the angler's skill.

These are the kings. The pulses thrill
To know such grace and beauty fill
        The streams that always seem the best
                Around the bend.

Cast in the line. Good luck or ill
Attend you, friend. This very hill
        May hide your goal, and so with zest
                Keep pushing forward in your quest—
The price is there in pool or rill,
                Around the bend.

The Burden

Apple bloom spread on the orchard floor,
Swept from the trees by the broom of the wind,
Bows down the tips of startled grass—
Grasses too young to have sinned.

And they must be for a little while
Content with the bloom of a foreign flower.
As a weight of love or gift from the wind,
It will fade and drift in an hour.

Then with a wave of running green
They'll swiftly wash the orchard floor,
And taunt blind roots on long hot days
With the pale pink bloom they bore.

The Contract

You may have my garden if you will give to me
The first pink blossom from its wild apple tree.
You may have the harvest and you may have the toil
If you will let me stretch in the black warm soil.

And all that I can say to you or you can say to me
Is, see how wide the sky is now that I am free
To cultivate my garden or investigate my soul;
Then you may play the gardener and I will play the troll.

And when you're gnarled and broken this of you I'll tell:
He had the best melons ever raised to sell.
When I am ripe and sleepy you must speak of me
As smooth bitter fruit from a wild apple tree.

The Experiment

You came and found me when the stars were blowing
      Like strewn petals flowering in the dark.
And throbbed against me in surrender, knowing,
      You only came to strike from me a spark.

The spark was struck and you were once more glowing.
      You laughed and left me here where all is still
Save for the sound roots make when they are growing
      And the rush of grasses on a windy hill.

In April

This I saw on an April day:
Warm rain spilt from a sun-lined cloud,
A sky-flung wave of gold at evening,
And a cock pheasant treading a dusty path
Shy and proud.

And this I found in an April field:
A new white calf in the sun at noon,
A flash of blue in a cool moss bank,
And tips of tulips promising flowers
To a blue-winged loon.

And this I tried to understand
As I scrubbed the rust from my brightening plow:
The movement of seed in furrowed earth,
And a blackbird whistling sweet and clear
From a green-sprayed bough.

The Reason for Stars

I never wonder a lot about stars.
I'm much too busy with things of this earth
That show when a season of labor is done
Just what the labor's been worth.

Stars are all right to admire like flowers,
I like to see pretty things when I'm done
Working in fields, but what do I care
Whether a star is a stone?

There's plenty to learn in the ways of a seed.
What do you get if you study the sky?
I'm greater for holding one fruit in my hand
Than a heaven of stars in my eye.

Beauty

I stayed in the field though the rain was beginning to fall
While the whips of lightning were cracking above my head
And watched the rain fingers lift my sun-beaten corn
Like Christ in a miracle bringing life to the dead.

It was none of my doing and yet I felt like a god
Bestowing his pity and strength in the way he designed.
Then the feeling passed and I stood there drenched to the skin
Trying to etch the picture deep in my mind.

Note: See variant of this poem, "Summer Rain," published in 1937.

Belief

My neighbor and I stood in the sun
And talked and left some work undone.

We could have spent the half of a day,
If we were not busy, this pleasant way.

For seldom it is that we can see
Each other when we both are free.

When we are working upon the land
Our speech is mostly a wave of hand

Except we shout across the fence
To give the gesture sustenance.

And I am certain we should do
More to encourage a word or two.

We should stand often against the sun—
And what of the work if it isn't done?

For we are two neighbors who like to share
A friendly word in the open air.

And we must talk swiftly against the time
When crops and men and women and rhyme

Shall be as quiet to us as stone—
The time of forever we spend alone.

NINETEEN THIRTY

Frost

Though nothing came that could be heard
Green turned yellow—and from no drouth
In my cornfield; and the last blackbird
Has swallowed his notes and drifted south.

If the change is death, then the color and all
Of blood in the leaves, of smoke in the sky,
Has deceived me with beauty; I heard no call
Of roots to the sap and no answering cry.

It is time, then, for me to walk alone,
To watch leaves fall, while thought runs slow
On the stubborn permanence found in stone,
On the sharp bright virtue of the plow.

The Body of One

Glad that at last the litter and waste of winter,
Drift ends of dirty snow and the icy splinter
Of eaves trough decoration, dissolve again,
I stand at the window watching the first spring rain.

Let it come down, let it come down in torrents,
I signal the clouds, so great is my abhorrence
For the sooty lives of houses, for the unkept
Complexions of fields dulled by the months they have slept.

Strike to the bone, let the earth again be clean
That willows and lilacs can line the air with green
And hold their color, that the least bird throat
Can point to the sun and form no tarnished note.

I would spare nothing the fresh birth of grass.
If rain by touch can make this come to pass
I will deploy my roots nor hold aloof
This body of one who is sheltered under a roof.

Country Men

The pussy willows show again
Along the boughs the furry rout,
And prove to watchful country men
The change they sensed has come about,

With one eye cocked upon the sun,
The other on their thawing hills,
They recognize the race begun
Between time and their fanning mills.

As if to snatch the day ahead
The spring comes on them leap by leap.
They drag the harrow from the shed,
The plow is roused from rusty sleep.

The horse resumes his halter rope,
The tractor shouts its fretful words,
While these men entertain no hope
Not voiced by line of singing birds.

Faster and faster roll the days,
The weeks slide down their shining tracks—
They move about in country ways
And hold the year against their backs.

NINETEEN THIRTY-TWO

Clover Swaths

My eyes are cloudy with death.

I saw thirty acres of clover fall over the sickle bar
today (not the Grim Reaper, but a bright steel sickle
out of IHC, guaranteed for sixty days against
faulty or defective workmanship).

Thirty acres of clover in full bloom died today,
besides such incidentals as a hen pheasant with
both legs cut off, her eggs decorating horses' hooves;
and only God can count the number of bobolinks
and meadowlarks that find their world leveled.

Thirty acres of clover just in its prime,
in its greatest flower, this field—
lusty, sweet smelling, the seed nodes filling . . .

Tonight when I go for the cows
I shall see it lying there in flat definite swaths.

(Only the young men go to war.)

Robin in the Straw

A robin scratches right and left
About the straw-embroidered hem
Of beds where flowers burst their shells
But he is not in search of them.

He kicks out gayly with his legs,
He thrusts in wildly with his beak,
I wish I might encourage him
But he would fly if I should speak.

I stop my day to watch him work.
He pulls and winks his head about,
And spreads his wings and stamps his feet
When worm resists his coming out.

When I go plowing in the field
With hat and coat hung on a limb,
And sweat to hold my plow and team,
I wonder how I look to him?

Seeding

The morning sun looks in on me
And gets me up and out to plow.
He does not know I grieve to see
The days come in so often now.

As though I did not lend an ear,
As though my eyes were half awake,
A sound haunts me I would not hear
And follows every step I make.

Have you the seed? Then sow it now.
Have you a plow? Come, here's the ground.
This is my answer to the low
Roar that time makes over sound.

And though I keep within my blood
The pulse of season and of field
There comes a time when field and wood
Must do without the flowers they yield.

And to oppose the coming dark
That steals upon us one by one—
I stand and hold my tiny arc
Against a circle of the sun.

The Grail

The snow falls like flakes of light—
Wherefore we come, Lord, bearing our promises.

Let the wind-lash curl the drifts and smother
the world in flying ice.

Frost knits the road into a carpet of iron
And locks the pond against the sun's finger.

We alone move through Death's false harmony
Saying:

If a tree drains its body of life,
Shall the root perish?
Who holds safely now the small seed?

Let it not vanish, Lord, let it seek haven
And if in the spring there remains one spark of growth,
Only enough for one pale blossom,

We shall come forward singing,
Our hands curved to the plow handles,
Our eyes raised to the light.

What greater praise canst thou have
Than that we seek the grail,
Not in the heavens, Lord, amid the stars' cold radiance.

But in the furrow, the plowed field, the meadow,
The places where it blooms for man in his short life.

Dead Crows

Early in the morning two crows abandoned wing
as a gun reported clear and sharp
that it had delivered two messages.

Each morning thereafter
until the feathers melted from the flesh
and the bones sang in the wind again
these two comrades inspired the flock
to wing dance, aerial maneuvers, sky acrobatics
to the excitement of low flying,
to hoarse barks and yells, to crow passion
greater than mating in the spring season.

But nothing was resurrected
and the crows returned to the grove.
Only people stare
each morning into the mirror
at their own dying faces.

Everything was just barely enough.

❧ MY SHADOW BELOW ME

Barns in November

Along an empty road I watched the barns
Crouched on the hillsides while the morning light
Poured in among the trees like mist and fitted
Panes to the windows now locked winter tight.

And overhead a birdless waste went streaming
Missed the sharp trees and mirrored with its own
Our rolling hills, but not in that grey country
Rise roofs like these, low bent and rooted in stone.

The bare and tattered fields have long been empty
Empty the pasture too of all save weather
Sowing his measure of snow where side by side
Fences and stone and furrows sleep together.

After the death of summer the barns inherit
Blossom and leaf and stem; granary and mow
Shoulder their loads in the darkness of timbers speaking
And pigeons sobbing, Winter is coming now.

And so the rafters arch to loosen the bony
Long fingers of the wind pressed toward the warm
And yellow pens where little calves lie sleeping
Rescued from their first snow. The heat of the farm

Beats in a slow beat and is steady, the pulse awakens
Strength in the beams and sills, and the haymow floors
Stretch their feet to the walls and a staring window
Discovers the farmer hastily starting his chores.

Thus shall the heart against a bitter season
Guard countless doors and windows, bring to bin
The crops of its own raising and gather in
The fruit and seed of love, the stalks of reason,

And stand alone among the vacant meadows
Calmly awaiting the age of winter weather
When, through the air, a chill and cloudy heaven
Drops from its mantle of snow the first fine feather.

Blue Again

We saw the horizon with stubborn clutch
Hold the clouds by their ragged edge—
Who had no right to restrain them thus
To rain and go is their privilege.

But late in the day the horizon slept
And loosed its hold and the west wind then
Roused up the clouds and gave them wings,
In an hour or two it was blue again.

And oh, what a chatter the birds set up
When the sun broke out on the trembling air,
We flung off our caps and the little red pigs
Were beside themselves and ran everywhere.

Cows Bawl on Sunday

The image of God
in a warm mackinaw and rubber boots
daily fights his way into the streaming barnyard
into a multitude of hungry, angry, playful and determined animals

through a cloud of raging sound
to bring order out of chaos.
Six times a week and rests not on the seventh—
and there fails his divinity.

Fall Plowing

The claim the stubble had no longer defends
This field, and mice laid bare in shallow burrows
Dart through the listless grass; a plow extends
Its shoulders of steel and the field goes back to furrows.

Slowly weeds stiffen to ash. All day the breeze
Cools the blazing sumach and rustles light
Syllables of death from frigidly burning trees
In each dry leaf that falls, in every blackbird's flight.

Autumn, Autumn, I can feel your harsh beauty
Closing around me as the end of the year
Moves into place to the sound of falling leaves,
I too have deaths to honor and the passion of death;
While grief sings in a shaking bush, while fear
Hunts in the furrow, my monuments arise
Like sudden shadows under October skies.

Farm on a Summer Night

From a clear sky at night the starlight
          flows down to the earth
And out from the eaves of the houses
          go prayers motioned skyward,

For better or worse the body resigns
        to the dream,
The work-tired the care-worn sigh
        softly an amen, their safe word.

And peace gropes over the valley
        to touch with blundering fingers
The wrinkled brow of the plowland,
        the cattle carved on the meadow,
The farmer bound to his wife where the
        ashes of beauty still smolder,
The children, the lovers, the old people
        wandering in shadow.

The starlight flows down to the earth
        and the prayers ascend skyward,
The cry of the earth rises up to be
        endlessly answered
By these bright shafts of starlight
        forever down raining
As drowsy folk turn in their beds
        and by sleep are swift lancered.

First Snow

The road and yard are full of dust
        That sifted from a cloud last night,
And I've come out because I must
        Review a brown world changed to white.
And lest I failed to understand
        The change that lies before my eyes,
I tramp about upon my land
        Examining each white surprise.

And I make new acquaintances
        Where I had left old friends before—
I shake the pump's protesting arm
        And knock upon my own back door.

The Forest

Within the forest of my heart
You came as lightly as a breeze
And singled out with simple art
The one old path among the trees.

You wandered on to the lonely place
Where I was happy many a year
And in a circle blessed with grace
You stood and bade the beasts appear.

The bright-haired tigers formed a ring,
The wolves sat down upon their right,
And a thunderbird with gloomy wing
Shadowed the moon to hide the light.

For back in the shadows were shadows found
That muttered and swayed them to and fro,
But you heard only my faithful hound
Crying the trail of an ancient foe.

And his bugle note now clear now dim
Swelled to you out of the forest deep
But when you would go to follow him
It was sleep again . . . and sleep . . . and sleep.

The Movers

The east wind whips the skirts of the snow
with a passing shower,
and over Iowa on the first of March
wheels churn hub-deep in the mud
or grit their teeth across the icy roads.

Home is only a shadow
flying down the wind in a
twisted swirl of snowflakes,
traveling down the road in an old lumber wagon
drawn by two shaggy horses
whose bones are too big for their flesh.

Even the wild goose
is not so homeless as these movers.
Peering ahead through the sliding curtain
of March rain they pass
with the furniture of home packed in a wagon.
Past corner, past grove to the hilltop they go
until only chair legs point from the skyline
like roots of trees torn from the earth.
And they are gone.
This, the parade of the landless, the tenants,
the dispossessed,
out of their Canaan they march
with Moses asleep in the Bible.

Who will call them back, who will ask:
are you the chosen people, do you inherit
only a backward glance and a cry and a heartbreak?
are you the meek?
But the early twilight
drops like a shawl on their shoulders
and sullen water
slowly fills the wagon ruts and the hoofprints.

Now I Have Taken to the Fields

Now I have taken to the fields
The secret of my own despair,
Down through the rows of moving corn
With the warm sunlight in my hair,

To let the cool wind hush my blood
And bring slow peace within my reach
That I may envy meadowlarks
The floating song that is their speech.

I think a song on this bright day
Could launch love from a soaring note
And my earned grief would drift away
Like those high hawks, black and remote.

And I would bring, when night returns
Its prophecy upon the land,
My chastened heart to lay again
Like clover bloom within your hand.

Plowman

This is plowing time and I am plowing,
Winding furrows like long black strings
Around a field that every day is growing
Smaller while the plowman sings.

For I am the plowman plowing my field,
Now is the time to turn it into furrows.
Plowing makes new land, new land makes new yield,
And turns into old land, plowed up tomorrow.

I am a plowman; I will plow the stars
And let them ring like stones against my plows.
I, a sky plowman!—Will you close the pasture bars,
Finish the chores, bring home the cows?

Reflection

I think I shall decide to stay
Here in a field with a fence around,
Sowing some wheat, making some hay
And learning the ways of a piece of ground.

There will be time to watch the birds
Perch on the sky, a wavering shelf,
While I am thinking important words
To say to men who are like myself.

I shall have this to recall when green
Seasons are grey and days are thin:
The infinite wonders that I have seen,
And the curious person I have been.

Seventy Times Seven

Let rain discover
Some other door
I shall not uncover
Mine any more.

The pale voices quicken
On the dark pane
Gather and thicken
In low refrain.

Bird and bee are lying
Under their leaf
My heart is crying
Its ancient grief.

Where under heaven
Can it be done—
Seventy times seven
Is only one.

Sparrows in Spring

The water falls drip . . . drip . . . drap
into a tin pail at the corner of the house
and the sparrows wink and teeter along the eaves
intoxicated with their own gossip.
They let fall
now a feather, now a ball of dung,
in their excitement.
They too are aware of the season,
they too dig in the ground, distribute fertilizer
and harvest seeds.
Now they ply the planting trade among themselves
while I select my corn for seed—
let us have no nonsense, they seem to say,
but be about our business
as briskly as possible.

Summer Rain

I stayed in the field though the rain was
        beginning to fall
While the whips of lightning were
        cracking above my head

And watched the rain fingers lift my
       sun-beaten corn
With the grace of a miracle bringing
       life to the dead.

It was none of my doing and yet I felt
       like a god
Bestowing his pity and strength in the
       way he designed.
Then the feeling passed and I stood
       there drenched to the skin
Trying to keep the picture deep in my
       mind.

Note: See variant of this poem, "Beauty," published in 1927.

Theology

When we were boys a man my father hired
Solemnly swore to us in broad daylight
He feared not God nor Devil; later our grove
Frightened him half to death one windy night.

He heard a tree go down, he felt the wind.
But God or Devil, who's seen one of these?—
Until we learned he'd never been to church
We thought he lied for not excepting trees.

The Warning Cry

The warning cry of wild geese from cold and cloudy roads
As they go winging over on a dripping March night
Stirs a stifled world, is an end to winter peace,
Turns me suddenly restless and sleep is broken and light.

Now, if ever, I reconcile my brother-to-stone body
When geese come spring honking through the misty air
With its own solid virtues, with the honor of its ways,
Lest my heart recall your flight and go dry with despair.

Winter Field

Whether or not the man who turned
These furrows and wondered if in spring
He would be here with his team and seed
Still lives, after all, is the major thing.

For a field can always grow up to seeds
If it isn't plowed and levelled for grain,
But a man who's dead has not such luck
He's done with things like growth and gain.

So I, the man who plowed the field,
Shall be relieved when they are gone,
This winter sleep, this snowy death,
I'm ready for work when the spring comes on.

NINETEEN THIRTY-EIGHT

Dark Flower

Oh, no, do not look too long
at the sky before dawn.
Do you wish to see the dark flower
spread its petals beyond the infinities
where even stars lose their memories of light?

The winter-naked tree may stretch stiff arms
expectantly toward heaven but its roots
clutch the frozen earth with knotted strength.
Do not stare your heart out, Oh, my dear.
Now is the time to let dreams lie softly,
to moan and turn and hide your head
as light reaches through the window for your eyelids
and reality comes in to say Good Morning.

Evening

Be quiet, Heart, the sun goes down
The sun goes down on the meadow.
As far to the east as the eye can reach
The cottonwood spreads its shadow.
A team in the field makes its last slow turn,
In a barn on the hill the windowpanes burn.

Be comforted, Heart, the sun goes down,
The sun bends down to harvest
The few remaining straws of light
That the roofs and the trees still cherish,
And a late-winged bird drops a falling bar
Of sleep notes to the evening star.

Be peaceful, Heart, though the sun goes down
Though the sun goes down and ever
It leaves to the pouring layers of dark
Our fields as it might forever,
This day our love, our labor and grief
Like the fiber of life have surpassed belief.

When a Neighbor Dies

Safe from loneliness, safe from storm,
Here he lies in his earthly form.
Here he lies in his last array
The neighbor who calls us in today.
He is our neighbor, he goes without
The grieving flags and the public's shout;
He is our neighbor and so he goes
Served by us in our solemn clothes.
This is his house, it was his home,
This is his land and its sandy loam
Has known him better than you or I
But he was our neighbor who came to die.
These fields of corn that line the road
Follow the fields his father sowed—
The gate is wide for his team and plow
But he must follow his father now.
What can you say to folks he knew
Of what he had done or tried to do?
What can you say that is the truth
Of a man you have known to age from youth?
We stand by the side of our neighbor dead
And only half hear what words are said.
We try to remember what he had been
And nod to a neighbor coming in.
He was our neighbor, we only know
That his hands were large and his temper slow.
We simply say as we stand and wait
That his fields were clean and his fences straight.
When a neighbor dies there is nothing to say
But we leave our field on a certain day
And offer our hands to lay him away.

Winter Solstice

This is the final day
And the last words have been spoken,
You shall not trouble me any more.

It is enough that winter is here
There is snow and ice to prepare for,
I shall not let you make me bare and cheerless too.

I shall search to the ends of the earth,
There must be something greater than love—
But how shall I find it by myself?

NINETEEN THIRTY-NINE

March Mourning

The late snow is a fungus
smothering the earth,
is white dust bringing sleep,
everywhere is as still as sleep or death.

Only the road shows black and living,
only the road shows that men still come and go,
but you passed down this road
and do not come again.

When the trees no longer grieve with the wind
and rust freezes the axles,
when at last the road too lies white and unbroken,
we shall sleep with our love safe forever.

On Relief

Our glances met as glances meet
And sharp as salt was my surprise,
I saw as I went down the street
A man with want-ads in his eyes.

For Sale he offered to my sight
Without the usual signboard's flash
A man's bewilderment and fright
Can mark down cheap when prices crash . . .

The factory quiet as a rock
And all around the heavy smell
Of men locked out as surplus stock—
His eyes like posters told it well.

And though his gestures still were staunch
With every glance his eyes returned
A man with no more ships to launch
With no more bridges to be burned.

Spring West of Town

A man who lives inside my head
Like a winter field in winter is dead.

Like fruit forgot on a windowsill
He shrinks in the cold and dark until

Comes widening from his winter cup
The sun who licks the shadows up.

And feathered clamors wake the hush
As spring comes on him with a rush.

As though he slept a month too late
He's now the man who cannot wait.

He is the man whose flesh is burned
With imaged furrows yet unturned.

He plants his corn and beans in rows
And hurries everywhere he goes.

If muscles ache from too much strain
He puts them all to work again.

Time is the only weight he feels
For spring has caught him by the heels.

He rolls an orbit like the sun
But who will be the soonest done?

Who will as still as his fields lie
While the brave sun still walks the sky?

He drops his life along a row
As though the years were seeds to sow.

And the faith that lives to keep
Will see him safe to bed and sleep.

NINETEEN FORTY

After the Son Died

The trees follow two sides of a square
and make a fine windbreak
in this snug corner
apple trees mount the earth and sift their petals

over the stone foundation
over a pile of measured stone
where no house stands
these are just the roots of a house
but there is no growth
here is a background for living
and no life but these trees
and the rabbits who spout from the stones
like furry ghosts
no dream even stands here on this foundation
for the dream went under another stone
and a rented house in town is good enough now.

False Warning

The meadow has lost its features and the grove
up to its knees in drifts is strangely still
after a season of seeing the fox squirrels shove
nuts in the leaf mold, after hearing the shrill
and bawdy japes of the jays, for a shroud of snow
like fire or flood or sudden desolate grief
has covered away the face of the land I know
under a mask as polar as unbelief.

Not that courage is ready to take to the trees,
nor the spirit retreat under a milk white fog,
knowing the trend of the seasons I know that these
thoughts will be scattered like beetles after the log
roofing their tunnels has rolled away, when the sun
say some day late in March when the buds are awake
and the maple sap is past the peak of its run
has filled the grove with creeks, the field with a lake.

But if this sheet of frost should fall on a man
and freeze him deep after his sun has run down
and leave him spinning in space too far for the span
of love's straining fingers to reach and be swiftly blown
out of his township done with his crops and their yield,
people like me would feel the false in the warning
by watching our neighbor tracking across the field
to see what the world is like on a winter morning.

Invocation

Come, you farmers, let us sing together
let us sing of the passion for planting
we the sowers and growers
live for the rising shoot and the spread root.

Let us sing a song of penance
for the ageless passion for crosses
staining the thick page of history
where we the peace lovers
fed and clothed the armies
where we the home lovers
milled like cows at the crossroads.
Let us sing low and sadly now
for the bellies not fed, the bare bed,
for rotten cotton and mouldy wheat
piled unfit to eat.

Let a Judas tree stand in every farmyard
to drip its bloody bloom at Eastertime
come, you farmers, Easter is also
the marriage of sun with the earth,
put a Judas tree in every garden
all you land lovers who lie down at night
on a bed spiked with mortgages,

you crazy farmers who trade a whole generation
for a piece of ground,
come, let us sing together under our Judas trees,
we of the strong backs and deep voices
let us sing about our farms.

Meeting a Pheasant Hunter in Our Grove

The bush's shape has been bent by the wind
from the bush in the seed from which it grew
though the leaves are the same and the flowering time
and bark and color are inherited true.

It set down its roots outside of the grove
where the northwest wind pushing up the hill
its load of weather could batter about
the shape of a bush it couldn't kill.

I've stood there myself and been glad for legs
to carry me into the shelter of trees
or behind the barn—is it something like wind
that makes one goose different from all other geese?

That makes me think it is wrong what you do?
I've a house to go into and so have you
when God ruffles the sky, what storm somewhere
has made this difference between us two?

Quarrel

In the angry silence
table and chair
kept domestic balance
with an everyday air

stayed close together
like two with their sorrow
but the sharp indictment
sped like an arrow.

Nobody screamed
but agony was there
in the fist on the table
in the grip on the chair

and the air was full of pain
more than heart could bear
that pushed aside the table
and overturned the chair.

The Same in This as Other Lands

He bows his head against the wind
that dries the muscles of his hands
and chills the poor and needy folk
the same in this as other lands.

Mud and the litter on his boots
witness the chores that he has done,
how many stables has he cleaned
and never owned a part of one?

His helpless eyes watch time unfold
vague leaves of promise everywhere
that are not written in his tongue
though he is often mentioned there.

The same in this as other lands
he grinds his labor for our bread
working the daily miracle
by which the multitude is fed.

The Sun at Noon

No country leads so softly to nowhere
as those slow shoulders that curtain the horizon
let us hold the sun at noon in this valley
for morning will not come again.
We will watch the trees grow up and the flowers stiffen
and brightly dressed desires
fade like women we have missed
no, morning will not come again
but here at noon I stand above my shadow
and balance on time's edge—
where is Joshua among us?
my shadow below me and I stand in the light.

Sweet sweet the night
not now spent sleeping
my love, I have been too long away
this is the sun at noon hanging in his arc
and morning past,
your breasts are like morning-glory trumpets,
this moment could live forever,
life full blown and the wheat ripening
let us draw the hills around our house
and kneel in the dust.

The morning dew has dried and the last seed planted
stretch up your arm, Prophet, and bid stand still
on this peak of light I rise and pass my shadow
on this peak of light I lay the morning down.
The compass draws its slow degrees toward the yellow west
and wisdom the white road follows its slow decline
but on this peak of light I rise and pass my shadow.

What really counted was the work I could do.
∽ MY SHADOW BELOW ME

After Chores

Close down, Night.
Henry Jensen has finished his chores
and his lantern goes bobblesway bobblesway
flick-flick-flickering through long determined legs
saying, what has been said and done today has been
           done and said forever.
The worn familiar doorknob reaches out to his hand
and the house draws him in.

Now is the time to relax under the lamp, to fall asleep
over the evening paper. Unroll muscles, and stretch.
Too soon you will stiffen into the last position.
What is this? porkpotatogravybread and butter
           standing ahead
of applesauce and three fat raisin cookies?
Reach out your hands, Henry Jensen, unleash your
           hunger . . .
tell me is anyone tireder than a tired man
eating his supper?

O sleep drugged head, staring endlessly
past murderers marriages crop reports and the
           stubborn fact of local items
hold up, hold up, the world confesses itself before
           your eyes
and you sink lower in deep clutched hands seeking
           the pillow.

These are the hours that no one counts when time
sneaks past your chair like a cat and the reluctant foot
has not yet found the stair
has not yet made
one quiet footstep further toward the night.

After Cornhusking

The last load ends the day
and the day the season
and a tired man leans on his courageous hands
locked on a shovel.

The stolid farmer has brought home his corn.

Time in a seed, a stalk, an ear
is the measure of his treasure,
the days of his convictions
lie yellowly heaped
in the low arch of autumn sunset.

Soon enough winter in a sheepskin coat
will back up his hunger wagon to the cribs
and yell, roll it down, you Hayseed,
can't you hear the steers bawling?

But now the stolid farmer patiently
shoulders his harvest to defy the lean
and leaping teeth of his old enemies
gathering all that his arms can hold
before the light fails
and the cold comes.

Note: See a different version of this poem under the same title published in 1951.

The Army

The pavements of the mind
carry out an army of hate,
close in ranks and black they walk
out of midnight's gate.

The people of the land
gape in fear and awe
to see the flags embroidered with
texts from the moral law.

The orderly traffic is broken
the wagons of thought are still,
while troop by troop the soldiers pass
led by an iron will.

They march in endless van
blood-brothers of the night
until the sun draws out his sword
and blinds them with his light.

Boundary Lines

The dog has a squirrel up a tree
I can call off the dog, he will obey me
but the squirrel will not let me relieve him of fright
he clings to his branch until I'm out of sight,
willing to let our separate worlds whirl
where one creature is man and another is squirrel.

Choosing

The stolid farmer took his hoe
instead of his plow and climbed the low
old wood gate with its wired latch
and made his way to the melon patch.
The sun was warm and the earth was wet
he thought it was one of the best springs yet
for a farm to show what a man can do

when he has the help of the weather too,
as much as he lives in this world alone
the man who feeds on himself eats stone,
both farm and the farmer had learned it plain
to nourish themselves on sun and rain.

The melon patch had taken the hint
and decked out itself in a live green tint
of feathery blades that covered the ground
not only this patch but for miles around.
Glad to find that his seeds were fertile
glad for one fear that he could hurdle
the stolid farmer stared at the maze
of form and color he seemed to raise,
most of them weeds that he did not want
for instance the wild tobacco plant
but if it's a right of growing there
which should he kill and which ones spare
they each of them grew in the self same way
and each of them offered its claim to stay
now how to choose between melon and felon—

But the farmer knew what answer to use
for he is no farmer who does not choose.

The Fencerow

A ripple of ground still shows the line where
a fence once divided this field in two—
the habit of being divided fades slowly
and may not be smoothed out in one growing season.

Here where two fields shared a common boundary
that kept corn from oats and the meadow from rye
the limit set to please some farmer's business
has now been plowed over and planted to crops.

There were stones here once and woodchuck burrows,
these things belong to the edge of a field,
where perhaps wild grapevine had looped protection
around the nest where the hen pheasant sat,

and rested its vines on the barbed wire fence
that stood for authority once in this place
till the wire went slack and the barbs grew rusty
and posts rotted off, and soon nothing was left,

in the wave of the ground but a few wild roses,
though lately I found a freshly dug den
where a fox of the old school loyal to his party
had refused to admit that the fencerow was gone.

Free Man

Hans Karen and debt were old friends until 1932
when he and his banker had insomnia
for the same reason.
Both now sleep sound
for no one will trust Hans
and since he did not shoot himself
he lives out mild unharassed days
and dreamless nights.

Good Friday

My neighbor plants potatoes on Good Friday
and feels himself blessed by tradition.
Plant potatoes, he says on Good Friday
like a man who knows what he is sure of.
It isn't just weather with him

and seed and black earth, it's a secret
of life that past farmers have lived by
and he only knows what's been told him—
let it be superstition, he says,
I get good crops of potatoes.

Guarding the Fire

The wind throws snow at the window
The frost furs over the pane
The hired girl clumps through the cold kitchen
And lights a fire in the range.

She watches the flame swell outward
On wings of kerosene
She leans on the stove and watches
Her thoughts flow past in a dream.

She feels the warmth over her body
Like the stroke of her lover's hands
And the light on her face winks rosily
From the flame and her heart's desire.

But the housewife late to the kitchen
Is shocked by no coffee in sight
No eggs sizzling hot in the skillet
And her words are impatient and sharp.

She shakes down the ashes with vengeance
The hired girl stirs in despair
At finding that time had betrayed her
While her dream lover was true.

When the breakfast dishes are heating
Both women guard the warm fire
The housewife's eyes on the damper
The girl's soft eyes full of fate.

They stand in silence together
Each feeding the thought of the flame
While the wind throws snow on the window
And the frost furs over the pane.

The Hammer and the Rat

The teetering carpenter sets his spike
and draws back his hammer cocked to strike
when he sees a rat poke out under the shed
so he aims the hammer at the rat instead.
But the rat draws back so he turns again
to wallop the nail on the studding when
the rat unabashed slides his whole body out
and the carpenter quick does a right-face-about
on the weaving ladder to get a good aim
with his poised hammer but spoiling the game
the rat ducks back in his hole and the nail
waits for the hammer still raised like a flail.
Released from the angle the carpenter veers
back toward the nail as the rat reappears
and freezes the movement he had just begun.
Here is the oldest play under the sun
the nail never driven, the rat never dead
because two ideas are in the man's head
opposed to each other but hopelessly wed.
The carpenter may be there twisting yet
though by this time no doubt the ladder has let
him fall from dilemma down into the mud—
O pray that at last he fell into the mud.

Homesickness

Marie Summers took a course in Commercial
and a diploma landed her in the city candling eggs
where the elevated's roar was like music
and pavements moved under her feet on rollers
until spring came without spring's features
and turned loose the lonesome hounds.
At last she dried her eyes and went home
and the boys clotting the drugstore
sniffed her sophistication eagerly.
But Marie only wept like a fool
at the sight of Monday's washing on the line
cookies cooling on the table
and a sun that walked like a giant
on everybody's grass.

How Many Shadows Has a Man

The dog looked into the water
and as he lost his daily meat
he found an essential truth—
I have never seen a man learn so easily.
I have seen a man walking toward the east
and his shadow was a giant coming to meet him,
I have seen a man walking toward the west
and his shadow was a giant coming to meet him,
I have seen a man stand in the sun at noon
and his shadow was a dwarf between his legs,
yet he was not in them himself and none of them
were what he knew himself to be.
A plowed field laid down in even furrows
in its appointed season reflects the careful farmer
but the image is not the man,

and what substance is there left in granite signals
in souvenirs of the dead
to say more than that a man passed by.
I have looked mainly into the sensitive eyes of women,
into the faces of friends and neighbors and those I love,
I have searched faces I tell you
and each one acknowledged a different man,
how could they name anything as definite
as an apple, an ear of corn or a greeting?
They have not counted black images
swooping silently from my heels like an old suit
with nobody in it.
In my study at night a black giant,
prisoner of the wall and evening lamp,
mocks my head and shoulders and supports them not at all,
a bobbing shape without emotion.
We must plow the long row
that turns the stalks of the old crop under
until we find the tree that grows
from the one root of the essential,
or we shall look to mountains for strength
and to sleep for deliverance.
Until we find the truths that grow
like a tree from our own lives
we will go on numbering shadows
until we are shadows to our sun,
blind to the steady bright reflection
that comes from a deed being done.

Logician

Pete Eversen was called four-eyed Pete
because he wore glasses
but he saw duty plain nevertheless.
When he found the hired man with his wife
he shot her instead
because help was hard to get
and anyway whose fault was it?

The Neighborhood

The neighborhood has a mind and heart of its own
that do not meet the stranger frankly.
Meanings run hidden like underground streams
which well up in pools and angry fountains
when a housewife takes a lover
or a man is smothered in debt
or becomes blasphemous
or when a young boy or girl is touched
by the finger of death.

The Old Dog

The old dog waits patiently for death
like a flower waiting to be folded into a seedpod,
curtains of age hang over his eyes
yet he starts a rabbit
or warns the fugitive sow
with the fury and joy of an image
created now only in memory.
He has lived a life of loyalty and obedience
to the authority from which his own derived

with a few minor lapses
and tried to keep his world
as orderly and well guarded as possible.
Now he seeks a corner that invites
the warm March sun
and with a cornmeal muffin between his paws
asks no description of the kingdom
he will inherit.

The Other Land

The strength and persuasion of the long slow turning
roll of the furrow modulates the fear
ever recurrent in the terrified senses
at the seasonal incest of the savage year.

Spring comes on with the cruelty of love
shattering the humble integrity of earth
so peacefully it lay and now forced to prove
the pain and the sorrow imminent in birth,

now forced to mirror the image of our Eden
where I am both Adam and the angel with the sword
terribly afraid and terrible in anger
lest the vine of transgressions should cover up the word.

Snake in the Strawberries

This lovely girl dressed in lambswool thoughts
dances a tune in the sunshine, a tune like a bright path
leading to that soft cloud curled up like a girl
in her sleep, but she stops at the strawberry bed
carrying nothing but joy in her basket and it falls

to the ground. Oh-h-h-h-h, her red lips round out
berries of sound but the berries under her feet are
not startled though they sway ever so slightly
as life long-striped and winding congeals into
form, driving its red tongue into her breast
forever marking its presence and turning into a shiver
barely a thread of motion in the clusters of green leaves.
She stands now as cold as marble now with the thought
coiled around her, the image of her thought holding her
tightly in its folds for it is part of her now and dimly
like faint sobbing she knows that part of her crawls
forever among green leaves and light grasses, it is the same
shiver that shakes her now and now her hair tumbles slightly
and now she feels disheveled but the spell breaks finally.
For the warm sun has not changed and maybe the tune
of her coming still floats in the air but the path
no longer ends in the cloud. She fills her basket taking
the richest ripe berries for this is what she came to do,
she touches her breast a minute and then the ground
feeling beneath her fingers the coiled muscles
of a cold fear that seems so dark and secret
beside the warm colors of the sunlight
splashing like blood on the heaped fruit in her basket.

Spring Barnyard

Pigeons circle the wet glossy mud
like a cloud of fancies
but the pigs and ducks immerse themselves
in a puddle of facts
and eye my rubber boots suspiciously
as fellow travelers.

Stranger

Following his father's footsteps
Clem Murphy retired at fifty
and left his boy on the farm—
but he is unhappy,
a stranger in a strange land.
The little Iowa town stares curiously
at Clem's ideas, its Chamber of Commerce
invokes the soot of factory chimneys
hoping to grow up into a second Chicago
out of the egg cases of the farmers.

Stolid Farmer to His Son

Choose your wife for straight legs and an honest tongue.
Take to market no more than you have to sell.
Be cautious with strangers and cover the top of your well
And teach your children virtue while they are young.
And when you are old be glad if you've learned to keep
Your wife's affection and memories of neighbors and friends
And had the sense to know that your comfort depends
On the money you saved and the grief you have put to sleep.

Time Like a Hand

The hardware merchant reaches back for the past
through the young girl's body
on a lonely road known as lovers' lane,

while the relentless hand of time at his back
pushes him down the street of middle age
where the picnic fires go out
and the green banks fade,
where he is trapped behind the counter
with his washing machines
and annual conventions,

to watch the fat jovial days
vanish in the mirror of a grey-skinned man
dressed in old promises.

The Vine

His wife and young son in his heart, the future riding his shoulders
he eagerly plowed up the weeds at the rate of four miles an hour,
shuttling across the field on his shiny bright red tractor.
The cornfield around him proudly shone in the sunlight
as he turned to look at it proudly reflecting his gaze
while the wind like a wave washed the field into motion.
A young farmer riding an engine could plow up the world
especially in June, in the morning, the sunshine thick in his pulses.
But he stopped at midmorning to stretch his legs and discover
a coiled vine snakelike climbing and choking a cornstalk,
he picked at it, tore it away, looped it tight in his knuckles
and saw that it made a green handle holding him to the earth.
He studied it for a moment as if he'd abruptly abandoned
his iron rooster to fight back the wilds with his hands.
He tested the torque of the vine, and the suck of the roots
tightening the strings in his forearm. As if they were equals
they faced each other, a man and a wild morning glory
each with his claim on the earth.
When the vine could hold on no longer it snapped off clean at the
    ground

the white root writhing as the taut green curls
slowly untwisted slackening their pull on his fingers
and he shook them off with the thought, it will grow back again,
the root got away from me and its life is still there.
He turned to the power tied to the ends of his levers
to his own ways and emotions as live and green as the cornfield's
thrusting into the air in bannered flowers of existence
while under his feet coiled a strength he had not overcome.

Winter Shower

This morning's miracle shakes my faith
So one who will not yet believe his eyes
Stares from behind the steamy wraith
Of breath and suspicion and rubs the lies

Of yesterday's memory out of his head,
And rousing the world that belongs to him
He walks from the house to his cattle shed
To scowl at the winter's latest whim.

For there is a threat in this chiseled tree,
The weighted fence, the shining path
The field now washed by a glassy sea,
A sudden and far gleaming aftermath

To the crystal wish of a winter shower
As if the lifeless, the songless, the doomed
Were the only things that could come to flower
Where the thrush once flew and the lilacs bloomed.

And I am glad that the chimney yonder
Throws some smoke the color of steel
Into the night or I might wonder
Which after all of these worlds is real.

The Young Old Timer

His hands seek each other under his overall bib,
his back arching against convenient corners,
but his eyes raise the question
and his throat repeats it—
why is it that nothing is the same?

Nobody worked so hard then and they had enough too,
and the crick's smaller than it used to be and
the ground ain't so rich.

We can't raise crops like they did,
and dust storms and floods, desert's creeping east,
no snow in winter, no thunder and lightning in June,
why is it like this?

Mildly he presses his quarrel with the times
at every meeting, at every corner-gathered group,
his anxious face sniffs
the wind of destiny and in his ears
the loudly rising storm of doom roars down
like the horn of Gabriel blown from his own barn ridge.

NINETEEN FORTY-FOUR

Burn the Cocoons

The sun waits in the sky for me
as I crawl slowly toward his feet
dragging the field I'm working in
that will be finished when we meet.

All day across the field I've come,
the seeder's whine my only note,
shivering as an east wind picks
the berry of flesh inside my coat.

The rising tide of sap has furred
the maple twigs with fires of green
burning away the grey cocoons
webbed on my eyes till I have seen

the land that I have got to sow
stretch like a plain into the sun
filled with crops I hope to grow
out of the seeding I've begun.

NINETEEN FORTY-FIVE

Inquiry

Now catch your breath and hear the softly rounded
Shoot thundering into the yielding air.
These are crocus blooms the root has hounded
Day after day to grow, to develop and bear.
Even though snow, now lying in strips defeated
Under the lilac bush, might strike like a snake
At the open ground, the sky has been plucked and depleted.
The cloth has been shaken—see the last twisting flake
Grope for a twig and miss and dissolve in the air!
Beat up the blood in your heart and bleed like a tree
For the scars you receive, O winter-bound sleeper—prepare
For the thrust of a leaf, for a glimpse of a sky like the sea!
I retreat from a room grown too small, and the indifferent page,

And listen to the voice of the creek now angry and swollen,
And see the sun arch his back like a bee in a rage
As he sparkles the air with clouds of his yellow pollen.
And I wonder if people are given the promise and bloom
That is given the root and all this slow-rolling land
As they come from their houses. Is there escape from the tomb?
Do people forget their mortality saying, The spring is at hand?

I learned resistance from a heart
of oak that lay charred in the grate,
it was in the fire from the very start
and still is solid.

⤳ Threat of Weather

Accident

The iron teeth of the harrow
gnaw the soft clods,
level the ridges,
and smooth the field,
rake through a killdeer's nest
without stopping,
and swallow the young birds.
The earth flows darkly past,
the tractor bone-jars on,
the heat waves wavering sing,
the killdeer build their nest again
low in the ground.

The Advantage

Three haystacks stood against the wind,
as best they could, while frozen mist
whirled through the farmyard from the fields.
The world contracted like a fist

where we were sawing winter wood,
I stooped and beat my hands together
and pulled my cap down past my ears
behind the haystacks. Any weather

surpasses none, I try to share
the gruff impulse of out of doors
unsheltered, but I go inside
as soon as I have finished chores.

After Cornhusking

The stolid farmer wipes away the sweat
of a whole year's work after the corn is in,
glad to leave the fields to their iron sleep,
such as it is, his crop is in the bin.

He sighs as if his faith was strained but solid
as square oak beams braced under his corncrib floor,
he moves his arms in tired deliberate gestures
as if to ask them who they are working for.

He prowls like a bear now, hunched in a dirty sheepskin,
gathering stray ears of corn that have fallen through,
and always alert for signs of thieving instincts
whether they come on four quick feet or two.

Some morning soon he knows the hunger wagon
that winter drives through countryside and town
will back up to his cribs: saying "You Hayseed,
the steers are bawling, come on, roll it down."

Note: See another version of this poem using the same title, published in 1943.

After the People Go

No one lives here any more, they all have moved away,
After the well went dry they left, no one wanted to stay
To watch the sun kill the maple trees after the crops were gone,
No one wanted to stare again into the blazing dawn.

Bitterness grows in the yard like weeds, bitterness rank and tall
Covers the bare and beaten ground where nothing will grow at all.
The sprinkler kneels by the sweet pea bed, rusty and black and bent,
Marking the place where the flowers died after the people went.

After the well went dry they left, nobody shed any tears
But like an oak tree each one bore the judgment of the years,
Records of birth and death and love, items of colts and corn,
Little odd packets for memory to keep—courage rings like a horn

Even in this burnt country. Let the rains come when they will
No one will feel their slanting strokes but the dead upon the hill.
And silence too of a human kind will let the cicadas' cry
Be the last prayers to a heaven veiled by the metal sky,

While nature sows with burning hands thistle and hemp and dock
To have some crop to harvest besides the crow and the rock.

After the fields are empty and after the people go,
She will not waste the season, she still has seeds to sow.

All Anyone Could Say

The children that we love are busy people
intent upon their work, though they will look
at fire engines and hear a ringing steeple.
At bedtime they will listen to a book
if monsters they have known by name are in it,
if sometimes they sit quiet for a minute
before you know what called them they are gone.

Their world is full of things that must be done,
so many roads to travel off they go
hopping the fence, inspired by feet and hands.
One little girl whose thoughtful face I know
decided to explore the ocean sands,
the soft exploding foam flowers led the way
to where the waves reached in with easy sweep
of their long arms and lulled her fast asleep.
And that's all she or anyone could say.

Analogy

It's like digging all day at a buried stone
And going home and nobody there
And lame from labor with no energy to spare
I find the house empty when I come alone.

A stone is like a stone, it won't wish away
Nor listen to reason, I get down in the dirt
And tug with my hands at its heavy rough skin
And limp home at night like a man who's been hurt.

I no longer kindle a useful fire,
I eat bread and milk standing up at the table
And each daylight hour as hard as I'm able
I work at the stone as if I had no more desire.

I know that at night the house for its part
Spies me while I sleep but I'm too tired to care,
I have too much to do to match it stare for stare,
I must dig up the stone though I destroy my heart.

Between Snow and Stars

The sun runs headlong down the sky
into a brush heap of dusk piled on the horizon
and the low winter day softly closes its door.
All along the feedbunks the hungry steers stand bawling,
the pigs like rustling shadows in the twilight
throng the empty troughs, their anxious cries
mix with the frosty stench and pillar of blue smoke
where the squat tank heater sweats against its ice,
the sounds and smells that roof the stamping barnyard.
                              The cows head for the barn
where bright green hay and mounds of yellow corn

are on the menu tonight, the little calves bucking
and bouncing, while wrapped in his serene
authority the bull climbs up the steep stone stairs.
The churning drive-wheels grind the tractor's way
ahead of the feed sled like a snowbound train
loaded with gifts for a crowded holiday
while the sentinel dog stands shouting in the gate.
And men with shovels, men with baskets, men with milk pails
stride down their evening paths, the patient network
that binds his facts to a man for life.

The barn doors close and the last man says good night,
turns toward the house and sees the sharp edged moon
already reaping the intervals of sleep,
thus the farm calls home its citizens and goes to bed.

Burning a Dead Heifer

This body burning here is not the fire I'd choose,
Though my grandmother said, they who have must lose,

And I must keep in step with things the way they are,
But she was a promising calf with deep red coat and star.

I found her stiff and cold in a corner of the shed
like everybody else we farmers claim our dead.

Now all is resigned to fire and the purifying air
Even the feed she ate and our labor and our care,

And the seed that grew the hay, the absence of another
Cow in her stanchion place, calves she will not mother.

Time will take them all, I watch the ashes blow
In a warm patient wind that worries the winter snow.

Construction

The hammer voices went on and on
telling the fields that the barn begun
would flourish under the winter sun.

The fields were frozen, the hills were bare,
the hammer music climbed the air
and echoes fell down stair by stair.

Rafters, when the time came, sprang
into their places. Storm clouds hang
over the ridgepole but we sang.

We nail and sing through wind and snow
as if we thought that ten below
is just the climate where barns grow.

The only visitors roundabout
are crows who view our work with doubt,
as critics do, they raise a shout.

What are you doing? they seem to say,
building is not the fashion today,
the wind is blowing the other way.

Crow's Impatience

After the hay was made and the threshing done,
One morning late in August when the arm
Did not begrudge the leisure of anyone
A crow spied me from a tree and gave alarm.

His carrion thought I'm not supposed to know,
But I was aware of what he craved that day,
Something of mine had died, a sickly sow,
And he was urging me to haul her away.

I meant to burn the sow and take no risk
Of illness spreading, to sterilize the ground
And leave no feast for solemn crows who frisk
Among my trees when they smell death around.

They seem to know that old age makes us colder,
We ought to tell ourselves as time goes by:
Remember the crow that lurks behind your shoulder,
Be careful of the things that you let die.

The Deacon Goes for His Sunday Paper

Good morning, good morning, it is a good morning,
We all ought to be in good spirits this morning.
The sky seems so peaceful, the sunshine is warm,
What's that? What's that? Oh, the fire alarm.

I like to get out and see how the town
Appears Sunday morning, why, as I came down
I thought what a friendly respectable air
Our Main Street has—Of course nobody's there

Trading today, but as I walked by
The window displays were a treat to the eye,
It made me thank heaven that I wasn't blind
To the best of the best little towns you can find.

Now what's in the paper . . . the news is our light:
"Town Marshal Shot in a Cafe Last Night."
What's the world coming to, shooting and churning . . .
You say that the Methodist Church is BURNING?

The Debtor

These leaden days when the sky is overcast
by a sharp-edged wind that turns the cattle home,
I keep my ledger open till the last
cornfield has been accounted for, I come

with pen behind my ear to check and close
the gates through which I hauled my hay and wheat,
I raised some calves and pigs the tally shows,
and these are pictured on the final sheet.

My estimates were often over-size,
I did not grow all I had hoped to grow
but something less, and now I realize
the difference is what I really owe.

Such debts would make me fat if I could tame
and eat them every day, instead my fare
is how to guard my roof against the claim
of the winter's landlord lien foreclosing there.

Fog

Waves of the sea's ghost
lap at my farmyard,
my neighbor has vanished
in a mouth of cloud,

I hear his dog bark
from another country
and the town has been crowned
with its smudge of smoke.
This is a moment of exile
I cherish, I am no stranger
to my own world,

With my permission I feed the hungry
in my denial there are no poor.
I lean against the morning
and watch the cows cluster
like daisy petals around the tank,
the warning cry of a far train
tightens your hand in mine
as the wind from outer space
brings its gust of news.

For a Neighbor Woman

Early this morning
as wind waked the grass,
she uncurled her fingers
and let life pass,
he took her, death did,
just as she was.

Early this morning,
after small disasters,
she put by her hollyhocks
and her bed of asters,
her Bible and spectacles
and the old chair with casters.

Early this morning
she left the drowsy farm,
she went too soon to hear
the alarm clock's alarm,
over rose and larkspur
she passed without harm.

Her weather-beaten basket
has nothing more to do,
the shoes that limped toward evening
and rest are empty too,
her gloves beneath the sweet peas
stain with heavy dew.

Maybe she died easy . . .
I think she bargained hard,
she borrowed all the earth would give
for flowers in the yard,
and mortgaged her own self to pay
for them afterward.

She was a farmer's wife
all of her days,
and wrung color bloom by bloom
from sour stoic clays,
she asked mercy from no one
nor God for praise.

The Great Coincidence

How strange that in the human flow,
And think of the people we have met,
That out of the many ways to go,
And think of those untraveled yet,
We should, enclosed in time and place
Like two in a dream, come face to face.

I marvel every day that we
With our own hearts escaped the fate
Of those who pass and do not see.
We stopped before it was too late
And tried the distance we could reach
Across the unknown each to each.

It is a wonder that we came
So close that we could learn together
The odds and pleasures of the game
We daily play with time and weather,
That we two joined in one defense
I call the great coincidence.

The Harvesters

Bright was the stubble, the sun that day
stalked through the sky and air disturbed
spun on the fork tines of two at bay
who lunged at each other without a word.

Blue denim let through so flesh folded in
three steel fingers to explore a heart
and clouds of anger dissolved in a thin
protest at taking a dead man's part.

The team on the hayrack dozed in the heat
a meadowlark flooded his mate with song
the field shouldered up its shocks of wheat
the tale of a woman was right or wrong.

Later the fall rains spread their hands
to cover a season's agony
but the clover field in future stands
bloomed for its own red ecstasy.

Impudence

Rowdy winter wind,
Slobbering snow,
unroofs a gaunt barn
and howls.
This old vacancy
like an empty grave
feels surprised
at nothing.
Even the fields
vowed to pity
close their clover lips
and sleep.
The wind snorts under
a loose wall
in his excitement,
while the old barn
chaste with age
gives him the welcome
of a cracked skull.

Late Spring

I tried to sow the oats and grass this year
as one who had learned from experience—
I see less springs ahead than I have lost
and what I've done the only recompense.

But it was a backward season, dry and cold
day after day, the air gritty with dust,
the ground too hard to cover all the seed,
yet I kept on because I felt I must.

I was late enough as it was, and when at last
I finished the field and looked the seeding over,
the sight of the work appalled me and I saw
dry weeds and clods instead of oats and clover.

My body numbed with fatigue, my stupid brain
wished only for some relief, like tears or rain.

Mad Dog

Like a great yellow dog, the sun
laps up the water in the creeks,
and his hot panting breath curls the corn
and sears the pasture brown.

He runs wild through the dry summer
as if no master could whistle him back
or drive him to cover
in a kennel of clouds.

Memorial Day

It puzzles me to see the stooping people
Bottling emotions in a vase of flowers,
The hurrying housewife and the stolid farmer,
The banker and the clerk, these friends of ours

All paying a respectful annual visit
To relatives tucked snugly underground
Who have no choice but entertain the callers
And hold the wilting blossoms on their mound.

There is no sign of welcome or refusal,
We set against each stone its sweet bouquet,
And satisfied at last with the arrangements
Solemnly start our cars and drive away.

No Leaves? No Apples?

No fruit bends the orchard trees
Waiting, patient, as the cold
Stretches beggar hands to seize
What could not be picked and sold.

Burning there against the sky
One gold leaf floats down and stirs
Anger's darkened pool lest I
Take for granted what occurs.

But though I protest in grief
All the ravages I found,
Stripped of blossom, fruit and leaf,
Rooted, the orchard stands its ground.

The Oracle

The oracle whose customer I am
Hides in the bottom drawer among my shirts
Or back of curtains, or upon the desk
Behind my unpaid bills, my solemn debts.

She won't take questions that aren't ready-made.
And neatly wrapped, delivered to my door,
She sends two answers, both ambiguous,
And I can choose the one on which I swear.

But still the morning seems like afternoon,
And floors I walk on echo underneath,
My oracle has told me I should take
Things just the way they are and save my breath.

The Orchard Man

Grandfather came from a town meeting country,
a meeting house man with no give to his morals,
who built his own home in the middle west frontier
homesick for New Hampshire, its mountains and laurels.

In Black Hawk county in the Red Cedar valley
he laid down his corners and sighting from these
to a slow roll of ground he raised up a farmhouse,
a simple white farmhouse surrounded by trees.

But he never understood soil quite so fertile,
these plains of abundance seemed almost a sin
to someone brought up on New England economy
where the spirit was strong but the living was thin.

He knew about stones and their place in foundations
and fields small enough to be planted by hand.
He wouldn't acknowledge the length of his corn rows,
he was awed by a farm that was nothing but land.

He withdrew to an orchard encrusted with beehives,
with man more than honey his theme of research,
where he taught his grandsons with rough righteous spirit
the difference in duty to state and to church.

He taught them the habit of steadily breathing
the clear air of freedom to nourish the blood,
he taught them to listen to contrary speeches
and not give an inch from the place where they stood.

His principles never spared anyone judgment
though his eyes were less stern than the words that he spoke
when he was correcting a neighbor's opinions—
he was mostly disliked by respectable folk.

He never had any expense with decision
his will kept paid up his conscience account
no debt ever languished for his want of action
no matter how large or how small the amount.

The man who came begging got more than he asked for
while Grandfather helped him chop wood for his food
he examined his faith and his concept of duty
the tramp usually left us as fast as he could.

He liked to bewilder the trees in the orchard
by grafting strange twigs on their staid humble boughs,
while his sons and his daughters nagged at the mortgage
by raising black pigs and by milking red cows.

Grandfather kept to his apples and beehives
where his praise and reproof were our fear and delight,
he made up small sermons to accent the labor
he spent in deciding his world's wrong and right.

When he took to his bed Grandfather requested
that his grave be marked by a New England stone
as if he and granite had habits in common—
he died as he'd lived, unafraid and alone.

Point of View

After a dark day low with clouds,
so cold the earth knocked underfoot
and struck me through my overshoes,
the mind's eye closed by falling soot,

far to the west a rising hill
thorny with branches caught and tore
a fold of cloud and bled the sun,
the snow stained like a butcher's floor.

Perhaps the accident of light
can only be redeemed by blood,
it came to claim the dark in me
the color found me where I stood.

I know the grace in what appears
depends upon your point of view.
I watched the sunset slowly clear
then did the chores I have to do.

Protest

Now as imperceptibly
As evening closing into night,
   As a young heart growing old
Is the wheatfield's sturdy green
   Shading into harvest gold.

The beauty of the color is
Not the thing which I protest,
   Gold is good when green is done—
But a summer in the sheaves
   Marks a season gone.

The Return

Shot from the cannon-barrelled wind the sleet
wrapped its weight on the electric wires until
the molecules of copper lost their hold
and the wires parted.
                              Henry Jensen did his milking
by hand under a smoky cobwebbed lantern
eyeing his dead motors skeptically
and when the chores were done and he had dealt with
an icy draft and latched the doors securely
he slowly ebbed back into speculation
beside his lantern and the milking machine.
As though he stepped down from the catwalk present
where balancing kept Henry, not too agile,
in a churned-up state of thought and indignation
he found a key to open a favorite door
into the sacred past where he went swiftly
past tractor, marriage, and twisting economics
into a wide green field of lasting summer
where fat crops overfilled both bin and haymow
and man was forever worthy of his hire.
His lips twitched as he recognized a straw hat
ragged and torn on a peg where he had thrown it
when he went to get the cows on old bay Bouncer.
Henry Jensen saw soaked shirts bending at harvest,
drank from a cool jug hidden beneath an oat shock,
learned again that day stretched into the twilight,
heard tired horses shake their harness—
Then the fields, contented men, the boy and pony,
summer sunshine, the glow and glory of memory
swept like a draft back into his smoky lantern
and utterly vanished in the smell of kerosene.
The lights had come back on and caught him dreaming
he blundered out of the past and squinted painfully
at the small sun screwed into his barn ceiling
and at the lantern sputtering by his side

and shook his head and then blew out the lantern
and resumed his way along the catwalk present.
He started a motor to separate the milk, he'd
get done now in time for supper.

Statement

It doesn't matter what the critics say,
I write what interests me in my own way.
I know they have to fill up the reviews
With what is called the literary news
But you and I have our own thoughts to please
And as my poems go by I hope you seize
On one or two that make you nod your head
As if you liked them. Poet Yeats once said
Of poetry and the critics' wailing wall,
"It's not a matter of literature at all."

The Thief

The fists of the summer sun
unclenched and I stole
the autumn weather.
Like a free spender
I traded the gold days
for colored woods
and ripe grapes.
Wild mallards
swarmed from their Arctic nests
along the sky's rivers
but I waved them back.
A foolish crow
with a thin bone of moon

stuck in his throat
coughed a warning.
Old Carrion, Old Evil,
I said and lay on my back laughing
until late one afternoon
the sky's militia
rose in their hooded shapes
and sighted me.

Threat of Weather

We know we can outlast the weather
the two of us, it has stormed before.
We have been through worse times together
and not turned back, ice seals the door

while the wind throws angry floods of snow
in malediction against our walls
and tries to blind a clear window
through which, we hope, the warm light falls,

such as it is, for you to see
if you are out in the dark. We give
what comfort there is in knowing we
are willing to show you where we live.

As if to defy the wind I poke
the burning logs, the rising cry
of a startled fire through the chimney's throat
drowns out for a moment the wind's reply.

Let the house shake, our fire and light
still prove to us, as the books contend,
that two in love can accept the night
and not be afraid how it will end.

I learned resistance from a heart
of oak that lay charred in the grate,
it was in the fire from the very start
and still is solid. It's getting late

but here I'll say at the risk of turning
a first rate farmer into a dunce,
it kept back enough for another burning
it didn't let everything go at once.

Three Old Horses

Returning to the gate at close of day
the horses walk together all the way,
one is a solemn roan, the others gray.

I watch their feet plunge softly in the snow
giving a plain account of where they go
but not revealing much of what they know.

The three of them are winter owners here
though who sold out to them is still not clear,
there's a farmer back behind it all, I fear.

They spend their day in nosing over some
problem beneath the snow, at dusk they come
as all do on a winter's eve, toward home.

They nuzzle at my sleeve and kiss my face,
and feel that they have said with this embrace
we welcome you to your accustomed place.

We walk together through the open gate
in quickstep for the early dark seems late
to those who know where food and shelter wait.

Heads deep in hay they soberly concur:
all grass is flesh, and nod as if it were
a truth with which I could make quite a stir.

And so in peace within their stoic shed
they let me choose at will what I am fed,
and while I watch the night they sleep instead.

What Was That?

Never was so much hubbub in the morning,
so many shouts and calls, so much expense
of sweat on busy faces, all of the farm
seemed to be pushing against its boundary fence.

It was the time to start the cultivators,
the corn rows crossed the fields serene and level,
we knew the weeds were growing to beat the devil.
we had the chores to do, the pigs got out—

The whole world seemed alert and full of sap.
It was one of those humid mornings late in May
when the leaves are out and the trees are full of motion
changing their shapes like clouds on a windy day,

when off in the grove huddled in some green darkness
cutting its silver note through the noisy birds
a phoebe repeated over and over its music
that seemed too sad and simple to put in words.

I wonder if there is time for plaintive sorrow,
in a working world, that questions our belief
in what we do today, that says tomorrow
will come to teach us more and more of grief.

His road is hard who bears within himself seeds of the sun,
who sees how patient earth cracks and strains to bring a flower
to bloom . . .
   ↜ Blind with Rainbows

Harvest Claim

The clover field in bloom seemed innocent
of any appetite except the urge to bloom
which loosed and fatted blossoms in the sun
as if there were no other months than June,
no other shade than purple, no response
but drift in waves under the wind's light hand
while bumblebees wrung honey from the land.

But I was sobered when the autumn rains
beat the earth to its bones and drove the roots
into their tunnels to hide what they could keep
of the bags of summer sap; the harvest plains
echo to sounds of metal and I weep
for the fields of summer lost and the end of play.
The crop, once sown, must learn what the sickles say.

Surprise

You seemed brave but lost in the ambush of clover,
The clover-thick valley spread out to the south
Of the wide-summer meadow, forlorn in the sunlight
Big-eyed and solemn with a sob in your mouth.

Perhaps you'd been sick with the fever of dreaming
And awakened alone? You pretended to be
When I called, an innocent, terrified youngster
Who had smelled of the flower and been stung by the bee.

Well, I came and I found you and pleased myself when you
Seemed touched by my word that the truth was what stung
Wherever you found it—then I felt the dagger!
You were old as deceit and I'd thought you were young.

Note: See also "Surprise," an entirely different poem, published in 1977.

Music for Seven Poems

I. THE HAPPY FARMER

This farm where I live
It's poor and it's small
But I'd rather live here
Than on no farm at all.

So here's where I live
With my cow and my hens,
In a tumbledown barn
And these rickety pens.

It's true I work hard
And the weeds they grow big,
They smothered my corn
And starved my poor pig.

This shiftless old barn
Had a sieve for a roof—
That the world it ain't perfect
My farm is the proof.

2. THE PLOWBOY

I'll plow myself a pillow,
I'll plow myself a bed,
Time goes by like a furrow
And soon I will be dead.

Then the field may wither,
Then the plow may rust,
And the gate sag on its hinges,
While I sleep because I must.

And I will not remember
That I was tamed for this:
To work in the yoke of summer
For the wage of winter's kiss.

3. THE SUPPLICANT

I try, when I awake, on a bright Sunday morning
Slowly, slowly, to open both my eyes
Just enough to see the clock, then sink down under
The clear waves of rectitude, a private exercise.

There time doesn't matter and nobody calls me,
I lie back and float on a summoning bell
That tells the other people—not me, but other people—
To gather up their pitchers and come to the well.

I sail into grace, half awake, half asleep,
Like an angel from a cloud, or a turtle from the sea,
And protect myself from evil, temptation and the devil
By offering up a morning's rest to hard-worked men like me.

4. THE HUNTER

You cannot kill the white-tailed deer
With tears in autumn when the mellow wind
Fingers the apples and pulls down the grapes
One by one from the cluster, blows the frost
On breathy mornings into a comet's shape.

You cannot kill the white-tailed deer
With kindness no matter how your hounds
Worry them with affection, you will find
Trails through the empty woodlands like the bare
Patterns of their hoofprints in your mind.

You must be ruthless, hunter, and stalk them down
From behind the trees, in covert, blind and mire,
And slaughter them one by one as the hunter's moon
Bloodies its face with clouds of drifting fire.

5. TRUANT

Little rowdy yellow duck, darting from your mother,
Scooting after water bugs, scorning warmth and shelter,
Wading in the mudbank, winking at the sun
With your shorty rumpled rump, running helter-skelter.

Little roly poly duck, sturdy for adventure,
Hiding in the tangled grass, diving in the middle
Of muddy weedy water dips, wavering for balance,
And flip-flop, somersault, tumble in puddle.

Little weary ragged duck, frightened of the shadows,
Streak and dimple in and out, stagger home to rest.
Oh, you droopy fuzzy head, snuggled in your pillow
Underneath your mother's wing, safe against her breast.

6. LOST

I hear a child crying
as lonesome as water
far off in the night
sobbing low over stone.

I hear a child crying
as lost as a kitten
out there in the wilderness
small and alone.

I hear a child crying
wild and forsaken
caught by the dark and
no way to go home.

7. EACH SPRING

When ducks print signs in the mud for the farmer to read,
And a thawing roof yields smoke in the sun at noon,
And a map of the earth's position shows through the snow,
The news becomes music to me like a newly made tune.

When the drying fields are ready for man to plow,
When pups tumble out of the barn like squirrels from a tree,
And a schoolgirl under her breath hums the sadness of love,
And plum blossoms shatter, like sap there rises in me

The excitement that comes with the promise of green-leaved earth,
With another day to wonder at heart-shaped flowers,
With another day to marvel how we are free
From the rules of winter—the season of hope is ours.

The Old Admonitions

The friend that I had
Marched away to the war
And the girl that I loved
Turned me out of her door,
And the taste of my life
Without friend, without wife
Went sour at the core.
The minister muttered
"Man reaps what he sowed."
But the old admonitions
Are dust in the road,
Are as useless to me
As the wind in the tree,
As the big-bellied, arrogant
Wind in the tree.

The Questioner

When evening bows its head so does the farmer,
I have seen him do it, haggard with sweat and fatigue
As he limps his way home to the daily chores,
I have been the man myself.

I have come to the lane that leads off toward the barns
And leaves the fields, and the streams of growing,
If one can think of earth as a moving tide
Where the flow is vertical.

I have stopped at the gates where maples lean on my shoulder
As confidential friends with nothing to say,
Staying to keep me company while the sunset
Squats on a burning hill.

Is this really the way it looks or is it seeming,
A distortion of the eye to fool the heart,
Collector of imitations, but still believing
It does not beat for nothing?

This is what I ask myself, is there a ledger
That adds this work and sweat to my account?
I know I do not fill my barns with dreaming,
But what's the accounting for?

Success

When I come home from work at close of day
Blind with the sunset, faced with the evening chores,
The hungry pigs, the unmilked cows, the hens
Restless for my attention, with feed and hay
To measure and lift, it seems the whole outdoors
Would let its need for order rest on me.
I hear the windmill's voice as I clean pens
But never the meadowlark's, a warning sign
I've meant to heed some day but never do.
Now I am old and stooped I've come to see
That such year charges interest for its use,
That life's a mortgage no one can renew,
I've found I traded even, farm for sweat
To justify the boast I'm master yet.
Shaky and cold under the wind's abuse
I read on the tax receipts the land is mine.

The Barn

It was like a house but larger and not so tame,
And smelled of harness and hay. We swung on the doors
And raced through the pens and stalls like frisky colts,
Hunted for kittens, and helped with the evening chores.

We made up adventures there—a small red calf
Was a princess under a spell, and the mother cow
Was the dragon that kept her enchanted. And so when she cried
We buckled on swords and sprang from our cave in the mow.

In summer vacation the barn was a circus tent,
But in winter we built a stockade where you could hide
From attacking tribes that howled in the wind and snow.
We knew that the walls would hold. You were safe inside.

The Cricket

If the sparrows would stop
their wrangling,
and the cardinal neglect
his morning news,
the garden muffle
tips of roots
and flowers diminish
their colors.

If the air bent down
to silence
worm twist, ant scurry, bee whisk,
grass sigh, leaves' excitement,

If the whole world held its breath
for just one second . . .
you could hear
the cheerful cricket in my heart.

Emerson's Page

His neighbors scratched
        stones from their land,
but Emerson with
        practiced hand

rifled their secrets
        as he read,
A stone is a granite
        book, he said.

Stones break plows
        hidden from sight
and farmers answer
        with dynamite.

But will by force
        is not the sun
to ripen truth,
        said Emerson,

a pine tree's wisdom
        speaks in cones.
He went on reading
        brooks and stones.

The Reminder

When the day finally ended I felt wet and cold
And hungry and tired for a drizzling rain had begun
While I was plowing that drove me in from the field,
The overcast brought the dark early with no setting sun.

It wasn't a storm, there was no thumping anger from clouds,
But the slate-colored light oppressed me and after the chores
I was glad to come into the house and shed my wet clothes,
I was glad to be warm at the fire and not out of doors.

The house smelled of love in the loaves of newly baked bread,
And my wife when I kissed her snuggled my hands to her breast,
When like a cry from the world, far off in the night
We heard a train whistle, wailing, sad and distressed.

It was nothing for us and yet we were painfully stirred
By the thought of our comfort, our house on earth, of our own,
And still be reminded of all who are homeless tonight,
Of the soldiers and prisoners and outcasts who cannot go home.

The Shadow

I have seen the butcher's shadow
Point like a finger where I live
Unguarded in my house of peace,
And I wept in fear.

I would rather sleep in desert places
Grow thin, unwanted, scorned, denied,
Bearded, strange, too dry for friendship,
Brother of bees and locusts,

Than be a sacrifice upon the altar
Built by the lust for self-destruction,
Where the smoke corrupts our breath
And prayers drip fat as the fire ascends.

Let me stand free, not chained by hate,
No bullock crowned with thorny flowers,
Brushed and sleeked by adoring eyes,
Led by the doomsday priests to a darkened room
Where the shaggy air rank with death
Hooks at my heart with an old dilemma.

Time of Contrition

Today I saw the gossip pack
That scours our town from end to end
Like dogs in search of hidden scraps
Scavenge the virtue of a friend.

They fell on him with tooth and nail,
They made his worth a gamey dish
On which to glut their appetites
And grant in fact their horrid wish.

With mounting cries in this bad spell
They stripped my friend from flesh to bone,
But when they had destroyed his truth
They wept at what they had done.

Time to Act

At last the revelation, a brisk wind peels
back the snow, unwraps the cold
from maple buds,
sweeps through the yard and piles the winter trash
against the gate.
The dog stretches and yawns, eyes the cat,
howls as the windmill turns to the south
with a rusty scream.
The henhouse awakes, the auxiliary cackles
confusion and strife without exacting duty,
till the practical housewife, shaking her rugs,
is seized with excitement and walks in the yard.
A bushel of sparrows erupts from the lilacs
scattering gossip in spite of the whip
of rhetorical flourish cracked from the elm
by a redbird. The farmer shells out of his coat
like a seed from the husk,
and marvels and feels
through his spread-fingered hands
the pulse of the sun.

I stand my ground and warm the air
with a man's presence . . .
　～ See How the Wind

First Signs

Today the wind trudged in from the south
and opened my door with eager fingers;
I lifted my head as if in a crowd
a friend had spoken my name.
I sniffed for rain and spoke to a bird
on the change in the weather; I looked at a cloud,
and behold, the cloud stirred! And out in the yard
a gander and goose were spreading by mouth
the news they had heard. Oh, excitement is starred
on the calendar's page when the little pigs come,
when cats sit in the sun, when drifts disappear,
when snowdrops and crocus—not yet named aloud
but only hoped for—are suddenly here!

See How the Wind

See how the wind repeats itself
and beats upon my door? Another gray November
come to remind me how the shrunken days
mumble and fret and shawl themselves from light.
Ducks drift down the sky like harried kites,
leaves scuttle under the oaks, apples lie still,
a crow talks to himself in an empty tree.
I stand my ground and warm the air
with a man's presence and let the cadging wind
back from the alleys of the world
whine on my steps. I am no humble vine to cringe
at a touch of frost nor a plowed field

humping my furrows against the snow.
I've looked at the hollow eyes of hunger
and faced them down, and before rust
sets the hinges of my door
I'll see again the falcon sun
poise and strike his golden spurs
into the green flanks of my land.

Time's Laggard

The house of summer closed its doors.
But like one fey or blind
I dreamed that I was still inside;
I kept it so in mind.

Now I am mocked by time's own truth;
A wild grapevine, far-flung,
Drops frosted fruit; at my campfire
The smoke sticks out its tongue.

The wind pelts me with colored leaves,
While in an oak a crow
Prophesies that an Arctic clock
Is striking the hour of snow.

Vigilance

Rocks grow expensive
when they squat on good Iowa land
and furnish their corner with
blackberry vines, sumac and even a few
crabapple trees. What's more, the woodchucks
dig under them and the whole brambly shambles

makes a mess in a clean, neat field.
Wilderness won't pay taxes,
it costs money to run a farm and I can't afford
the luxury of wildflowers where corn ought to grow.
So let's dig this stuff out, and level the ground,
dammit, watch out for wild bees,
keep nature tame and in her place,
I don't know how this patch got started,
you have to keep a lookout all the time.

Weed Solitude

Machines worn out, embalmed in rust,
Lie here abandoned to the weeds,
As will beneath time's acid dust
The farmer and the farmer's needs.

A binder flakes to ash, a mower
Sinks by a tree, the wild bee hums
And tastes the nettle's bitter flower
Where nothing goes and no one comes.

NINETEEN SIXTY-ONE

Advice to Farmers

You trimmed the wilderness to size
now keep it docile,
a sharp plow and harrow
will do the job for you,
those wild roses, that patch there,

plow them under before
they get the jump on you,
thick, crooked, thorny stems
wasting good black ground
that costs you taxes.
You don't tip your cap to nature
because she looks nice,
roses will take that whole field
with flat-faced blossoms
if you don't keep the land
cultivated.
Dig them out, don't leave one root.

Animal Tracks

There is a tiger hid
    in each seed's growth
and in its flower a lamb,
    I see them both

Frolic on lawns of love
    and I feel bound
to learn how they contend
    in flesh as ground.

I find a jungle still
    unmapped in the blood
where outside the stockade wall
    my heelprints stamp the mud.

The Bird

One day in the bleak month of March
while the ice crackled underfoot,
I held her in my arms under a thin arch
of honeysuckle branches rimmed with frost
and when I kissed her I looked up
and there a bird, a robin, one of the first,
watched us as the wind puffed out its breast
red with sunset like a berry ready to burst.
Since then years have tumbled into the abyss
and many roads have known my feet,
I've never returned to that place again in spring.
I have forgotten her, if you should ask I would say,
I have forgotten and it would be the truth.
Her face somehow escapes me and the kiss
is all I can recall where the honeysuckles
are doubtless dead by the time I remember this.
Even the kiss I'm sure I wouldn't remember
except for the robin resting himself there—
it was years ago but it fluffed out its feathers
and the low light drifted in from the west
and for a moment it seemed to glow like fire.
March still comes with threats of spring, I suppose,
the girl has probably married and raised her kids,
the bird burned there in the sun and then took wing.

Cross Purposes

The farmer sun
forked the clouds over the horizon
blunted the edge of the wind
and stroked the fields of grain
until they ached for harvest.

But I wanted rain.
Though signs of need have never made
the sky weep for my sake,
I wore my rubber boots to tempt
the clouds and worked inside
at rainy day chores.

Love

Love hungers, a cruel eye
stalking from the cliffs of cloud
the trembling sign—a meadow heart
is pinned beneath its plunging shadow;
goes with a rush of wings
into thick cedars at dusk
fiercely and no cry is lent
the wind where talons
struck.

A Matter of Fact

All through the summer I failed to wring truth out of words,
I crumpled my notebook and set the pages on fire,
Walked out the door and started north, then south,
Stopped undecided and leaned on the fence's wire.

In this barren land directions went nowhere of course,
The signposts added miles in a column of noughts,
My shoulders ached with their weight, I stared at a field
Already threshed and tried to stand out of my thought.

And there in the stubble a bird's step focused my eyes
On truth as it is, I forgot the past and the crops
That did not mature, absorbed in a matter of fact:
On the ground a meadowlark walks but a catbird hops.

My Father's Care

The binder glittered in the sun,
Its new paint fed our hungry eyes,
The servant hid beneath the lies—
My father was the honest one.

He sat high up upon the seat
And rode the binder, saw it thrust
Its sickle teeth through clouds of dust
To cut and bind the field of wheat.

It was a noisy tireless thing
That mocked the frailty of our flesh,
Though chains would break and cogs unmesh
My father ruled it like a king.

He always kept it in a shed
To save it from the rusty touch
Of time; he would not do as much
To save himself; I wish he had.

Owner

The morning sun surveys the time for me,
Sets the stakes, guides me to the meadow,
Shows me green acres of unmarked land,
Opens my eyes with the fire of farmer's lust.

I draw the first furrow as if I had signed
A blank check or taken a strange wife,
Indelible marks of beginnings point out
A rule of thumb I use to set my sights,

As I straddle the field, on the crop to come.
I sidestep the tractor at a killdeer's nest,
Then shear off the heads of a million worms,
Running my lines as if I owned the future.

Quiet Sunday

The old dog sleeps on the porch.
The farm dreams a summer Sunday morning
spreading the benediction of shade
for dozing hens and peaceful cows—
only pigs root as if it were Wednesday.
My serenity rises from pious knees
to bagged feet on the graveled path of chores
while my hushed vision rocks the bees
to sleep in tulip bells, ties a spider's web
across the furrows.

Tired of Earth

Wind bites dust from the furrows
and clouds your eyes, runs through the yard
in a gust of feathers, chills the early dusk,
summer is gone, slipped through our fingers
so precious we did not know how to keep it.

Gossamer threads stream from fence wires
spun out of nowhere to catch at your face
like veils worn to shadow grief;
a brown leaf flutters reluctantly
like a flag lowered after a holiday.

Roadsides breathe the heavy smell
of dead weeds, across the fence
smoking manure piles ripen the air
as days shrink and empty rows
of cornstalks kneel on broken knees.

Cows trample the vines, pigs run
over the garden where bursted cabbage rots
after frost. The gardener has gone away,
stooped with harvest, tired of fertile earth,
and left the gate wide open to the world.

The Waster

The stalks still stand erect and the tassels wave,
But the milky ears are ripped and fouled, I am able
To guess a masked raccoon as the night marauder
Who makes my sweet corn patch his private table.

All crops approved by a farm (and this is the truth)
Have an enemy with a prosperous eye to catch
The auspicious moment, when time is ripe, to dishonor
Whatever eggs have been put in the nest to hatch.

When weeks of fog rot corn, or the scorching sun
Wilts grass, I accept the heavens' rebuke, the hurt
Wills no deliberate malice, but this is a waster
Who tramples my sweet corn with animal feet in the dirt.

Autumn Love

When you stood smiling under a roof of leaves
Stained by the frost, a huntress eager to start
Her quarry, I froze transfixed and heard the forest
Sing with an arrow softly claimed by my heart.

Other folk passed and spoke as if they saw only
An everyday street post the notice of autumn again,
But I was mortally struck and even the shadows
Seemed burning, and flowers grew from my wound and pain.

Beggared

The quietness with which I watch you go
Deceives myself, the fact is past belief
That I cannot by calling on your name
Hear your light step and feel your hand touch mine.

But you move toward a valley where the wind
No longer stirs the waters, you inherit
Green pastures tongued with spring's antiphonies
Far from my barren field the dust describes.

Sunflowers touched by frost shake out their seeds,
And wither in dry creeks the wild blue flags,
And I spendthrift of love beyond my means
Find myself beggared in an empty house.

I do not know the man who prospered here.

Birthplace

This is the heart of the farm where I was born,
This farmhouse framed in remembered feelings of home,
Here is the window where first the sun spied me,
Here are the elm trees that told me about the wind.

I stand in the yard where once in imitation
Of my father's six-horse team on the big gang plow
I hitched our collie dog to my baby cart
Which he overturned and licked my face when I cried.

I think how many autumns the leaves have fallen,
How my folk have fallen, and friends and neighbors too
Have loosened their hold on time and drifted away
Leaving the work of their hands for me to remember.

Here is the hoe my grandfather often used
Until it wore down thin as an iron shaving,
Here is the rug grandmother wove and kept
When she went upstairs to die on her walnut bed.

And the rose an aunt had painted, the raffia wreaths
Hung on the walls to be used as picture frames,
The copy of "Snowbound" faded and gently worn
That belonged with the apples and fire to a winter night.

I lay my hands on the Bible, heavy and black,
That spoke to me sternly on Sundays about my sins,
So that I had a solemn face as I did the chores
And wondered if I could be trusted another week.

The hitching post is gone and the stepping block.
The view from the window is changed, the trees have grown,
They bury in shade the porch where mother planted
A rambler rose to surround each ornate post.

The lawn seems shrunken where once my cousins played
At forbidden games as well as hide-and-seek,
And how they admired my father who let them ride
An old plow horse that was very suspicious of children.

The horse has melted to earth but the mouldy saddle
Still hangs in the barn, I tremble to think how things
Outlive the hands that used them, they speak to me
In the voice of a teacher echoing down the years.

The fields remember the past where children knee-deep
In shooting stars saw ditches drain the sloughs
Now fenced and fertile but rimmed by the same horizons,
A land known by the signature of the plow.

If the roots of the present seem reaching down to the past,
The upthrusting plants insert their tips in my heart,
For this is the earth where I grew in sunshine and storm
And learned from rocks to bear time's leveling blows.

My sister and brothers and I mocked the farm's slow pulse
Locked deep in our veins when the sun awarded us shadows,
But it keeps its account in stray sheaves pledged to the gleaner
From a stubble field green-leaved in our early season.

Blind with Rainbows

Man wakes in the morning and builds a fire. He walks up and down the world seeking food and shelter. He is the hunter, the keeper of sheep, the head of a family. But in the evening when the shadows close around him, he fits a hollow reed to his mouth and pipes his song.

Man is a shaper, a maker. He takes the air in his mouth and warms it and shapes a tune. He himself becomes the song. As if it were signed with his name it shows the face of his spirit in anguish, love, triumph and sorrow. It is something new in nature, not known before. The artificial bird is more true than the robin. Listen:

> Let's make a song for winter sorrow
> > A song to melt the ice of care
> A song to tell it upon the mountain
> > That where flowers bloom the spring is there.

> A tune of hope, now and tomorrow,
> > I beg the sun bring one who grieves
> For the frozen tones of the silver fountain
> > The green crescendo of the leaves.

> Listen, a voice is awake in the branches,
> > A color like blood fills the tulip bells,
> The vineyard hope uncurls its tendrils,
> > And no one cares where the torment dwells.

> Heavy with dream we float on water
> > And watch the reflections of the sky
> Promise a country of floating meadows,
> > But the wind springs up and the pictures die.

Sing of the time when blind with rainbows
      And torn by our need to flower we come
Thrusting our way toward light, our voices
      Mount on the beat of the sun's great drum.

Come turn away from dream's bright mirror
      Broken by waves on shores of sound,
Praise deep roots, seek earth's own fountain
      Where streams of life lift from the ground.

PART II

Man is a shaper, a maker. In his workshop where imagination
comes to terms with life, he shapes dream to reality. The harp
strings of nature are tuned by hazard but man waits on form for
a pattern of meaning. He shakes the air with purpose and finds
harmonies in waves of sound. He is haunted in the forest of
experience until he snares the bird in his heart's net. He sweats
at his forge until the cage is wrought. He hangs it in a tower built
from simple stones.

His road is hard who bears within himself seeds of the
sun, who sees how patient earth cracks and strains to
bring a flower to bloom, how apple buds are mauled by
the tiger growth into their ripened fruit, how forcing
sap shoulders its way when April stirs the trees, how we
are born in pain and feel the scar all our lives who carve
stones from our hearts.

Out of despair and discontent,
      Lost for days in a tangled wood,
Out of the midnight of our toil
      We shaped the dream as best we could.

God does not let us harvest fields
      We do not sow, nor train our hands
For easy tasks, the doors we force
      Are hammered brass and only the strong
See from the gate the promised lands.

Still it will come, the day with the flower face,
when tall among your fields you walk the path
that leads you where they grow, the signs of faith
turning to gold, you will sing the inspired place.

Smells of the earth will remind you how blind roots
possess the need to transform hill and plain
as they purple the meadows with clover, once again
you will feel the vernal passion of willow shoots.

But it will come to you, peace in flesh and bone,
from the burning seeds that pierced you day and night
till your sun was spent, now in the autumn light
you are bruised by love as the plowshare breaks on stone.

PART III

Man is a shaper, a maker. He constructs a pattern of meaning to
give purpose to his life. He is tormented by a rage for order, a
hunger for design. He peers into the mysteries of creation for signs
to reassure him.

He walks a short road from dawn to dusk but the path is marked
with monuments of his struggle. He repeats his vision in a song, a
picture, a stone jar, and by this art makes our lives memorable and
provides a stay against confusion.

The sleepers in their hidden caves awake,
roused by the rapture in their blood,
they shout toward heaven their impassioned cries.
The air resounds with deathless names.

Aeschylus, Plato, Pythagoras, Homer and Virgil,
Demosthenes, Praxiteles, Anonymous the First,
Chaucer, Dante, Shakespeare, Milton,
Anonymous the Second, the Third, the Fourth,
Giotto, Raphael, Leonardo, Michelangelo,
Benvenuto Cellini, Palestrina, Johann Sebastian Bach,

Johann Chrysostom, Wolfgang Amadeus Mozart,
Beethoven, Mendelssohn, Brahms,
Wagner, Tolstoy, Pushkin,
Rimsky-Korsakov, Rabindranath Tagore,
Columbus, John Smith and Pocahantas,
Cotton Mather, Washington, Jefferson, Lincoln,
Tom Paine, Benjamin Franklin, William Billings,
Hopkinson, Foster, MacDowell, Emerson, Whitman, Frost,
And Phineas T. Barnum.

And back, far back, Egyptian priests, Brahmins, Hebrews,
Persian chanters, singers, makers, pipers, dreamers,
now they shine like leaves on the immortal tree,
flames of gold upon the sacred boughs.

Keepers of our great rose tree,
guardians of the mystery,
we serve your honor as we pour
wine from our hearts to feed the roots

in that country of eternity,
our love, our pain, our joy, our tears,
like flowers of song,
blossom where the great tree blooms
on the cliffs of night
where name by name each leaf is light.

Note: Written as the text for a cantata in collaboration with composer William Latham.

Change toward Certainty

The afternoon closed in until it seemed
No larger than a room of snow and cloud,
The small March sun glowed dimly in its socket,
The window of the air looked out on mist.

I met you there among the apple trees
Close to the feedlot where the playful steers
Rumpled the bedding in their narrow pen,
And starlings searched the ground for spilled-out grain
Like careful business men, the fog was a wall.
Oh, we were all prisoners of the day
Though some found fences more substantial than
The feeling. I was centered in my mood,
Your warm appraising look slid off my back.
Like quicksand underneath our boots the snow
Shifted as we sank deeper in our coats.
Look, and you pointed to a maple tree
Where swollen buds now showed a waxy red,
I looked from where bare ground defied the frayed
Snow carpet, then you said, There's not much yet.
I felt the wind, not freezing, raw and wet.
A ghostly crow in the fog spoke his short piece
With nothing new to say, I looked at you
And saw your hair curl lively from your scarf
Framing your face where the excitement grew
Out of an anxious frown as if a light
Had come to light blind eyes, your mittened hand
Turned snug in mine like a child's while a shadow went
Away from your face, and the actual bodies of things
Filled up the space where their shadows had seemed to be.
Nothing seemed changed and yet the change was there
In the tree, in the bird, in you and I felt your love
Beat in me like a pulse I had always known.

Farmhand

A mule with fork and shovel breeds no honey
for spring-triggered girls to buzz around
though he wear overalls and hate his muscles.

Sweat marks name me, not the moth
that longs for perfume in white bells
and dusts love pollen after dark.

The cracked and aching heart
of my desire, plain on my face
as a smear of fresh-dug earth,

bleeds foolishly while sleight-of-hand
salesmen with instructed mirrors
make me pay for what I see.

So sober I, tied to my stake,
chew the grass within my circle
and shake my long ears at the moon.

Grandfather's Farm

The worn scythe hangs in the box-elder tree,
The wheelbarrow lies on its side by the shed,
The grindstone tips forward to kneel on the ground,
Aged beyond use, they recall the unsaid

Promise I made when I was a boy
And worshipped Grandfather to equal some day
The skill of his hands and walk in his stride—
I look at my soft hands. What would he say?

His Daily Pack

Come here and let me tell you about this man
Who always crossed his t's and dotted his i's
In what he said or thought or tried to do,
Convinced his addiction to order was enterprise.

He carefully drew to scale each map he planned
To account for a world that ran on a wobbly wheel,
The roads he surveyed all lay straight and true,
His facts were obedient, taught like a dog to heel.

But the grain he harvested always invited rats,
And his purebred heifer wasted from scours when
He doctored her feed, he promised his wife to attend
Her funeral at half-past nine and the clock struck ten.

One day a spark from a trash pile leveled his barn.
I'm through with farming, he yelled. He never came back.
It's sad when you stop to think how the rules he made
Kept breaking like straps when he shouldered his daily pack.

Landmark

The road wound back among the hills of mind
Rutted and worn, in a wagon with my father
Who wore a horsehide coat and knew the way
Toward home, I saw him and the tree together.

For me now fields are whirling in a wheel
And the spokes are many paths in all directions,
Each day I come to crossroads after dark
No place to stay, no aunts, no close connections.

Calendars shed their leaves, mark down a time
When chrome danced brightly. The roadside tree is rotten,
I told a circling hawk, widen the gate
For the new machine, a landmark's soon forgotten.

You say the word, he mocked, I'm used to exile.
But the furrow's tongue never tells the harvest true,
When my engine saw had redesigned the landscape
For a tractor's path, the stump bled what I knew.

Late Meadowlark

We know the meaning when we read the signs
in sumac leaves but still abides the wish
to halt leaf fall, to sweep the frost from grass,
and beckon back the winging flocks
that waver from sight.

But look, look here, here in the yard,
alone, unafraid, in a stack of straw,
a meadowlark crouches and tries its tune
as if one voice whose truth is summer
could strike its pitch and sing back days
born of the sun. I smile, of course,
for birdlike faith, but even I,
calendar read and learned in texts,
hearing this song find my taste hungers
on autumn's table for a peach out of season.

Limited View

The clutter and ruck of the stubble publish the time
That prompts my steps, I know what I have to do
For my bread before frost locks the land against
My hand, and fire shoulders the chimney flue.

Rocks have a word that crows repeat over and over
On the cold slopes of winter where the picking is poor,
It echoes in empty granaries and I learn by heart
To say in the hard days to come, endure, endure.

But now I straddle the field and break its back
In the vise of my plow, while a thresh of weather streams by
Sweeping up clouds and birds, leaves, banners of smoke;
I gouge out furrows, a starved wind ransacks the sky.

Many Hens Do Not Make Light Work

The drake has too many hens
and he knows it.
They squat meekly
supplicating favors
with sleepy eyes
and soft necks.
He bows loyally many times
and shakes his tail
up and down like a
salt sifter to put himself
in the mood. But, alas,
he treads the warm
willing backs with
every hope of achievement
but his promise wavers
and he falls back,
waddling off like a man
late for a committee meeting.

Mexico
(San Miguel de Allende)

Fresh from the slow hills of Iowa
milky with corn, I stand aghast
where sharp-toothed mountains tear at the sky,
the feathers of Montezuma shadow
the cactus, the thin trails, the lonely cross.
A pink stone church praises God
from a fold in the hills, but the dry light
prods my eye with burro and vulture
lest I look too long at the flowers' radiance.

Blue grace pours from heaven
on proud heads and kind shoulders
risen from the stone altars
as a smile shines in the doorways
and love welcomes you in.

Moment toward Spring

This is the day when on the hills of noon
The winter's towers burn, the torchman sun
Makes virtue of destruction as he strikes
Flame to the drifts and melts them one by one.

And everywhere the tyranny is broken,
The shining fields appear, the poplars stand
Ready to publish leaves, the messenger pigeons
Rise from the barn and circle over the land.

I stare from my door amazed at the resurrection
Of rising life where the snowbank burned, I note
A fire more fierce and strange than ever I set
Under a kettle to pulse in the chimney's throat.

Need for Grass

Yes, there it was,
the raw mound of a grave
hungry for grass.
He had come up the hill under the dark trees
determined to be brave,
with vigor in his knees,
he knew it was there,
the center of his landscape everywhere.

He often dreamed it was not there.
He looked down at the rim
of yellow clay and knew,
he knew there was a final closing
to everything but pain,
his love in earth's soft arms reposing
would not come back again.

There was no grass to grow over the scars
these moments stenciled upon his heart.
Without a tremor he put up the bars
to his emotion and resumed his face and hat,
a middle-aged romantic playing his part
as best he can alone. He will do that
because he knows she would expect him to.

Alone, erect, with a brisk nervous trot
he goes back to his car like me or you
showing the world mostly what he is not,
afraid to ever admit that he is afraid
of being alone, alone, alone, sad and dismayed.

Need of Solid Ground

He hadn't offended God nor failed His Word
The way he worked, for there were only a few
Could match his efforts, he felt that so much sweat
Deserved return, a soaking rain, not dew.

He looked at the fields the frost had spit upon,
How much was a man called on these days to bear?
The black and wilted vines, the withered stalks,
He doubled up his fist and pummeled the air

Lamenting, then growled indifference to the threat
of ruined crops and shouldered his hurt aside.
Let God pile it on, he would make no more complaint
But laugh at the spear defeat thrust in his side.

He needed some solid ground on which to stand
Or a text to sustain him, but nothing he knew seemed pat.
He thought, Most men get along as best they can,
Well, it's something, I guess, just to stand on that.

The Red Flower

The day sagged under heavy wind
Piling up drifts on lawn and street,
Colder than iron the air complained
In clouds of breath. Beneath my feet

The path toward home renewed itself
And fired with hope I pushed my way
Into your arms, the ice bound door
Closed on the dusk of a winter day.

Then in your face I saw the light,
The deep June hour when nothing said
Among wild strawberries searching hands
Touched and clung while the berries bled.

This summer love melts winter fear
Because your kiss has made it so,
As if inside our window bloomed
Some great red flower against the snow.

Scatter the Petals

She sleeps as if the mouths of buds,
About to utter their gentle bloom,
Suspended breath lest an echo darken
The silence where she keeps her room,

And sleeps. The warm October sunlight
Holds in its hands the troubled year's
Moments of grace before they wither
The asters, and leaves rain down like tears.

She seems to dream in the early shadow
Where a fountain trembles, she does not start
At the blackbird's whistle above the cedars
Nor the tiptoe steps of my anxious heart.

I bow my head as the prayers attend her,
But heart, poor innocent, swells to make
A sudden gesture of warning to tell me
At the last farewell, she will not wake.

Spring Gymnastics

The puppy threatens the sleeping cat
from a safe distance, growls at a rosebush,
mauls a tattered overshoe and wrestles with
a worn carpet too tired to struggle.

The little calf leaps in the sun,
bounces back, shies at a thistle,
jumps clean over nothing, or maybe
a bird's shadow on the grass.

My thoughts turn handsprings and I'd show the world
a trick or two upon the old trapeze
hung from a maple limb behind the house
if I could break the tether tied by duty.

Spring Lament

The season has sounded its call to the farm's sleepy ears,
The snow has flooded the ditches and gone from the land,
The meadowlark lifts from a fence post her bubble of song,
And here at the edge of the field I am with my plow.

The wind is a bastard for chill and whips at my eyes
Till tears wink out like tears I have honored and saved
To weep at my leisure over the losses I bear,
I see the sun pale on the stubble and think of past years.

The sun is the same, the birds and the weight of my plow,
The strength of my arms is the same and the skill of my hands,
But you are not here, my friends who will not return.
The sigh in my breath is tuned by the grey bell of time.

As winds tear the blossom my heart is torn by these thoughts.
The field to be plowed can wait while I bleed from my wounds.
I came here to open a furrow but deaf to spring's music
I listen for voices though no ear will hear them again.

Let me cradle my sorrow a moment before I begin,
And remember with grief the faces I will not forget,
And cherish the thought I can keep them till death buckles me,
And I strong as the great colt yet though broke to the plow.

Spring on the Farm

The mixed emotions which I hold this spring
Grow from the farm's offense
Of tracking muddy footprints where the inward eye
Supposes dreams but finds that common sense

Will be more use to me out in the slush,
The wet March cold,
Where I hang my breathy wreaths of flowering sweat,
Trying to get the mare inside before her colt is foaled.

I know the sap is running, the maple trunks
Shine black as mud
Where I am spreading straw to give her footing
And get her to the barn, like all flesh and blood.

I'm a fool in some ways, but I know that spring
Comes down to this:
For me, O Lord, the chores, always the chores of birth,
Calves, pigs and colts, with kittens on their own
And chickens in my lap as frost heaves from the earth
And skies drip down, and patience and pain are sisters.
I gawk in relief at a rippling wedge of geese—
The farm isn't always like this but today it is.

A Stray

Neighbors, neighbors, help me find
My breachy heifer, snatched or strayed.
Last night I closed her in her stall,
Bedded her down and fed her hay,
Today no answer when I call,
it sticks like thistles in my mind
To think what voice teased her away.
She had a barn secure and made
Safe from dogs, fresh yellow corn
To pad her ribs, since she was born
I've favored her and yet she's gone.
Neighbors, have we spooked a thief,
somewhere a scrounger who has done
Vengeance with my heifer's loss?
Still, if she's wanton she might roam
The Lord knows where, it's my belief
she'd not go far unless by force.
But where she went . . . I jig and toss
The same old coin: what sank the spur
To madden her—Oh, if you see,
neighbors, a track or sign of her
Publish the news, don't spare your horse
But hurry and bring the word to me.

To an Old Sow

Whoa there, you crazy sow, where do you think you're going?
Charging through the garden like the devil's on your tail,
Did I forget to lock the gate or did you force the latches?
Someday I'll skin you for your hide and hang it on a nail.

Hey quit dodging back there, sniffing the air for mischief,
Turn around, behave yourself, get back into your pen.
Don't stop to smell the daffodils or cultivate the roses,
You've rooted up the pansy bed to prove you're loose again.

Let me catch my breath now before you test me further,
Easy . . . easy . . . that's a girl, walk right through that gate.
Let me offer you a hand so we won't take all morning,
As if I'd nothing else to do but pass the time and wait.

At times I see in you, old sow, ways like mine too clearly,
You won't jump to attention when someone blows his horn
As if he ran the township—don't chomp your jaws at me!
The Lord had trouble with nature the day you were born.

Look . . . it's almost twelve o'clock, quit your crazy fooling,
Move . . . or take what's coming, I'm ready to throw the switch,
Come on, you've raised hell, let's have peace and order,
Come on, this is my last word, you big black slippery bitch.

Truth

How the devil do I know
if there are rocks in your field,
plow it and find out.
If the plow strikes something
harder than earth, the point
shatters at a sudden blow,
and the tractor jerks sidewise
and dumps you off the seat—
because the spring hitch
isn't set to trip quickly enough
and it never is—probably
you hit a rock. That means

the glacier emptied his pocket
in your field as well as mine,
but the connection with a thing
is the only truth that I know of,
so plow it.

The Unprotected

The sun at noon
stirs a scurry of ants
to autumn's business.
I wear my owner's look today
and charge the bins and granaries
with the field's account. I'm trustee of
a township in my heart where summer joy
and spring expectancy depend on schools
of singers, cheepers, chirpers, clowns in grass
and pool and air, who chorus, caper alive
the spirit's moments. And now I must provide
against the day when snow lies deep,
the sun shrinks south, and no kind neighbor comes
breaking the drifts to say the year has turned.

The Visit

FOR ROBERT FROST

The little world of the garden bare,
Swept by the frost from wall to wall,
We carry our roots to the cellar's bin
When, look! a brown thrush comes to call.

The short day runs on frozen feet,
Its shadows lengthen out ahead,
But today a gentleman in brown
Sings in our hedge, pecks at our bread.

All through the night we hear the surge
And ebb of wind against the panes,
Housed in his twigs and straw our guest
Startles us with his summer strains.

The morning climbs its shrunken arch,
The sundial wakes, but the bird is gone
As if he had told us all he dared
Of life renewed by the grace of song.

The Well

By accident one day I found a well,
Someone had dug and bricked it years ago
And used it and moved away, the water stayed sweet
As if it tapped a vein with a steady flow.

I cleaned it out, I know the roots of life
Are thirsty every day, there's seldom enough
Water to waste, sometimes not even to drink
All you would like and then it becomes precious stuff.

And when sand under your eyelids truly describes
The hope of harvest withered beyond control,
Then a drink from Moses' fountain cupped in your hand
Restoreth the spirit and the spirit makes us whole.

I bring you a gift of apples now
mellowed past spring's desire . . .

ॐ Indian Summer

Discovery

The wind swept the yard, wrinkled the pond,
ruffled a robin, tapped on my window
and called me out to the sunshine.
I ran past the blue eyes of wildflowers
shining in a wide meadow,
past green waves of grass, past white lambs
chasing cloud shadows,
to a tall maple where a solemn crow
spoke three times and flew away.
I leaned against the tree
and felt the deep strength of roots.

Home

The house sags like it's grieving, paint
Peels off in spots, you can't find much
Grass in the yard, the barn doors ain't
Tight to the wind, guess my eye don't touch

On nothing beyond my patch of corn
Where plagued by weeds and bowed by debt
I look for luck where I was born
And the old folks wrote my name in sweat.

But like I'm rooted hoe in hand
To red clay hills I'm here to stay
Where cockleburs cover the cut-over land
And my wife lies sleeping one valley away.

Utopia

When early dark and chilly rains
Shake down the leaves and warn the roots,
I am obliged to tramp the fields
In mackinaw and rubber boots

To round up the inhabitants
Who pay no taxes for their keep,
I search the farm and bring them in,
The pig and cow, the hen and sheep.

To keep them warm, I spread the straw,
And fill the tanks their thirst to slake,
I shovel corn for hungry mouths
Lest their cries make my conscience ache.

They tread my heels from stall to bin,
Wrapped in their appetites like coats,
As if I were the governor
Who came to office by their votes.

The Wasted Corner

She was a higglety, pigglety hen,
one wing askew, tail ragged,
stranger to the rooster,
under a board pile
she nested a clutch of eggs
that decay ripened.
She fought off rats and crows,
comb bloody, eyes blazing,
feathers loose on her basket of bones—
a daft old woman
snug in a wasted corner.

Buried Seeds

The buried seeds drink up the snow,
wheat from the tomb promises bread,
and through the roots of April flow
the green destroyers of the dead.

Wait, wait, hear the flood of frogs
waken night's desert, streams of sun
water day's field, dry rotted logs
blossom with mushrooms, one by one.

Up from earth's dark and hairy floor
rise stalks flame-tipped whose stamens burn
with pollen's rage until seeds pour
fire through the veins of flesh and fern.

The Captain Ashore

I know a man whose twisted wife
Feeds him each day on humble pie,
She sews her hands in his pocketbook
And pours tears on his Sunday tie.

His children crowd a different table,
Shrewd as squirrels they gnaw the store
Of kernels saved to pay their winter,
Each has a key to the secret door.

And yet his eyes like sun on water
Sparkle, and he stands straight as a mast,
His footsteps ring to a martial music,
We stand at salute when he goes past.

Karma

Still, cries of hunting shake the grove
where as a boy I with my gun
betrayed a rabbit shy as love
who made no leap to hide or run.

Deep in the cleft where time returns
the man and weasel to one shape
and no star for those shadows burns,
the hands of love were claws of rape.

And I who walk convinced of grace
should flee in terror day and night,
prey to the hunter I must face
who will not loose me from his sight.

Love's Apostate

I shoulder my bag, slink through
the fog, hide in the hold of a
foreign ship while the storm watches.
Overboard, rocked in the ever-
lasting arms, I cling to a
raft of frail promises.

Without his whale Jonah lacked
redemption, I listen for the
watery steps and swear my heart
hostage if I am cast out on
the shores of your forgiveness.

Reprieve

I too have gone
with a cracked jug for water,
wept by a wall,
felt neglected in church,
I too have wintered
alone like a rabbit,
starved on my pride, been
storm-whipped like a birch,
wandered a hillside
where thieving crows plundered
a lark's nest, been locked out
of my house at night,
heard a harsh word where
a kind one was needed,
waited for day through
a long anxious night.
I too have watched for
delayed buds to open,
begged clouds for rain
when drought struck my land,
then wept like a fool
when frost's teeth loosen
their hold on my heart
at the touch of your hand.

The Return Flight

Evening spreads fingers of shadow
down empty corn rows as I stand
and scan the sky, five wild geese
plow the air in furrows of light.
I stare and drift slowly backwards

from their moving sky, they have not changed
these trumpeters whose spring salute
aroused us from sleep though now
the blood excuses what the mind recalls.
Toward the arrow's notch they burn
in autumn's fire, the steady beat
of wings stirs me to wonder what dark desire
once turned me from my anchored roofs.

Tasters

The summer sun made blood like sap
rise till her lily face blushed red,
he felt the swell and wash of love
nuzzle his veins from toe to head.

In Eden's garden ripened fruit
dripped sweet between the lips, alas
birds sang a warning soft as breath,
the smart snakes gossiped in the grass.

Unearned Gift

Shut the door,
blind the windows,
leave me alone with my joy.
Stay away dogs, cats, birds;
keep outside trees, flowers, grass;
turn back roads and paths; people
don't come near; I'm a threat with good news.
The cupped hands of my heart carry
a new wonder, strange beyond all

telling that fills my room with flame
and sings in the weather of my age
where no birds sang lately, as if grace
on wings descended, and I think of you,
and love, and how you said love is not earned
but only deserved, and my heart swears
to bear its burden in your honor.

Wilderness Token

Wild grapes tied their vines
in a loose knot to the branches
of haw trees strung with berries,
spiced the air with broken clusters
swelled by rains, plundered by bees.

Dry paths led the boy with a gun
through tangled sumac to the creek's
edge where a pool hugged the roots
of leaning trees and handsful of yellow
leaves sprinkled the black water.

Indian still he stood, two wild ducks,
a mallard drake and hen, filled his
hunter's eyes, iridescent and shining
they kissed the black water—the wilderness
held its breath, the gun kept silent,
the pair started a single ripple

and swam deep in a boy's October memory,
honey clear air and gold leaved sky,
until a cold November wind shriveled
the last grapes, and love fell with broken wings
after a short flight through a man's heart.

Apple Harvest

The wind knocks on my door,
I must pick my apples now
or let them rot.
The wind straddles my back,
I set the ladder carefully
lest more than apples fall.
Someday the tree will die
and with stalks and men, towers,
birds and fruit seek earth's
level. We support our shapes
while our strength lasts. I store
the barrels inside the shed
and with my thoughts I watch
the clouds, gray membrane of wind
across the eye's vision.

The Balance

I bathed in the tender welter
of Spring's tide and tried to learn
the sap's secrets. I joined the willows
in their leaf birth to find a calyx
of myself taut with blossom,
but time rides the sun and my green
faded. Across wide fields I saw the wind
snatch up color without mercy
and bleach the wheat stalks bowed
with yellow heads.

My summer ended bankrupt and I
felt myself impoverished but leaf
by molten leaf gold fell into
the vault of memory to be spent
like a prodigal's in the bare season.

Behind the Stove

It takes more than wind and sleet to
snuff my candle, my god, at my age, a
kitchen intrigue, to be installed among
the pots and pans, not the parlor where
the owner sits, and she's no nymph.
A broken basket of odds and ends,
a dark square owl thick in the shoulders,
blowsy hair, sprung thighs, pads on
flat feet between her cupboards, hoots
from her chair, blows coffee in a saucer,
hoards affection, tires from intercourse
with words. Sure, I know all this, I'm
not blind, but, hell, she charms me and
I decorate her wall, chair tipped back,
a kettle still of use, but not worth
polish, I pat her rump as she goes
past and get a dull poke from an elbow
or knife handle as she scrapes the carrots.
I'm an adulterous bastard, while her
husband cuts wood for my fire I
scratch her itch as hooked by love
as any rooster who has caught his hen,
glad to find a spark among the ashes
and make the time seem warm.

A Chance Meeting

A chance day opened a door
on the street, and you came out,
thin autumn sunlight faded
and trees choked a crimson shout.

We stood on a point of time
transfixed, the silence broke
with a sigh as slight as the life
of an empty joke.

A jet black beetle tunneled
the dusty space at our feet,
its ball of fluff like words
our mouths will not repeat.

We left red clover warmth
behind, and ahead of us snow.
You said, the birds are leaving
and soon the leaves will go.

Claim of Two Countries

My native land finds its map
rolled up in a seed where signs
of the sea still linger,
jungles of tiger buds stalk
through the clover-tame meadows.
I too swam into light and
each foot felt rootlike for earth,
I fled the hunter wounded
by arrows of shine and wet
under blue space and rose again

and again blind to the mystery
of my journey.
And become a citizen of the country
known for hard knocks where soft words
drown in the echoes of the clank
of machines. I haul manure to the tune
of meadowlarks, drive my plow through
wildflowers, blast the breath of lilacs
with a tractor's exhaust, crush my path
through squatter's rights to a donkey's harvest.
I stretch barbed wire to guard the land
where wild plum blossoms gather me
in clouds of delight but still I walk
backward through the fields I own
at the boundary of two countries.

Cold Snap

The winter night in your face
darkened, and sparkling stars of frost
enameled your eyes. My words
caught on a splinter of ice
and bled to death. As their last heartbeat
sang to the music of the band
my ears felt empty and now
I can't dance with anyone else
with my blood frozen by
your white hands.

Common Ground

Two neighbors lived across a road,
One on a side, I knew them both
And how each was his neighbor's foe,
And why they bore this secret load
With diligence I do not know.

One raised his crops by luck and wish.
When he felt tired, called it a day,
Not superstitious, saw no ghost
Of duty when he went to fish;
Leisure was what he cherished most.

The other treated play with scorn,
Bound as he was to field and chores,
He sweat in earnest, found the sin
Of loafing was not to be borne;
Work as salvation kept him thin.

Neighbors they were, each with the knack
Of holding his nose for the other's lack—
And one carried milk in a leaky pail,
The other a mortgage on his back,
Each found Sears Roebuck in his mail.

The Farmer's Season

Yeah, spring, I know spring, the vernal season,
the chores of birth bathed with lilac's perfume,
but the lily's gilt rubs off for the farmer's son
who keeps night-time vigils with mud and rain
and cold. Lord, what a way to inherit the earth,
aren't there other paths to life and the fullness
thereof? All this pain and blood and struggle

for a new start, all this sweat and moan to bring
forth, all this care, to clean nostrils and
let in air, to dry the body and warm the blood,
to teach wobbly legs to stand, the mouth to suck.
Here I am alone at midnight with the rain
for music, a bale of hay for my bed, a lantern
for light, and for company an old sow with
a basket of pigs in her belly ready to deliver.

For God's Sake

Why don't you clean up your place,
can't you see that crummy pile of
tin cans crouched under the lilac bush,
that chair sagging on the porch,
those broken flowerpots climbing
the back steps, branches all over
the lawn, papers everywhere—do you
have to be told to get this junk
the hell-and-gone to the dump? Rake
the stalks and litter off the tulip bed,
this garden used to be quite a sight
in the spring—but I can hardly bear
to see it now because it looks so much
like I feel.

Forsythia

You said, take a few dry
sticks, cut the ends slantwise
to let in water, stick them
in the old silver cup on the
dresser in the spare room and

wait for the touch of Easter.
But a cold wave protected the
snow, and the sap's pulse beat
so low underground I felt no
answer in myself except silence.
You said, winter breaks out in
flowers for the faithful and
today when I opened the door
the dry sticks spoke in little
yellow stars and I thought
of you.

Hen Pheasant

Dusk fills the grove and seeps
to the fence where my barnyard flock
clamors for attention, but on the
sunset side, light flames briefly
toward the stubble on the meadow's
face—look, no, only a bush shivers,
the clucking fowl scratch toward
their roosts. A tree breathes, leaves
peck at the wind, wait, again,
see, I think this time the view
has spoken. Is it? oh, look,
unbidden as beatitude, delicately
parting coarse grass, sleek-satin shy,
the brown bird, folded in her dignity,
as delight comes through the slow
beating heart, leaves the wilderness
for an instant's home in my eye.

Hog Economy

The little pig stuck his nose in the trough
But the big pig moved him over,
He started again where he left off
But the big pig moved him over,
He squealed and shivered, his whole intent
Was to find a place for himself—he meant
To give no offense—and protesting he went
As the big pigs moved him over.

He bristled with signs of a small pig's right
But the big pigs moved him over.
He struggled and bit with a small pig's might
But the big pigs moved him over.
In the trough was his dinner without fork or plate,
His hunger's edge warned him not to wait
(Though the pig was little, his need was great),
But the big pigs moved him over.

He trembled, the little pig did, in despair
As the big pigs moved him over,
He pushed for the trough like everyone there
But the big pigs moved him over,
He panted and wrinkled his small pig's face
There was plenty to eat, was size his disgrace?
But the length of the trough, in place after place,
The big pigs moved him over.

Home Place

This is the way it was:
the cold warned my feet,
the wind urged me to leave,
the snowfield blinded my paths,

but a buried stump and a straight fence
told me their names.
I listened carefully lest the voice
of the season confuse their speech
and leave me lost in a land
of unknown tongues.
But when their names were said
I knew what landscape lay hidden
under the winter folds,
and while a vagrant wind
stole leaves from a sleeping oak,
I stood my ground.

Indian Summer

The sun drops honey-colored days
into the valley of November, bare
twigs hold up the sky, winds keep
still, grief hides its face, a slow
pulse opens the last chrysanthemum.
I bring you a gift of apples now
mellowed past spring's desire while
the gold light falling through maples
turns us from aftermaths of frost.

Note: See "November," a poem with similar lines, published in 1979.

Marred

This headache of a morning
is split wide open with birdsong,
such yipping and piping
and shrill whistling from the lawn,

the cardinal gloats in the elm's top
and drives his sharp treble
like a nail into my eardrums.
And the sun bursts unannounced
into my bedroom, squats on the floor
in a yellow uniform and stares
at my eyes until they hurt.
Show me a door I can back out of
in my sullen clothes and come back in
dressed as I should be to delight
my wife's eyes this summer morning.

Noisy Morning

Decisions not yet made parade past me
this morning with pounding drums and
shrill cornets. Let them wait. I
run from the shriek of traffic, the
baying of power mowers, the report
of a delinquent motor—a bluebottle fly
in the window fills the leftover chinks
of silence. My ears cower between the
doorbell and telephone, retreat cut off
as the parade reforms and the drums
applaud. I escape down the path of
deafness to my mind's cove where even
the sun speaks softly and I sit in a
pool of time and let the ripples spread.

A Place to Sit

Come in, come in, Neighbor, please come in,
I feel so tired this morning I don't know
if I'm still Emma Brown wife of Pete Brown
or just a worn-out farmwife who won't see
fifty again, and never having had
children won't start having any now.
Today I guess the house has got too big
for me to handle, my working power's drained off,
and here I set, the morning work not done.
All of my married life I've tried to do
more than I could, you know, fix up the house
with rugs and curtains, have flowers in a vase,
wear bright fresh dresses in the afternoon,
hoe out my row with the ladies' group at church,
but the farm just sat there like a hungry frog
and gulped down every cent that we could make.
This morning Pete came in—I know the plow
was old—to get my chicken money, he said,
"Another iron carcass for the boneyard."
He's got a place, weed high and hid away,
where he piles worn-out tools, machines and wire,
he calls it "boneyard," it's a place for junk.
"Where is your money, Em, I've got to buy
or rent a plow, God how the work piles up."
I never put no store on money's face,
not having any, but this time I'd saved
for something special. All my married life
I've thought how nice linoleum would look
on the kitchen floor, you see how worn and stained
the boards are, just this once I hoped we might
spend something on the house and not the farm.
I guess it ain't to be though, it's hard to save,
you don't get rich tending a flock of hens
that roost in an open shed and scrounge for food.
Why, let the chickens scratch, Pete says, he gives
corn to the hogs, sometimes he laughs and says

the hogs eat better than we eat ourselves.
He works real hard and yet he's kind enough.
You're only tired, he says, I'll get Maybelle
to come and help you—she's the neighbor girl
who isn't worth her salt except to prance
and wiggle herself at Pete when she serves dinner.
What? . . . No, he laughs . . . Oh, Lord, I wish he would
show interest in something beside the bank account,
or tiling a slough or putting in new fence,
just to show he's human with a touch of sin.
He don't know yet how gray my sickness is,
he don't know my gray hair means gray all through
my skin and bones and heart, hope's all leaked out
and I've dried up like asters after frost.
I had a garden once, once I liked flowers,
when first we married I was fond of flowers . . .
My goodness, see that clock, it's dinnertime
and here comes Maybelle dressed up fit to kill
in a fancy apron, see now what I mean?
I have one comfort, a day or two ago
I walked out past the barns for some fresh air
and forget the kitchen chores, see if I could,
and look at things, I've always felt the need
to be with trees, they seem so rooted—like
in being what they are, well, pretty soon
I came to Pete's old boneyard hid by weeds
where discards quietly rust themselves away.
I thought I'd bring my rocking chair sometime
and sit among 'em, they look so peaceful-like
and quiet, they wouldn't begrudge my joining them,
it was a thought I took real comfort in.
Oh, must you go? Well, if you come again
and please do, it's good to talk and lose
myself in conversation and forget
how tired I am, if you can't find me here
and my rocking chair is gone, at least you'll know
where you can find me hid among the weeds.

The Quarrel

The front steps seemed not
to remember my tread as if
she had told them to treat
me like a stranger. I pushed
the bell and felt the echo
of an empty house. I rang the
bell again but the locks obeyed
their orders and silence spoke
for the closed door. I turned
my back on the blank features
and wished the steps good day;
and my wish not to be salt kept
me from the sight of her pale
face hiding in a window, while
two sparrows in the eaves
bickered over a half-built nest.

Second Look

Lord, let me be patient without rancor
and spit my gritty words into an old
bottle which can be emptied surreptitiously.
Though I am used to nature's paraphrase,
these wilted, reclining clover blooms
cut down in their prime and filling the air
with the soft, sticky smell of resignation
seem to me the lost edges of self-respect
and I see in their repose a vacuous face
full of intensive submission like a
southern rose laid on the dark casket
of an old perversion. The worship of decay
calls us everywhere but we don't
have to kneel and we can tear the wreaths
apart with our bare hands.

Shortcut

A shortcut, so we said, a different road,
we never saw it until this afternoon,
it serves the back country and folk like us
who try to save some miles, but the new moon

had risen before we made it home, your wish
whatever it was forgotten, the road dug through
clay hills and sand and we got good and lost,
wild blackberries, weeds and sumach mocked us too.

A shaggy man with a gun came out when we
turned around in his yard, we were scared to stop,
we met a girl with jet-black piggy eyes
who wouldn't talk—I guess this was the crop

of people we saw. The chipmunks seemed more tame
and friendly, we fed them crumbs. After several hours
we found the highway again and took a deep breath
of relief to see the signs, we dumped the flowers

we gathered at a crossroads where we'd stopped
to call on instinct for directions, the change
from numbered streets confused us, we felt safe
with pavement under us, in the country strange.

The Storm

A storm struck down the old willow
last night, and morning saw it laid
out on the lawn. I touch the tangled
branches where a child I knew lived
in their green world and flew
to its shelter on summer's wings.

An empty bird's nest cast aside
like a tattered cap bids good-bye
to the boy who rode in innocence
above the familiar yard on rough
barked boughs. With his pie-plate shield
and barrel-stave sword he galloped
through a wood of unaccountable terrors
and one still lives with me and moves
like wind through dry leaves, whispers
the hours, as I remember my brother
at arms felled by a storm like the willow.

Undertow

The bay of morning shines through
night's thicket, no windpuffs ruffle
the surface, I swim a straight course
from breakfast table to desk and
survey the solitary beach where I work.
The storm dwindles in my mind to a
passing cloud, all about me lie the
signs of calm, the fresh odor of a
new day rises like a breeze through
pines, the instruments read steady,
direction north, temperature mild.
I settle myself for the day among
the cargo of my thoughts, stamping them
to ship out, when like a shell half
buried in the sand, I find the
handkerchief crumpled by your hands
behind my bookshelf. A sigh sends up
a wave so huge the undertow sucks me
from my mooring and floats me out to sea.

Wilderness Ways

The rabbit knows the hawk is there,
the hawk sees where the rabbit hides,
the wilderness sustains the pair
with no pretense of choosing sides.

Nor does the deer choose hunter's ways
though hunter tracks a heart to death,
but hunted nor the hunter stays
the talon's plunge, the arrow's breath.

NINETEEN SIXTY-SIX

Conservative

The wilderness sleeps in seed and furrow,
Plow it or scorch it, it will not die,
I train my hands to profits domestic
And fence my fields with a circling eye.

Today I found thistles alive in the meadow,
Killing the clover, the homemade latch
Failed on the gate and some grunting scroungers
Rooting like pigs spoiled my garden patch.

My corn grows in rows each straight as the other
Like the text of a deacon repeated each week,
But weeds spread seeds with the strength of a forest
I hear, as I hoe them, the wilderness speak.

Day's Routine

A day of simple duties
ends with the hours' flight
into the lake of sunset
under the mountain night.
I keep the path until I see
your face framed in the light.

You hoed the housewife's garden,
I traded strength for bread,
and we must tell each other
what we have done and said
before the dying embers
before the drowsy evening
send us all to bed.

Elegy

Listen, my friend, shuttered in
your small room, winter is gone.
I tell you spring now wakens
furred buds on the boughs of pussy
willows, at the field's edge a lark
nests among weed stalks harsh with
the wind's whistle. Maples unfold
new leaves, oaks wait for the warm
May sun, violets rise from the curled
clusters and wild plums cover thorns
with white blossoms, even watercress
shows color at the spring's mouth.
You have seen flocks of geese print
their flight on the wide innocent sky
over Iowa, and bundled farmers on bright

red tractors smooth the fields for sowing.
Listen, you can hear the cock pheasant's
cry while April rain sends up shooting
stars and jack-in-the-pulpits. Fill your
mind's eye with the hill beyond the big
barn where she last watched an autumn sunset.

Line between Seasons

The rollicking whinny of the wind
tunnels the arches of the trees,
itinerant snowdrifts hug the ground
and find diminished comfort there.

Buds are bundled tight as bulbs
as out of its pattern the grass unfolds
and deep roots pump through veins the sap
to carry the news of a maple's virtue.

My neighbor, I know, has seen the signs
but he, by god, serves the commonplace,
go draw the line yourself, he says,
he keeps his pace but will not hurry.

Not being a willow, he only sees
(and knows what he sees, or thinks he does)
enough to follow his own concern
he won't change more than the change around him.

He studies the wintry clouds and waits
firmly convinced the sun's in season,
knee-deep in the mud with a hold on March
he notes that a heifer has taken the bull.

Out of Bounds

Black asphalt abides between unbroken curbs of cement,
and orderly rows of streets control their crop
of sprouting traffic by signs of whistle and light,
if schoolchildren push a button, all the cars stop.

A spade defines my lawn at the edge of the walk,
and light poles accept a distance named on a map
in the city's files, and here the permits live
which allow a house to locate upon the earth's lap.

In the garden, arranged in beds, the flowers grow
chosen for size, the short stems down in front,
a canary, hemmed in a cage, still likes to sing,
space invites boundaries—as a contrasting stunt

a sunflower, wind-seeded and rowdy, crowds in a plot
of innocent lilies and nods its great yellow head
as if it was pleased to be breaking domestic accord,
as if its seed by chance would be widely spread.

A stroke of the scythe or hoe will empty the space
it usurps and restore the lilies' prestige. I've found
a word from the jungle confounding my patterns of thought
and won't be dug out where I give it such fertile ground.

Potencies

Earth, sun-plowed, rain-swept, trembles
at seed stir, thrust of root and foot,
summer sweats in birth and growth,
I in overalls as judge's robes sentence
tares from wheat, weevils from bins,
rats from stored boxes but the

judgment word is final. Behind
my back I know a thistle fouls the
lily bed, a quick tail whisks beneath
the cellar wall, on some clear nights
a ring frames the moon.

Retired

He sulks in his garden,
pouts on his lawn, resents the
enterprise of phlox and daisies,
relishes his hatred of crabgrass,
mopes on the backsteps of his failure
to join the season as a partner
in production. Also he neglects
the rim of prairie beyond the frontiers
of his discontent where sunsets bloom
in crimson success. Slowly his vision
draws in to regard nothing outside
the curb—as for the atom bomb, the
fire truck bellowing up the street
will not cause him to lose a moment
of his hoe's rhythm.

Tornado

The cornfield felt a need to write
its truth in growing green, to lend
syntax and order to each row.
Where ragweed tried to blur the sense,
it punctuated ends of speech
with a tall, straight logic designed
to harvest meaning . . . till the sky

turned black before the vacant mind
of wind, a roaring funnel shape
that clawed stalks and rows and field
into one blotted garbled word
only an idiot could read.

Words of a Season

Bundled in scarfs the kids ride their bikes,
clouds surround the patches of sky,
a dry leaf makes room on a branch for a robin,
a snowbank bleeds into a fringe of grass.

The wind picks up grit from the street
cold enough to deny the sun's intentions,
outside of town fields shine with muddy streams
that turn the roadside ditches into rivers.

The mind gags on its debris and smothers
the dull pulse of boredom in its pain,
you called me yesterday but today were silent,
a bluejay squawks as if it knew the reason.

. . . a vision turns stones of fact to miraculous bread.
∾ Plea for Single Focus

Before Frost

Now summer's golden bell is mute,
the muffled tones of autumn sound,
this is the day we store the fruit
and search the ridges of the ground

for pockets of potatoes. Vines
of melon, squash, piled by the fence,
a zodiac of garden signs,
confirm the gardener's common sense

in recognizing portents, hot
odors of rotting cabbages stir
him as he watches mares' tails blot
the sky and chestnut burst its burr.

Before frost speaks the final word,
he shapes the furrow to the plow
turning the earth whose harvest stored
in sack and basket waits him now,

as in the cellar of the heart
the roots of love lie safe and cherished,
the gardener sighs to end his part
with seeds and seasons that have perished.

Bowed Strength

The winter sun had set
As I walked through a field
Seeking a newborn calf
Its mother had concealed,

It being too bitter a night
For a calf to spend alone
And as I walked I noted
The sleep of tree and stone,

And thought, my work goes on
With chores astride my back
As day after every day
I circle the same old track.

But frost flakes blinded me
From following cattle signs
And stopped me when I entered
A grove of snow bent pines,

And there I stood and stared
Unmindful of the cold
And half afraid to breathe
Lest I appear too bold

At the tall dark trees,
Humble before the slow
Strength of their needled branches
Bowed by a weight of snow.

The Change

The same plowed field and
gold-leaved woods, calling crows,
mice in stiff grass mark
the same season,
a hawk wheels on the wind
as hawks wheel each fall.

The same hunter slides his gun
under his arm and stalks
the pheasant, unmated now, in
meadows where grass lies curled
in brown balls just the same.

A pale sun views the same harsh
landscape, I close the gates
and leave the fields to hawk
and hunter in the same way.

November wraps its days
in a cloak of dry leaves,
nothing seems changed,
frosted windfalls lie underfoot
in the same decay,
but a spring sun stirred
love's roots to grow and
I am not the same.

Close the Accounts

The putting-away time shows up
on the calendar after frost prompts me
to turn the page, I grease sickles,

back the mower into the shed beside
the plow and planter, coil the hayrope
on a hook inside the barn, turn off
the water at the pump that runs to
the pasture, drain the tanks there.
This is the day to straighten barn doors
with new hooks and hinges, fold back gates
to the fields and let the cattle glean
the empty rows, to file away spring's
expectations with heart's discontent.
Labor has dried its sweat and written
its sum under the year's account. I
read what the granaries say, walk
through my autumn thoughts under a shower
of yellow leaves, my gains less than I'd
hoped, my losses more than I planned.

Cold's Verdict

Anger wraps me in a mantle of yellow
leaves dropped from the old maple
wedged in a corner of the yard, I live
with the earth mostly as I go about
my chores, turning off water in
pasture tanks, draining hoses and pipes,
I nailed new hinges on a sagging barn door.
My neighbor washes storm windows, the
ladder he borrowed propped against the
porch, I grease the plow's moldboard,
cut dead grass from the rake's axle,
fasten a board on the corncrib and
pick up the spilled grain. But I know
the sky shows an empty blue face and
warm deceptive air stirs sleeping buds,

a pin oak flames in the sun to light the
world to some unknown exultation. All this
color and warmth to mask cold's verdict
mocks me and I throw it back in the day's face—
I who saw you wrestle with pain till death,
your courage tested like a twisted pine
on a cliff battered by the sea's wind.

Forewarned

Now when the breath of frost has chilled
The waiting aspens, when the sky
Has floated the birds to another country
And summer's brook goes dry,

I can review and list my losses
Without complaint, shoulder my grief
While the cold-fingered wind strips
My heart of its last leaf,

And watch time's plow turn under days
Like stubble, I must lace my boots
And fill the cellar bins—they winter,
Trees, in their roots.

In Doubt

Perhaps the fields are doubtful too in spring,
the early spring I mean, when the air's still cold
and only the straw and stalks of last year's crop
mottle the earth's wet skin with webs of mold.

Nothing has shown the slightest tinge of green,
the buds look dead, the grass lies thin and brown,
the lack of singing birds almost suggests
a serious question answered with a frown.

There seems to be no movement where the tips
of tulips last year pushed the earth aside
and hoisted up thick stems designed for cups
of color, as if the lips of the season died.

Perhaps this moment's chill serves to revive
in seeds of men and crops doubts almost lost
as eyes peer out through memory's windowpane
at sparrows, hungry, distracted by husks of frost.

Intruder

The morning flowered in
petals of cool air, serene sky,
bees thick in the honeysuckle,
the sun's dance on the table,
on such a morning
my thoughts bathed in light,
coffee and toast dispatched
to their duty, hands
warm in their skin,
the sense of being alive
comfortable as a loose jacket,
who would have guessed
before I could close the windows
or lock the doors,
an immense sorrow would
curl round and round in me
like a bear in a barrel
and trample the petals
from the morning.

It Was Like This

It was neither the Herod in me
nor the Pilate that spoke, it was
the mob's mocking voice, no wonder
you cried out as if a spear tipped
with anger touched love's flesh
this autumn day. How dare I call
for the judgment? After three weary
days (who breaks faith lives with
guilt), the bright spirit hid in the
crypt, you mourned as Martha but as
the angel rolled the stone away and
love rose up in time for me to ask
forgiveness.

Little Bull

The . . . poor . . . little . . . bull
behind the gate calls to
cows knee-deep in clover,
the wind smells of cows in clover,
the sun stains his back with
sweat where flies gather,
he bangs the gate, barbed wire
sinks its teeth into his hide
and he bleeds, down in the dust
he kneels and bawls, red-eyed,
furious, his groin aches and swells,
the steel sings in its muscle,
he's just a little black bull
butting his horns against the
damnedest bull-tight gate
you ever saw.

Love in Autumn

Do you remember the meadow
when clover bloom brushed your knees
and bumblebees arched their backs
to plunder flowers, your eyes
dreamy with sunlight as you tasted the honey
of late love? The air trembled with
your low song and the meadowlark
listened to catch the tune and clouds
kept their shade from you, your hands with
the signs of work on them lay loose in your lap.
Autumn turned mellow with gold light
and each day set a crown of sweet
purpose on your hair.
It was then I came from my work with the
stains of sweat still on me, ears alive to catch
my name, my hands eager for your touch,
and the hard lines smoothed from my face and
labor turned light and the stony ground
softened for the plow and even the plow handles
themselves seemed hung with tiny bells.

Love's Survival

The blind fingertips of longing
feel for the edge of summer as it
slips away over the roller time winds
the days on to the music of the cicada,
the fellow with the rasping voice
who saws the hush of evening into
fragments from his perch in the
poplar trees, as lovers stretch
hands across lonely boundaries
that divide the country of identity.

Stone sentences written
across berry-rich land can be erased
in one breath of annunciation, eyes have
seen feathery branches rocket into leaf
from the memory of a bare tree, and wide
margins of air defy emptiness with one
bird winging north and love? Well,
love may face itself in a reflection
of earth to learn how a root survives
the season.

Love's Ways

Almost as if you hungered to be free
of clothes you strip your pulsing body bare,
under your feet or pulled off overhead
you shed a husk of garments till you wear
corollas of velvet flesh and with your lips,
as warm as your avowals, pressed on mine
the cradle of my arms rocks you to bed.

Later you stretch and yawn and take a shower
hidden from sight behind the fuzzy glass,
shut in a cell where water clothes your skin,
you wrap a towel around you when you pass
across my sight to find the dress you want,
then distant as a nun in her retreat
construct a private mood I can't come in.

The Meeting

This is the curb where
the car stood, see the dry

square on the rain-wet pavement,
and here the elm tree dripped
its tears. This is the very ground
she stood on as she fled
(in her mind, her step
slow and reluctant), this air
for all I know is what they
breathed, this sun broke through
to mist the windows of the car,
this bird sang, this grass
must have heard the news, but
something's gone, lost, dissolved,
vanished, frightened away by sobs
and anger, X marks the spot on the map
of a make-believe country where she
gave back to him what she had never
had although he said she would not
pledge a straw to keep it hers. So
the tears she shed so piteously for
her release blamed him for what he was,
yet lacked his signature, as money
spent on grief or love never
exceeds the debt.

Men Give More Than Promises

You'd let me walk barefoot on
broken glass while you wore shoes,
you'd wring the necks of baby birds,
if the mother bird was watching,
to show how strong your muscle is,
I might have died and if I had
you'd have bought paper flowers and
thought you showed off big, you in a
new suit and straight face just long

enough to get me stuck away. Boy, when
you said, "You got yourself in this, now
work it out," I knew how much you cared.
I'd like to get you in a trap that
closed a little tighter every day
and watch you gnaw the bars, I'd take
you to that phony doc who cuts your
heart out while he springs you free,
and let you hobble down the street so
bugged with shame you hope the garbage
truck will pick you up—don't come near
me, snowing me with them words, you don't
love me, I'm just a doll, rag one at
that to play with. I'll nail my door
so tight death can't get in if you
come around again.

Metamorphosis

I starved for the honey you
promised in the flower of afternoon
and watched a spider crouched
in a hole, wound up like a tight
spring, motionless as a stone.
I saw a lone fly circle the hole
then buzz away, an ant started
to enter and turned back, a moth
hovered low but floated past,
I breathed the crisis of a
baited trap—I did not hear you
until you called my name. Did
you see my fingers quiver at
your approach, feel teeth poised
to strike your veins?

The Molehill

The molehill became a mountain
before we could stop it and
here we are with all this landscape
on our hands and no map to guide us.
We can pretend to go some other way
but to test our hearts we must
climb it and no matter where we turn
there it is waiting to see what
we will do.

The lower slopes are alive with flowers
but what about that stone frown on the
precipice? Well, it's ours so let's buy
some rope and spiked shoes and see
how far we get. Not being mountain
bred we may not hold out all the way,
we can stop when our strength stops,
and build a house and save the top
for another day, or lease it for
its clear view to other couples.

Morning Walk

The first thing after breakfast
he walks downtown for a paper
past the grocery clerk with bananas
on his shoulder, past the banker
parked in the shade, past the minister
busy with his flowerbed, past a woman,
bare-legged, bent over her shoelace.
He tears a smile in two and leaves her
half, but his steps never stutter as they

speak out, one-two, they repeat one-two
one-two against concrete indifference.
His feet keep their rhythm over curbs,
across alleys, over gravel-lined driveways.
One-two, one-two they say plainly.
In step with his determination he walks
through sunlight, under tree shade,
against the flicker of cloud shadows,
he walks into traffic unmoved by horns
bawling Me First, he walks in scallops
of motion, through billows of grass,
in wing dip, leaf sway, water over stones,
he walks alone and turns aside for
fifteen cents' worth of news at the post office.

The New Calf

In the basement by the furnace lies
a newborn calf I found, chilled and wet,
in the barn this morning, its mother
a wild-eyed young heifer frantic in
the pain of her first birth didn't
lick it off to dry its hair and kicked
it in the gutter when it tried to suck.
I picked it up, rubbed it down and
fed it from a bottle. Here it lies
in a basket lined with straw while
I watch its heart tremble, flanks quiver,
muzzle twitch, eyes flicker. It sucked
so feebly on my finger I had to spoon
the milk (mixed with a little brandy)
in its mouth and stroke its throat
to make it swallow. Now it waits for life
to decide whether to go or stay—and

I think of deserted innocence everywhere,
a child locked out of the house,
a woman dirtied in love,
a father betrayed by his son, all of us
sometime abandoned, lonely, denied.

Ownership

Old neighbors of my people
sleep beneath this knoll
who hungered in their bones
for earth the owner owns,
the ample field plowed over
is their warm bedcover.

The church steeple is down
and vines grow up again,
worship has moved to town
and left this plot to men,
markers along the fence
make no more pretense
to identify the claims
asserted once by names.
Neat in stacks are pressed
the crumbling half-blind stones,
since by land possessed
no longer need old bones
be honored row by row.
The farmer with his plow
unroofs each sunken mound
as if folk lying there
had asked for rain and air.
Indentured to the ground

they worked so hard to keep
when underneath their boots,
they serve now in their sleep.
There through oats and clover
the winds go nosing over
boundaries the birds neglect,
where grasses genuflect
the owners reap their faith
in a harvest bones bequeath,
and chosen by the roots
they make their presence seen
in the meadow's darker green.

Penance for Anger

Many times you have fed me, my dear,
but not this morning when I fast on
my imagined pillar with real crows
for company. They do not pretend to
be ravens wandered from a story I have
almost forgotten, these carrion eaters
who live on death and prey on corruption.
They will not feed me, I who have eaten
my own death and pray for resurrection
at your hands, nor will manna from heaven,
my woe is not so high, my need more humble.
My penance pleads my faith, hands that
touch, lips that speak, bodies that join
are not deceived by dark words gathered
like crows to wait the end of love.

Plea for Single Focus

You saw double today when you said you saw the wind
riffle the tree tops while the waters lay still—
there's always a child playing house or going up in a swing,
and an old man, lame or blind, going downhill.

Though the sun invades the summer burning with pollen,
the dark nights of winter lie heavy like flesh in pain,
there's always a picnic with a full moon on the river,
there's always hay to be made before the rain.

A farmer plants apple trees, his young son watches
from the stump of an old one cut down by an ax or time,
lilies bloom sweet in their beds before they fester,
bells describe weddings or funerals by their chime.

A man lifts walls of a new house set on a hillside,
sows grass to hide a raw grave with its feathery touch,
on a rickety porch in the valley a small helpless woman
rocks slowly, finds even that effort almost too much.

Oh, see with now's round-eyed appeal, hold and cherish
love's warm hands like wheat grains at harvest, sweet apples and red,
remember how water dissolves the dry desert's rancor,
that a vision turns stones of fact to miraculous bread.

Progress

Own all the land you can get,
tile the sloughs, blast the rocks,
burn the trees in the grove,
level the hills and bury the creek,

you bought it to make it pay, didn't you?
Fence it, fence it, heavy gauge woven wire
with three barbed wires on top—show
who's the owner. You can act like
a king and say, by god, what shall
be done and not done, what field plowed
(even the old sod pasture) and which
one souped up with fertilizer. It's
your land, isn't it? Poison the gophers,
trap the raccoons, shoot the crows,
all enemies of profit, whose farm is it
anyway? You give it the works and get
used to the mortgage on your back.
        And won't you be surprised some
morning, oh, who knows when, but later on
some fine morning a man like you with a
gimp in his leg, and a tricky heart and
shaky hands will pound in a stake and nail
a board on it that says FOR SALE.

Propped Apple Tree

Its branches bowed with fruit, the tree
affirms its stations of growth at the altar
of ripeness, each apple a witness to its
miracle, beyond all mischief now except the
schism of broken boughs. I bring
sticks and boards to defend the tree
in its virtue. How ridiculous it looks
shored up against the wind's temptation,
dead wood propped under living limbs,
heresies supporting the true faith.

Revival

The anxious hours numb me
but day's clock counts a low
November sun still warm at noon,
fields with the smell of damp decay,
a hawk fetters mice to their furrows,
wind bends the stiff weeds. I write
the record on odds and ends of mind,
shaken by leaf-fall I would have
tramped through in happier years.
Now in a whirl of dry grass I read
the signs that end love, but the sun
throws its web over my face, blinds me
to shadows, and I see how wind speaks
in bare trees, the hawk lives his way
in the sky, mice stuff their burrows
with seeds, a man reads autumn's words
like a text for his thought and remembers
the sharp taste of salt on his tongue.

The Search

Here on the hillside is a square of ground
marked off by two fences and a row of apple trees
that stretches to the south and lets out frost
the earliest of any field we know.

Here I open the first furrow with joyful abandon
while the point of the plow
seeks its way among the roots like a mole.

I walk through the air with the sun's steady hand
on my shoulder.

Wagon wheels speak to me from the road and a bird overhead
sings Free Free Free but I can't wait today.

My neighbor stops to tell me how busy he is but his words
float here and there and settle nowhere in the mind,
a salesman flashes his polished sedan but my stride
says sternly, Let me alone, I don't want anything today.

I plow and plant this field to say what shall come up,
a field won't wait on you this time of year,
in a world aflame with hate and hater's fury
a man walks down a furrow and sows spring seeds
seeking truth on the only path he knows.

Signed by Your Kiss

We came too late, we found the trees
bereft of leaves, the birds were mute,
there was no answer to our pleas,
we stood beneath a vine whose fruit

littered the ground, the sun's pale eye
fattened no flocks, a strong barred gate
stood in our way—I heard you sigh
as if you guessed who made us wait.

To shame the lock, you turned your face
to mine, and faith signed by your kiss
defied the chill of the troubled place,
led us away on a path from this

withering season and let us pass
into the memory of summer's day
where only the wind high over the grass
spied on the trespass where we lay,

and strung love's purple clover bells
across a valley wedged in June,
far from the croak of toads in wells,
to the peak of light of sun at noon.

Three Sides to a Farm

So now he wants to buy my farm, he's got
The girl—young squirt showing off how smart he is.
He tries to be casual, offhand, man to man,
"An old bachelor like you," he says, "could move to town
And take it easy, what do you want for your farm?"
I spurred him a little, just to see him jump.
"What do you want with a farm? You just got married.
With a wife like that you won't have time to work."
He cocked his head, a grin on his big mouth
(I'd like to knock it back into his teeth),
"Marriage won't bother me none, she's a good girl
But she's got to learn to work, money ain't free."
(Work? That child? Like putting a fawn in harness.)
"One hundred and sixty acres will do to start with."
He boasted. Start with? My God, does that boob know
It took me forty years to get it paid for?
"I know you wouldn't cheat me, you've known me
Since I was knee-high to a grasshopper
So I guess we can trust each other." Did
You ever hear such bleat? A milk-fed lamb
Sassing an old buck? "My wife has money,
A little, I ought to be able to borrow the rest."
All right, you borrow and give me the mortgage, Boy.
I'll show you a trick or two (that girl, that girl,
She shouldn't have let this young pup lick her hand).
"Me sell my farm? I might at that. Stiff price
On easy terms. Sure we've been neighbors, friends,

Since you were born, a contract signed by you
Would suit my book, with yearly payments made
Of interest and principal." Then let him squirm
When he hits a year when he can't make the payments.
He'll treat her like a slave and let her sink
Into a dreary round of kids and chores.
(Oh God, if I had that girl I'd build a tower
Out of my love so deep and high and strong
She could only see the love and heart it's torn from.
I'd walk barefoot through glass to touch her hand.)
Listen and hear him stretch his yapping voice.
"It's all I need to start with, a quarter section,
Make out the papers and show me where to sign."
Did you ever see such a fool? Like his father was
Who always trusted the man who cheated him.
Born as a sheep who wanted to lose his wool,
Well, I was glad to shear him and be obliging.
Let the boy sign, I'll hold him prisoner
To that signature like a vise, I'll let him see
(She had the softest hair when a little girl)
Once more how an old fraud leaves a line of tracks
In the snow of the new year.

Time's Flail

A scraggly corner, maimed by brush and weeds,
a broken maple, rolls of rusty wire,
a hay rake on bent wheels, a surly box,
a confusion of rotten boards,
the ground stirred up in mounds
as if a giant gopher out of spite
had marred earth's body.
Here I come for comfort, to repent
my need for order, here where weeds

cover the skeletons bedded in decay.
My ax and scythe lie naked by my side
while in my veins I feel the pull
earth makes on trunk and stem.
It feeds a hunger or delight, this rage for rest.
Time hammers bones to dust as I dull blades
and wear my muscles thin to raise new towers,
glue eyes to fences as if faith in lines
kept guard and made the boundaries permanent.
Plows eager for their furrows find soft earth
wears down stiff tongues of steel, so all our plans
dissolve like webs under the massive flail.
I grow tired of making sense of my own words,
I crouch and wait, my rust-found tools
deep in the assurance of the grass,
in a junkyard corner listening to the wind
for sounds of an older language.

Trials of Ownership

The title to the land's a piece of paper,
a piece of paper's no match for the wind
smearing a summer sky with signs of wrath,
a wind that takes shape in a crest of clouds,
the many-bladed wind scoops dirt and moves
topsoil from fields to saturate the air,
piles purple mountains lined with branching fire,
rips into tender corn with hail and pours
rivers of rain across the moving edge
of weather fronts, swells waterways with floods
to wash away the best black fertile earth
a man can own this side the grave and shoves
whole farms downstream into the Mississippi.

There went my farm and crops, the deed asleep
in the town bank's lock box, all I had to find
out now was if my wife had lost her way
among the pots and pans and furniture.
What do you really own, I asked myself,
searching the house to see if she was gone—
she wasn't but she could have if she would—
how many storms can I survive and still
say what I own is mine? Sometimes I feel
bereft of anything the wind picks at
on a stormy day, sometimes I kick myself
for never having learned to do without.

We All Bear the Mark

The mark of Cain is hard to spot
these days, what with the hairstyles
and hat brims, and mirrors in most houses
don't see more than skin-deep, or maybe
we get so used to faces we don't inspect
them any more. I walk through the meadow
where a shrike hangs a mouse on a thorn tree,
a snake steals meadowlark's eggs, a hawk
rides off with a baby rabbit, blackbirds
across the fence find worms in the plowed
ground, even a spider on a fence post
grabs a fly—nobody makes any bones about
survival, and downs his prey unmoved by
headlines, so the meadow basks in the
peace of true hunger. Even the President,
they say, pulls down his nightcap when
he prays.

What Shall We Do?

It is really a small matter,
hardly worth official notice,
but a citizen of our village
walks his own path.

He has been known to uphold a friend
behind his back;
He has been known to mention the death
of an old tree;
He has been known to handle facts
without gloves;
He has been known to cancel the debt
of a mortgaged boy;
He has been known to enjoy walking
against the wind;
He has been known to feed crows
in a hungry winter;
He has been known to sit in the sun
on a working day.

What shall we do with this man,
would he be safe on a committee?
Even our children beg
to follow him.

Wren in the Vervain

Sprung from the sacred verbena family
it is a small bush to be the pulpit for
the piercing exhortations of this
pert-tailed demagogue who counterpoints
his transport with shrill repetitions of

the text. Under a spray of leaves, veined
and translucent as stained glass,
sun-dappled and light-stirring in the
slow air of noon, he bubbles out his strain
in repeated cascades of tremolo until
the flowers over his choir loft, the tiny
purple, tube-shaped spikes, that resemble
a miniature candelabrum, shake and quiver
with his fervor. His brown feathers
swell and diminish in the paroxysm of
his faith, the white clerical bib at his
throat trembles over the full cup of
treble notes he sprinkles on the heads
of his congregation. He memorizes by
recitation as the hours drift slowly past,
the summer apostle entranced with his tune.

. . . bury the work in its old clothes,
let's go inside to learn how fire lives
on top of ashes and watch shadows of light
leap to the windows.

    ↄ Let's Go Inside

After Years Apart

The town moved on its streets
in familiar sunshine, storefronts
beamed, the quiet stare of traffic lights
kept automobiles lively, a corner bank
hoisted an impartial awning for debtors
and creditors, somewhere a bell clapped
for attention, the town's small boy and
dog searched the gutter, the market
wore a friendly gloved smile. But I
was a stranger seen by faceless glances,
jostled by a scurrying people at stores
and corners, an arrival too new to know
my neighbors. Then you and I at an
intersection met face-to-face after
years apart as if I had found at the
end of a journey a clear cool lake
hid in a grove, and looking at you
saw not the features I was bound to
but the path your feet made on my
heart's highway.

The Call

The call burst into the room
sweet but shrill, brought me
outdoors into naked air,
washed down space, the door
clicked shut by itself and left
me afraid to listen. The cry

all around me—all around?
Houses sprang up, fitted with
locked doors just like mine,
blocked vision wherever it looked,
leaned into height, said nothing
to my question. I ran in my mind
on hobbled feet, rabbit-dodging
into blind doorways, no one
returned my hand touch, always the
terrible conclusion of the song,
far from the country of my tongue,
not even notes I could live with.

End of April

A grey sky roofs the morning
and just when I have decided
it is the only color the
day will wear, a tulip
bursts in my face, a boy
across the street hoists a
purple kite, a neighbor lady
arranges a clothesline with
plaid shirts and checked aprons,
an angleworm turns red on the
sidewalk, I flinch from the glance
of polished chrome.
If you were here, we would not
gawk at these flash cards but
follow the example of May baskets
and decorate our door with
surprise tendrils of love.

Fear of Renewal

Snow rotted at the sun's touch,
sloughed into dirty gutters,
slid from the bank where summer
had bedded down in long grass,
caught time's disease for change
and disappeared among dead stalks
into memory's roots. A green signal
made hearts jump, people danced
in the streets of their hopes,
saw mountains move like clouds
and counted on the promise they
inherit. Like an old woodpecker
I stayed in my tree to peek out
at the sound of hoarse-voiced wishes,
wise with the wisdom of many seasons,
glad in such crazy company to be lost
in loneliness of the mind's winter.

Fourth of July at Aspen

The color-striped day
moved me to look up where
the mountain stood aloof
from the valley nor did the
rainbow rockets and hearty bombs
change its habit. By midday the valley
boiled with people breathing the fumes
of cars clotting the streets far from
the thin vapor circling the mountain's peak.
Music sang, faces mirrored the heat,
rigors of vacation rocked the valley,

people leaned toward one more swim, climb,
walk, meal, drink, acquaintance. I watched
us bustle about the level where we stand
but no tremor shook the mountain which
gathers the first and last banners
of the sun.

Games Are Never Free

The city park still draws children
to its shabby ambush, leaves and
papers soak in the bird-stained
fountain, grass dies along swing
runaways, trees scratch at clouds,
cries scalp Indian-hearted boys,
girls swing at the sky, small fry
clot the slide and scream their wonder.

      Lord, what a sight!
How many games ago I raced through
the forest until a father's voice
harried me home. Stern-faced houses
still surround the park, still frown
at my search through leaf-fall for
the path to my wilderness, remind me
games are never free, scold a
running boy who has forgiven me
many broken promises.

Giant Fear

The day overwhelmed him with its size,
he read the book of duties marked
tomorrow, unable to comprehend letters
too huge for words. The mountain
with a thundershower barred the path
to its top, horizons raced away,
sky stretched out forever. He searched
for a crevasse to hide his fear
but the book gave no directions for
his return, blocked by a precipice
he felt emptiness swell within him
until he burst into nothing large
enough to be a man.

Let's Go Inside

The furrowed field sleeps
in the cold November rain,
stalks of weeds in the fencerow
crumple in decay, the rusty call
of a crow sweeps through
an empty sky,
my shivering breath clouds the air
protesting the absent-minded weather.

I say, bury the work in its old clothes,
let's go inside to learn how fire lives
on top of ashes and watch shadows of light
leap to the windows.

The Oldest Season

The eye's doors blown open
swing in a cold wind,
feeling's empty rooms reflect
the vacant yard filled with
debris of summer stalks,
the snow runs in white tongues
along the fence to silence
the stooped grass with blizzard
talk. Familiar guideposts
sink in this Arctic smother, only
poplar trees signal directions I can
be sure of. A strange snowfield
empties the mind of all but
an oak leaf tumbling downwind,
nothing else moves in this
wildfire of winter storm.
Chickadees shelter in husks of
thought, heedless of doors
swung wide on a barren season.

The Rescue

She piled harsh weeds under the wheel,
the spinning tires chewed them up
and spit them out, the car sank
in its tracks, a sound like a sob
boiled over in the winter dusk.
The road waited, a lone tree
leered at her, she felt fingering eyes
from fields and ditch strip her
naked to her fear. A hoarse voice
mocked her muddy thoughts, blasphemed
her virgin's sweat, the oracle

of the day shaped like a crow
bowed as it sang. The car died
in its breath, quivered at the shout
of another engine . . . suddenly lights
seized her and held her and a shape
moved from behind them like a
shadow on a wall.

Sadness Weeps

In my day hate clouds skies
that promise fair, and knives
hidden in words slash at the claims
of the meek to inherit the earth.
I sit in a comfortable house that
walls out cries of pain and hunger
along a street of lawns as tame as
well-bred faces. If rain falls
like tears it is because sadness
weeps in words praising our roses
and their fragrance while the wheat I grew
for my neighbors' bread
sours in the bin.

Saturday Morning

This morning wrapped in my indolence
I sat by a pool of sunshine
while two wrens discussed their affairs
and a small boy argued with himself,
dandelions broke the news of slow growth,
wind nudged the grass and laughed
up a drainpipe. I hid the pencil

that adds up work and turned my mind
out to pasture when a woodpecker
on my steel ridgepole raised such a
whooping-tattoo I wondered why
what I heard made me feel guilty.

Spring Fever

Sun-touched I sit on a
frail box beside the garden
tools waiting for the noon
whistle.

All around me spring sweats
in labor, I hear roots push
in deep tunnels, stir in a
bird's egg, smell dew on a
thrust of buds, feel thorns
of a climbing rose.

How many springs lie piled in
the cellar of my mind, in baskets
of unplanted bulbs, dried seeds,
a litter of odds and ends of
withered trials? Now spring shines
again from green wisteria vines.

Sun-touched I sprawl, in slow motion
on honeysuckle clouds, deaf to the
growl of accusing bees.

Spring Rain

An early frost last fall
caught the syringa bush
full of sap and burst its twigs,
I planned to dig it up.

Wait, you said, for one warm rain
the bush still lives if its wounds
bleed, and then broken bark will be
transfigured by white flowers.

The Strongest Magic

Anger pens me in a sty,
shapes me bestial with snout
and tail, bathes me in filth
when I wallow in stale pride,
flies torment me, dungsmell
fills my nose, I sleep in sour
straw, eat from a trough, squeal
when the prod strikes. Light
glazes my red eyes, a cold wind
brings me bad dreams, I grunt
hairy thoughts crazed by blood
surges, until you laugh the beast
into its shadow when your kiss
turns me to a man again.

The Test

This guy walking down the street
with his ego on a leash never learned
to do without diapers and he sucks his
rubber tit for the last drop of sympathy,
hunts for a shoulder to hang over while
he belches. He is windy with alienation
and hates his father-and-mother, my god
at his age he still hates his parents.
Oh, he sobs inside as he talks to himself
about the big L (you know, life) and feels
sorely about gravel inside his shoes which
he insists on keeping, look at him, he minces
down the sidewalk in a half-assed trot,
cuddling little ego in his arms, keeps up
a perfectly unintelligible chatter to which
no one listens, and hopes to feel lonely enough
to have one solid-silver hammered-out
emotion to talk about—let's hit him in the
teeth with a couple of hard facts and see
if he runs . . .

Warm-Eyed Memory

While I wait for my next student
the morning lies around like
a sloppy nude that the sky strokes
with sunshine. A thicket of aspens
sprouts from a knoll, glitters in
the mountain's breath, birds play
hide-and-seek behind a veil of clouds
draped from two peaks. I am too
absent-minded to notice the lounging

slut on my doorstep who tries
to wish me with wren songs and
a black-and-yellow caterpillar.
Your neat, warm-eyed memory moves
in and out of my thoughts until
a crunch on the gravel walk
turns me to my day.

A Way to Measure

How stupid to try to measure
life by time like yard goods
in a store, so much plaid and
gingham and chintz, so many percale
sheets 70 inches long, piled on
memory's shelf to be added up
on inventory day or cut down or
sewed together to fit the occasion.
Maybe the clear sound of a bell
on a quiet morning, or the taste
of a lobster claw as you suck the
meat out, or the slick arch of a
cat's back under your hand, or the
breath of a cornfield on a hot day
in midsummer, or the kiss from a
young girl when you are too old to
expect it, should mark your sundial,
or maybe a loop-worm should just
measure you for a new suit.

A cow is a completely automatic milk manufacturing machine.
It is encased in untanned leather and mounted on four
vertical movable supports, one on each corner.

    ꩜ What Is a Cow?

Bluejay and I

The bluejay perches on the
ear of corn stuck on a post,
he's blue, white, black with a
topknot sticking up as if he
hadn't combed his hair. He's harsh
at his singing but now he works
his beak against the corn until
he digs out a kernel, flies
to the oak tree, holds the grain
between his toes and hammers it
to pieces and eats it.
It's the hard way, all right, but
so do I work hard for my bread.
He takes corn earth gave me
as if he owned it, and so do I.
He fattens his guts on my labor
and I do too.

The Chipmunk and I

The chipmunk sits upright
(as some men do not)
and opens the peanut shell
at one end and with tiny hands
presses the nut into a cheek
swollen like mumps—the chipmunk
sequesters every nut he finds,
dim in all our veins rides the
spectre hunger. His stripes

(the chipmunk's) run up his back
to the end of his nose, his fur
is flecked with gold, his bushy tail
stands straight up, he jerks
like a wound-up toy. I watch him
sniff his way to the windfalls
I throw him and expect no thanks
or greetings. He eyes me as
nature's neighbor to be neighbored
at a formal distance. We know where
the line is drawn and keep
our own places.

Cry Shame

Stones outlast weather,
horses sleep standing up,
flies never bother pigs—
how can I endure the tears
of a woman whose husband died
in a jungle?
I have my own wailing wall
to weep against for the many
murders I have planned, and
what sleep is there for any of us
when our hearts cry shame?
I too have sent planes, bombs, poison
to burn and rape the country
of brotherhood, and who can tell me
what to say when my own anger
calls me to account.

Destruction

The barn stood for shelter
on squared corners with a tight roof
until the wind sucked it up
and split it out in a shambles
of splintered boards. I tried
to salvage the ruins. While I
pulled nails and sorted out
split studding, citizens of the
barnyard clustered around—pigeons
fluttered where once the ridgepole
hung, sparrows frisked through
broken window frames—and let me
sweat over the collapse of order.
I lit my pipe and tossed the match
toward the tumbled hay and let
chance decide if it lived or went out.
The flame caught, winked among the stems,
then tongued the air until
the draft formed a chimney and the
fire went mad. I leaned against a
corner post, the roar of the fire like music,
the lunge of its appetite now
beyond control.

Dogma

Sucked and bitten I shake
puppy questions from dry dugs
of thought, leave the kennel
classroom to the litter of students
and trot down the street alone.
Store windows shelter my reflection

as my eyes tiptoe around crowded faces,
I shrink at the call of a familiar voice,
gallop away from a proffered greeting,
pad on stealthy notions toward a cave,
lest I am caught without my collar
and no one calls my owner.

A Green Voice

Whatever cold tones
an empty sky echoes
after birds vanish
from meadow and tree,
and bright hues of color
fade as the flowers lie
buried in snow above
roots sealed in frost,
if the tunes grow faint
in the ear of your memory
and the country of your silence
seems windswept and bare,
give sun to this plant
that I bring you for Easter,
this small tree risen
with love from its earth,
and listen as soft leaves
unfold note by note,
it will add a green voice
to the time you need singing.

Hard Words

Hard words married to
burnt toast scar the morning,
spilt coffee spreads a Rorschach
on the tablecloth after a
clenched fist made the table
jump and a knife stuck in
thin-skinned answers filled ears
grown deaf from clocktick with
blood as the stove swallowed its
flame and the refrigerator held
its breath. The wax doll strutted
her pins, pretending doors were
locked and no one had the key.
Your sobs begged me to run the reel
backward but the machine stuck
on the present scene so we threw
the film in the sink and choked
our words on a fishbone kiss
but they never finally died.

Leaves Like Tears

FOR JESSIE

You say the leaves fall
like tears, a dry vine trembles
on the wall, the wind mourns
in weeds by the fence, drifted
in windows with the whisper
weeds make before snow?
The thin piping of chickadees
fades in an immense echo of sky,
the messages all read, low

pale sun, wind north, earth
frozen, her hands quiet?
Then stand bare to grief
and be silent, throw a shawl
over sorrow's head and lead her
home, we've heard enough
sobbing for one day.

Names for an Obstacle

This iceberg of granite
with its heft underground
lodges in my field and dooms
my way. It won't budge for chains,
stone hammers or dynamite, so
I go around it with my plow and
no crops grow where it lies,
this glacial snag, dotted with
bird stains, circled by weeds,
seamed with scars, this exile
from time, ancient as grief,
a tusk thrust from the depths
of earth's ocean.

Not Floods but Emptiness

This morning I stepped outdoors
and found earth firm, a solid back
I share with two elm trees, a dog,
some daisies, a flight of steps,
an empty pail, a stone too large to move,
a snake, a robin, two rabbits, angleworms,

a chain, lawn mower, doll dishes, a shoe
marked with puppy teeth, and grass.
I move sure of support on earth's
broad shoulders where names, round as a
pebble, match with things, keep us aware
of our footprints in rocks, sand and
running streams.

The wedge of time splits us apart
from origins written in our blood,
left untranslated as we climb the path
to clouds of thought, to lose our way
in the mist of new vocabularies
as we try to read ghost words on signs
we took for directions. Spellbound
by what we say, we understand nothing
that shows us what we are and what
wind blows.

We look in a still pool and think we see
mountain and valley and plain as solid facts
until a pebble, a drop of water from a bird's
beak, stirs the surface and makes the
picture blur. We build schools from bricks
of jargon, shape colleges from a fog of
words disguised as pain, love, loneliness,
disguised as truth.

I wade through sunshine to lean against a tree
owned by its citizenry of birds, watch buds
grace green stems, smell decay in old leaves.
I name the facts I live with one by one.
My dog knows this home where I was born,
learned love, where we will die, he knows
but does not speak to prove it, lets my tribe
turn hostile to meadows and clear streams,

tear out the guts of forests and pile up
slag heaps from mines and used car lots.
We vent our spleen with abstract nouns and
verbs—we kill the enemy, never an actual
man, orient our viewpoint, maximize security,
elevate the personnel, provide sanitary
facilities (my dog and a tree), endure
subjective compulsions, discover dynamic
forces, harmonize adjustments, identify
aggressions and sublimate our instincts.
I roll my thought around and wonder how
we lost our way in this dark abstract wood.
We hate our world with words and atomize
experience, boast nuclear fission as prestige,
yet the earth holds us, feeds us, cradles us
when we die, friendly and most beautiful.

I walk and scuff earth with my toe,
a small stone makes me lame, I empty
my shoe without one word to tell me how.
It may be our fate to die by language,
to become extinct and never understand
why we were doomed to disappear in space
where no rain falls, nor snow, nor flowers
bloom, nor bluejays call, nor young folk
mate, nor all the gusty days of our delight
will dawn again. Then who will know what Eden
we rejected, we the people rose too soon
in triumph of our tongue to live the day out
in the garden to live the day in, and
catastrophes will not be floods and
earthquakes but a spellbound emptiness,
concepts never furnished, never felt.
I watch a leaf fall as if there fell the
star I stand on into the mulch of time.

Once Glimpsed

Once I thought I saw it
at the edge of my path,
but underbrush builds a wall
of twigs and leaves, keeps you
half-blind back of the wood's
lattice. But it was there,
a stir different from wind's breath,
a beckon for me to notice,
no dream, it vanished almost
before I saw it go. Now frost
has shrunk the leaves, matted
the grass, opened thickets,
but nothing shows, my eyes
remember the hunger of something
longed for, deeply craved,
once glimpsed, never known.

Stranger, Share Our Fire

Stranger, share our fire,
Here's bread, a sop of stew,
It's all we have ourselves,
It's what we offer you.

The sky swells out with stars
We stare to see the view,
It's all we have ourselves,
It's what we offer you.

The ground beneath our backs
Holds us and warms us too,
It's all we have ourselves,
It's what we offer you.

The road tomorrow sends
May be the worst we knew,
It's all we have ourselves,
It's what we offer you.

Tonight the fire is yours,
And yours the morning dew,
It's all we have ourselves,
It's what we offer you.

Valley and Mountain

The valley floor crawls with streets
and utters the sound of traffic,
I talk to myself to hear a human voice,
the mountain waits with its wisdom.
My daily path from square to square
traps me in the facts of footsteps
while the day's meaning seems to ride
like a hawk, small and soaring,
over the mountain's silence.

View by View

Poplars mark the limit of the yard,
in front the house is bounded by a street,
smoke rises from the chimney, snow falls down,
Saturday afternoons is when we meet.

One clock is silent but the other strikes,
even the stealth we practice has its rules,
your car's in plain sight but we lock the door,
wise men leave their tracks the same as fools.

Fast in the web spun by the spider love
you and I so entangled in what we do
and bound to each other wait on what's ahead
helpless before time's change from view by view.

Weeds of Anger

A man who plowed America's future
for a money crop had milked him dry,
he had his garden left. He thought
of roots to match his anger and
planted the toughest weeds he knew;
bull thistle, ragweed, mustard and tansy,
dogfennel, spiderwort, burdock and
wild morning glory. He'd fought them
all his life to keep his farm clean
and now he planted them! They grew,
god, how they grew, a forest of stalks,
flower explosions and pollen everywhere.
The neighbors scolded him but he felt saved
from something, from diminished rights,
as he gained a freehold on the
estate of man.

What Is a Cow?

A cow is a completely automatic milk manufacturing machine.
It is encased in untanned leather and mounted on four
vertical movable supports, one on each corner.

The front end contains the cutting and grinding mechanism,
as well as the headlights, air inlet, and exhaust, a bumper
and a fog horn.

The central portion houses a hydro-chemical conversion plant.
This consists of four fermentation and storage tanks
connected in series by an intricate network of flexible
plumbing. This section also contains the heating plant
complete with automatic temperature controls, pumping station
and main ventilating system. The waste disposal apparatus
is located at the rear of this central section.

In brief, the externally visible features are: two lookers,
two hookers, four stander-uppers, four hanger-downers, and
a swishy-wishy.

There is a similar machine known as a bull, which should not
be confused with the cow. It produces no milk but has other
interesting uses.

Wish for a Season

Today you said you would not sigh
for blood in the maples, for the flat
faces of sunflowers, the lonely cry
of a goose in flight, ignore the splat
of walnuts falling, the bared thorn
of haw trees, not think flowers were born
for frost to fade; and wish that I
turn back with you, retrace our path
to violet beds where we used to lie
before we heard time's mocking laugh.

Don't bring any more naked questions
for me to clothe with answers.
Styles change too fast to keep up with
and I'm going out of business.
    ~ Don't Ask the Professor

Between Neighbors

A raw nerve jumped in our
neighborhood when your dog
upset my garbage can three days
in a row and I shot at him with
my BB gun to scare him away.
Red face, loud voice, slammed door
probed the ache and locked your
"Good day" behind
tight lips.
Now I sit in the sun on my
back porch and watch my thoughts
dig up your garden.

The Blame

It is difficult to explain
yourself to a woman who is
explaining herself to you
after you have both agreed
the affair has petered out
and you try to excuse each
other from the blame you feel
you each deserve. The words
cluster around your mouths
like a flock of birds on a
telephone wire that sits there
momently, then flies away
leaving the perch empty but
the wire alive with its
throbbing tongues.

Come On, Let's Go

Wake up, dope head, wake up,
the first warm day catches you napping,
you sit sun-struck on a sheltered stone,
my god, the fence post will shoot a bud
before you do, look at the wheel ruts,
the same marks you left last fall
when you came through the gate, remember?
Mist and fog in the air, pheasants
snug in the grove, the lungs of space
sucking in the air to blow out that
cold north wind and you, old achingbones,
driving home the last load of corn.
Well, where is it now? And you, where
are you? The gate lies right where you
left it, no one cut down the willow tree,
but now the sun wrings the chill
out of the day's breath, routs out frost,
sends rain fingers deep—break out
the plow and turn the field over,
shake out a few seeds, start dreaming
of those big fat ears of corn you
love like money, come on, sleeping jesus,
get off your butt and see if you can rise again.

The Day of the Hawk

I went to the city
and ate my loneliness
where everybody is nobody
who cried in a loud voice,
"reject him."
The rivers smelled of decay
and air blinded my eyes

with the dust from chimneys.
I went to the country
and listened to solitude
but the man who killed the deer
cried, "I am a man and this
is only an animal."
He offered to feed me but
the bloody flesh sealed my mouth.
I walked beside a small stream
that led me into the mountain
and found a strange woman
nursing a dead fire.
"My white cape is soiled,"
she told me, "and the spirit
no longer comes when I wear it."
I looked at the sky and saw
a huge hawk in the wind,
his eyes brighter than fire,
his talons curved scimitars,
his wings shadowed the world.

Day's Facts

There came a morning when
machines defied her and the work
piled up—dishes unwashed, dirty
clothes, even the oven refused
to bake bread—perhaps a fuse blew.
What blew in her broke circuits
of old promises joined by her
to years of service. Now she sits
and dreams of formal gardens
shaped by flowers, brighter than
love's colorbook, far from the
toothless mumble of day's facts.

Deaf Ear

You said you would come and
your promise filled the day with
wings of light. The sky stripped
itself for frost, a stonechill gripped
the earth and a few snapdragons spoke
for the garden's faded pride. But I
was like spring in my joy for the tune
I made from your words and when the phone
rang I sang the louder to drown out
the tolling of any bell.

Discarded

I tried to open a drawer in
the old desk but something inside
braced against the frame, a book perhaps,
or a bundle of papers, or half-closed
ruler. I pushed and pried and jerked.
My thoughts said, Forget it! Nothing there!
But my clattering heart shouted,
Not so, Not so, there's an old letter
(pink fragile paper smelling of
rose petals) you used to read when
you were lonely . . .
Today when the Goodwill truck
came for the desk I remembered
the words "you" and "always" and "love."

Don't Ask the Professor

Don't bring any more naked questions
for me to clothe with answers.
Styles change too fast to keep up with
and I'm going out of business.
For one thing, I can't get material
I can depend on, it's shoddy, shrinks
when wet, won't hold a press. It's hard
to match with thread, seams gap,
alterations show, bias ravels,
an uneven weave spoils the pattern . . .
Perhaps my eye isn't what it was,
the scissors don't cut true along
the chalk line, when I pin pieces
together the shape won't hold and
the pins fall out. I say the situation
is out of hand and you better try
ready-made styles. I'm tired of trying
to please customers who don't want
my kind of truth anymore, let them shop
for answers in some other place.

The Face of Things

The creek retreats from flood rage
to its summer voice, trees
shake out leaves, turn the page
from dark and cold to seize
on green directions, how
blackbirds float from bough to bough.

Sap's rise wakes an old tune.
Almost persuaded now I hear
rustle, whisper, sigh and soon
flowers burst from bud, queer
to return again to this new start
where violence detonates and bursts the heart.

Yet for the moment I stand caught
in the web spread by morning's sun
where time hangs beckoning, I ought
dig deep, plant seed and feel begun
faith in my roots, that my sweat brings
truth again to the face of things.

The Farmstead

The farmstead lies in the angle
of pine and spruce trees set to break
the rush of winter winds, a few
young apple trees lean north
so buds won't wake too soon
if a March thaw stirs their roots.
The house from its knoll squares
with the compass points above
the feedyard flanked by an open barn
and feedbunks filled with
bright ground corn where cattle crowd
and drift away, and a water tank
with its skim of ice. In clear air barns
shine red against the white-walled house,
a road loops through two gates
(come in for coffee or go out with trucks).
Steers bawl, pigs squeal, dogs bark,
sparrows whirl from a bush, a cat
waits on a robin, a salesman starts his car,

and braced against confusion the farmer
stands in the sun and wills his world
to order. He notes a change of wind,
reviews his plans, grins at his hopes,
helps his wife in the garden after chores
to burn dead stalks and stems, remembers seeds'
soft burst above the highway's rumble,
and trusts a newborn calf to keep
his sky from falling.

Frustration

Thoughts run like mice
in the pantry and if I
catch one the trap squeezes out
eyes and dung. I save the bait
and throw away the body—what use
is a dead thought to a man
whose house won't keep out
mice that aren't thoughts
and whose head can't keep in
thoughts that aren't mice?

Let's Not Fool Ourselves

While you wait, time digs at you
with tiny claws, the itch bleeds,
you find lifting a sandwich and a
glass of milk almost beyond effort,
and if you try to take a nap,
the ceiling makes faces at you
until you roll to a sitting position
limp in your mind.

What is there to say, you ask
yourself, what password do I know?
But you aren't bugged for answers
and you know it. You want her to
come and wring the neck of your
anxiety and throw it in the garbage can,
and she doesn't come.

Moment Like Love

To see the shine, the glimmer of light,
the lift of stalk and leaf, to be aware
of crisp petals, wing stir, a soft note,
to feel underfoot dew-fresh grass,
to bathe in the warm flood, the urgent pour
of our yellow star, to taste cold drops
from lilac boughs, a breath from morning's
deep, to be awake in this moment between
waves of hush, to share the expectancy
of one dip and sway of a willow branch.

News of Your Coming

broke open the day like a flower
where bees wallow in pollen
and petals wear the colors
of a fresh morning. The frown
on my face smoothed as the news
spread through the house, doors
spoke softly, rugs embraced floors,
walls beamed at rooms, even windows
opened their eyes to the sun

while the slow hands of the clock
wound up the time of your return
and green tips woke the dormant plant
in my shuttered heart.

Resort to Calm

No protest, just the door's soft sigh,
but the house shocked me with its
closed blinds and stale breath.
I touched your hand, you smiled
and said, Let's go outside and sit
behind the hedge in sheltered privacy.
You rolled your stockings down,
thrust out your legs, I shed my shirt,
we bathed in pools of sunshine.
The afternoon beamed on us, forsythia
lit its yellow fire, urgent odors
smelled of earth, spring's warm river
flowed through us, over us, around us,
and we talked as neighbors met by accident
who swap news in neighbors' fashion.

Routine Keeps Me

I make water in the morning
before I eat breakfast because
one need is greater than another
but I don't shave unless I want to
until noon—routine keeps me
trimmed, neat, clean and fairly
comfortable, a credit to my profession,

a relief to my wife, a plus sign
to my banker and a recognition
by the neighbors that I will keep
my lawn mowed and dog tied.
But sometimes when I put on
my work clothes on Saturday and
my church clothes on Sunday, when I
see the dentist every six months,
the doctor once a year, and pay my
bills the first of each month,
buy Christmas presents before Christmas,
birthday presents a day late,
buy a suit in the middle price range,
a new car every third year, avoid
women at parties who seem too friendly,
and men who seem too cold, as I count
the expense of each risk and decide
it's too much, then sometimes I think
(not in working hours) of the mountain
ground-squirrel who hibernates eight
months of the year and wonder if
he ever wakes up out of season.

The Smile

You smiled and waved as you drove
past. I look out the window now
at a yellow rosebush starred with
buds, at silver backs of leaves
turned by the wind, at an oriole
in a treetop, two boys on tricycles
racing downhill, a man on a ladder
mending a shutter—but none of this
says what I feel.

Sounds around a Man

It's late, late in the year
to hear a plowman sing, he yells
his tune above the tractor's clatter
mocked by a crow from its perch
in the grove. I listen to air shaped
to sound, a hunter shoots, a pheasant
squawks from the meadow and flashes
bronze and scarlet as he sails downwind,
a dog barks, somewhere a cow bawls,
two boys shout from a farmyard.
I grew up with this language hoping
to find what signs warn me what I
stand for, for whom I speak.
These bugle notes ring out in a
bowl of sky bound by horizon's
ring to solid earth, the plowman
rides over the hill with his song,
wind mutters among the dead weeds,
the power line overhead vibrates
its monotone, I am caught in a web
of voices anchored as far
as their echo.

Stormbound

Whipped by the blizzard I fled
inside and looked out at the
whirling snow. A junco flew
to the windowsill beside me,
tipped his black cap to one side,
bright eyes wary, breast fluffed out,
stayed there behind the wind.

An Arctic wall closed the yard,
shut out terrace and hedge,
drifts stood out in a frieze
carved by the wind's chisel.

The bird on the windowsill
crouched in his snowy nest,
through glass in darkened air
I saw flakes swirl and settle,
strangely paired we stormbound
travelers shared our shelter.

To a Loquacious Friend

Either you bleat like a moth-eaten
sheep that knows only one argument,
or you make a whip of words to
jump the quick brown fox over the fence
of logic to bewilder your audience.
Sometime just shut up and listen
to a pin drop, or take your ears
into the woods and in human solitude
among chattering squirrels, quarreling
bluejays, the buzz and whine of insects
learn silence from a dark still pool.

To Run or Sit

Today, he said, the sky bends down
where I look out and grips the ground,
it's welded to the horizon's lip
so tight I can't escape through it.

I've tried with cars alive with power,
or airplanes that outfly the hour,
I've walked the compass day and night
but sky to earth is fastened tight.

I've tried to sneak up from behind
but back becomes the front, my mind
labors to break the horizon's trap
but each new plan but turns me back.

If action will not set me free
I'll sit and meditate, said he.
He placed a board across two stones
and on his butt as one who owns
the right to wait he sat his bones.

Vacations

What do people do for vacations
who live by mountains and lakes?
Do they go to the neon-glazed
avenues of the city to stand on
street corners, sniff the ozone
from diesel trucks, listen to the
warble of traffic, eat the billionth
chain hamburger, go to a western
movie and see real imitation Indians
and cowboys, not like those at home?
While their city cousins run to the
mountains, set fire to the forests,
throw beer cans on the banks of streams,
clog the roads with cars and motorcycles,
spread refuse in any yard and park
knowing this is a free country where
all men are equal in the amount of litter
they can distribute.

What Wind

crept in to slam the door
when you went out, to thrust
an elbow in the kitchen's face,
open the cupboard door to black
my eye, and leave me with spilled
coffee to remember you by?

Anger and hate find new voices
each generation for blasphemies
not dreamed of under the big trees.
  ∽ Comfort in an Old Tune

Bitter Taste

I ate the sour grapes and tried
to forget them as I walked to the
field, kicking the dust, the smell
of smartweed hot in my nostrils.
A striped gopher whistled,
grasshoppers snapped from the grass,
a bullsnake pulled his spotted rope
across my path, a bobolink rode
a timothy stalk, grain ripened
under the wind. I breathed
deeply, unclenched my hands,
spread them to the sun, felt
comforted by facts, but my mouth
tasted bitter all afternoon.

Caveat Emptor

I meant to take a quiet walk
into the woods and hear the talk
of squirrels and jays and be alone
under a tree, perched on a stone,

and think my own thought for a while
in privacy and my own style.
My fault it seemed was innocence,
I found the woods caged by a fence,

a breast-high fence that had been built
to keep folk out, respect, not guilt,
for someone's right to close a door
held me from what I'd claimed before.

But where in silence I once stood
a sound of traffic shook the wood,
and where I sought the leafy tree
a billboard rose in front of me,

and word and picture said I ought
to be glad to buy what can be bought,
a world where barbed wire holds the line
beside a No Trespassing sign.

Comfort in an Old Tune

The fields echo an old tune
without words—a music beyond
memory, even of trees that hear
whispered hints from the wind.
The sound of growing things,
clover bloom, corn tassels,
cries of mating birds,
silence of passing clouds,
comfort the ear in waves.
Not the snarl of headlines,
fists of machine guns,
clack of helicopters,
nor the squeak of poverty
as it turns on the dry axles
of city streets.
Anger and hate find new voices
each generation for blasphemies
not dreamed of under the big trees.
Only a green tongue thrust from
a clod of earth sings for a fresh
start no war ever promised.

Every Teacher Has One

This morning I cleaned out
my closet and found a skeleton.
The bones huddled in a corner
flaky with age and dust, I gathered
them in a basket and buried them
in my private cemetery.
Now let the grass have them
and the tree roots, let them
go back to earth and nourish
the present as the past has
always done. I can't remember
why I hid them nor from what fear
these remnants remain.

The Farmer's Bride

Dry weeds wait for snow,
trees creak, the road's skin
turns gray, a pale sun throws
pale shadows, cold air wraps the day.
I see a bundled man in work clothes
walk across the yard, head bowed
to mark icy spots where a man
might fall, his mittened hands
hang like boards. The dog leaps
to lick his face, cats arch and
weave between his legs, the cows
moo softly at his approach, even
sparrows follow behind his back.
He does the chores before dark,
and locks the barn doors, warm in a
faith he shoulders with all he owns

that a spring sun will sometime
break the winter's back. I stand
and wait where a wound of light
bleeds through the window.

The Gardener

When in the sun and armed with shears
and gloves I now begin to strip
the garden's bed where frost has lain
this autumn day and snip by snip

I trim the hedge, I rake the leaves,
I dig bulbs, pile dead vine and stalk
in basket after basket full
to carry and burn, I turn and walk

past clumps of asters still in bloom
as still blooms grief I have to keep—
I wish I knew how I could choose
what heart will need when love's asleep.

I spy a patch of grass still green,
a hawk draws circles in the sky,
but slant rays of the sun at noon
warn me to put the summer by.

Spring seems to shimmer in the air
no farther than the coat I shed,
but in my bones I feel a chill
not of today but what's ahead.

The Hard Sell

The spangles in his talk glitter
as he stares us down and cracks
his order book to make us jump
to elevated promises. He feeds us
candy words to tempt us to leap
through the hoop of hopes then ends
his act with a silverplated bow
and a smile that cheshires in the air.
Dazed from the show, still cowed
by the cocked pen, the tilted chair,
we retreat to a corner with our
check stubs and shiver while balloons
burst on the figures of fact.

The Morning Paper

The morning paper told
of gains made by our side,
and the number of killed and wounded
(but these were men that died,

a nightmare round of facts),
but statistics do not bleed
so we find comfort in adding
the score to the news we read.

The morning stands in my window,
a sparrow chirps in the eaves,
I think of the wonder a child has
for the dance of sun on leaves.

Order in the Grove

The small grove has been let go,
looks ragged as worn cuffs
on an old coat, a hodge-podge
of thickets, raspberry bushes,
dead limbs, fallen trees,
it invites rabbits, squirrels,
skunks, one beaver, chipmunks
to become citizens. Birds loiter
and litter tawdry taverns
of branches.
The fence I built is straight,
wires trim, taut, posts vertical,
next door my cornfield maintains
a decorous pattern of squares.
So with ax and saw and scythe
I whacked at the grove until
it became a little park, all
neat and trimmed and mowed—
but not one squirrel came to say
thank you, not one bird composed
a song for the occasion.

Out of Season

Half of the elms along the street looked dead,
a smell in the air like garbage starting to rot,
crabgrass muscled through lawns and army worms,
and no one mowed the weeds in the vacant lot.

Enough to make your stomach turn inside out,
everything running down and going to seed,
a world at war with itself, hell bent to die,
people so stingy I doubt if cut they'd bleed.

This nymph appears. I'm old, slack-spirited.
She struts by short skirt almost to her crotch
and smiles at me and time breaks out in flowers—
in dreams I cut on my gun another notch.

Poverty

The field of clover sowed last fall
takes the March sun, glitters in its bed,
it will be nip-and-tuck if they make it,
the young plants smothered under ice.
I've seen them when frost heaves
the crowns and breaks roots, perch
above ground like crows around
a rabbit's body. This is the time
to worry when one turn of weather
will favor foxtail where
I'd hoped for clover.

Pressed Flowers

The flowers we picked last summer
and pressed in your ladies' magazine
have crumbled to dry blossoms
and feed a winter fire. But they
remind me how you walked in sunlight,
red clovers in your hand, laughing,
while time turned cartwheels and
on a single spike of timothy
two bobolinks fluttered together.

Pride in Love

The neighbors laugh up their sleeve
at our wildflowers, quick to wither.
Their tame delphiniums last longer,
survive dogs, children and envious hands
in plots spaded, sowed and weeded
and even watered in a dry season.

Our flowers grew untended
and bless us with their presence
as they bloom in the innocence
of the pure in heart.

We learn to endure our pride
in what is freely given even
a scanty crop on stony ground—
if that were all-knowing
this land is loved by none
but those vowed to live there.

The Problem Comes

With the new schedule
time draws up after
the farewell party when
you see what you are down for
after years of marking off
days by hours, hours by bells,
to wash and shave and dress,
for ten-minute breakfasts,
bells for doors, for customers
at lunch, memos, appointments,
golf on Saturday . . .
But now in silence

you listen for skipped heartbeats,
a cough, shallow breath, nod off
in the sun, avoid stairs, take pills
at night, remove your teeth.
Clocks join the calendar in
a conspiracy behind your back.
The pages turn blank you once
filled with plans, starred and
amended to confirm
your prophecies.

Queer People

Queer people eat soup
with a spoon just as I do
and burn their mouths
if it is too hot.
I know a man who sits
in a swivel chair so when
his phone rings he can whirl
until it stops ringing
on the theory that bells
make him dizzy.

Reflection in a Dimestore Window

It's not that men are never
ridiculous in the public eye,
but their tailor-made assurance
makes them less vulnerable than
Mistress Overplump downtown
on a summer afternoon,
her bulging behind plainly

showing each hitch and jiggle
through baby-pink stretch pants,
tight as the hair stuffed in
the metal rings around her head.
I glimpse in the dimestore window
her naked face
smouldering in cosmetic fire.

Sharers

        You grieved so for a rosebush
frost killed, I brought you
a cinquefoil to grow in its place
and light with small yellow blooms
the gray space, we planted it in
fresh earth, tamped and watered it
with a gardener's pride, blessed it
with spring hope.
        Now in the autumn wind
we wrap the bush against the cold,
lest the sight we shared of small
yellow flowers desert us in
a barren spring.

Spring Rites

We celebrate the rites of spring
with cross and circle, see green flames
leap from the earth, baptize with sap
our kneeling wishes and their names.

We live the energy of ants,
feel need of vines to wind around
a maple's trunk, we flow with creeks,
with roots we burrow underground.

We wait upon the season, nights
we pray in hope the harvest yields
redeem the sowing and beg the sun
mornings to stir the flesh of fields.

We join the rites to fill the cup
of bloom with fruit and eat the bread
of body's earth to invoke the clouds
to send up rain and raise our dead.

Stunted Root

A season without rain, he saw the stalks
wilt down and saw corn tassels scalded white,
and in himself he knew a kind of drought
that wilted him on many a sleepless night.

He leaned against the gate and shut his eyes,
not much crop here to see—he could not blame
her for desires he did not satisfy
that seemed too strange for him to speak the name.

He dreamed of clouds, he thirsted for a storm
to blind the sun, to shade his withering love,
but no break in the sultry weather came,
and heat waves rose as from a red hot stove.

Even if rain came now he could not hope
for much new growth of heart or stunted root,
scorched earth had burned his seed, the woman too
had sowed the land he plowed with dead sea fruit.

Thought of Bluebells

Along the banks
back from the water's edge,
beds of bluebells lie ready
to transform the earth.
They sleep in their roots
until the spring sun
calls on them to bloom.
How many times you and I
have assumed their blue
assurance when our love
survived a cold season
with only its roots alive.

Undone by Frost

While once again you must accept
the sumach's scarlet, the silky fur
the milkweed wears, the gossamer threads
waving from wires, the lily beds
undone by frost where summer kept
them bright with sun, you still demur
as ghosts in smoke show how time treads
like trodden leaves the child you were
who smiled to wake and dark hours wept.

Vacation Cottage

Dandelion clumps flourish
between flagstones, a window latch
loose above a rain-soaked chair,

spiders and wounded bees clutter
bathtub and floor, dust waits on
shelves and drawers as we enter
our promised land.

A spade and spray can
announce our will for order,
we sweep out dead bodies and
fill the trash barrel and stink up
the air with clouds of dust,
while beneath thought's floor,
the basement creatures plague me
for the homestead I dreamed
I inherited.

Weltschmerz

I

Saturday, late November sunshine
wilts frost from grass and roofs,
a robin hops from seed to seed,
dirty, rough, a stupid stayer,
looks ragged as my thought.
I'll sell this day on easy terms,
promissory note? Futures contract?
Trade? But one condition for you
if you buy it, let me deliver the day
and perhaps your word, touch, gesture,
laugh will warm a man so wintry
in his mood his green shoots
might not make it until spring.

II

A misery bleeds inside me
today and will not let me be,
it is a day like any day,
subtract or add a small degree.
There must be something ails a man
to plague himself on this bright day
when what he wants is what he has
but what he has he will not say.

NINETEEN SEVENTY-TWO

At Least One Step

It was a night to stay inside,
not cold, but rainy, clouds hung low;
a simple man would speak for faith,
my friends told me I ought to go.

So from a shelf I took the hat
I seldom wear and braved the weather,
to hear a man supposed to add
more than two-plus-two together.

From judgments moral and pulpit-stained
I try to keep deaf as a post,
but this man coaxed my ears to learn
hunger far more than bread or roast.

. . . I'm older now, but something woke
my appetite for what he meant.
Though I've forgotten what he said
it changed the way by which I went.

Cloud over the Sun

It's a surprise to find you
seated in your mind's cemetery
eating crow among the tombstones.
I thought the street of your thoughts
was a lively place, crowded with
eager friends to prove your faith
in the company a man keeps.
I suppose rain falls in the
cemetery and muffles birdsong,
keeps the sky low and trees dark,
I've walked those paths myself.
I'd like to show you a hidden valley
where a mountain stream talks
water words, birds wink in and out
of aspen trees, sky flowers collect
in clumps of color, and a
chipmunk welcomes me if I
feed him, and no one but me
makes any human cry.

Cock Pheasant

The pool of morning lay cool
and quiet behind the garden gate,
earth broke from its winter skin,
a white-faced moon retreated
down the sky, a shaggy oak kept
its dead leaves, if roots uncurled
from tulip bulbs and sap swelled
lilac buds they made no stir, even
the air warmed quietly in the sun.

Along Dry Run trees held bare twigs
without a sigh, arches of dead weeds
looped over the garden's edge, rotted stumps
of cabbage exhaled a sour breath, a row
of cornstalks crouched on stiff knees.

From a clump of thick grass
a cock pheasant shattered the
morning surface, exploded in purple
and gold as he rocketed through
sunlight, his hoarse yell broke open
the silence and suddenly color and
passion recovered the day for us all.

Come Back, Come Back

You emptied the house
of your footsteps,
silenced the mornings
without your voice,
left me my reflection
for company—what a world
to live in!
I'll mow down the miles,
sack up the wasted hours,
shut out the wind that
blew up the storm.
Listen, the garden's weedy,
the lawn unkempt,
birds sing off-key . . .
Come back, come back,
raise the shades, make the beds,
throw out the withered flowers,
tie the shoestrings
of my footloose heart.

Con Man

The gifts I buy and offer you, my dear,
may seem installments on a payment plan
devised to ease you, an impoverished heart
finds purse more open than the inner man.

When you unwrap them I hope you can find
forgiveness for the way I try to meet
the promissory notes you hold, my name
proved to your eyes I walk on honest feet.

Bankrupt, burglar, forger, I confess
the signature I swore to write in sand
you witnessed when I opened love's account,
I bring you gifts to hide my empty hand.

A Curious Critter

Man is both good and kind
if you do not trust his mind,

he will play the better part
if he answers with his heart.

Think how cruel he can be,
he hung Christ upon a tree,

and he will not keep his word
in this world of the absurd.

When he works or when he plays
he corrupts his nights and days

by using tricks and sleight of hand
to live in castles built on sand.

He dirties love by making whores
of victims of his sexual wars.

And real wars he will righteous fight
his son as soldier, boasts his might.

When proven the cheat he has denied
he sneaks away and tries to hide,

but if he's caught and sent to prison
he weeps for innocence that's his'n.

Oh, what a rogue and what a fool,
a king of clowns, the devil's tool,

yet if he's praised for his own worth
he will do anything on this earth

to heal a child, to feed the poor,
to build a school, a church, a sewer,

and spend his money, time and thought
on earthquake victims, for folk caught

in floods, in drought, he sweetens bitter,
oh, man, he is a curious critter.

Dirge for an Old Wound

Any root worth its salt
tries to stay alive in spite of
stony ground, drought or lack
of sun, the push for growth
wakes a need that takes what
nourishment it can with greedy mouth.
Notice how gnarled, twisted,

turned back on itself a root can be
and yet deliver the goods.
I've seen a tree cut by an ax,
marred by a fence, rubbed raw
by an animal, bleed while its roots
pumped up sap to break out leaves
in their usual glory so birds
could sing in its green house.
It still stood against the wind.
If too much attention to pain
neglects the morning of a new day,
better let the inner man bleed
than bind up an old wound when
there is work to be done.

Discord

After the accident
(what's a bent fender!)
people crowd around to see
a bit of shambles on display.
But if you trip in church
and spill the collection plate
what a carnival it makes as you
sweat through confetti grins.
Or if you fail to mow your lawn
or forget to shovel your walk,
the neglect makes you No. 1
man in the neighborhood.
But the pay-off is when
you're all thumbs on the
keyboard of your bed and the
discord makes her shiver
her way from the place where
once you had a rapt audience.

A Field You Cannot Own

You thought there was a For Sale sign
on her heart and decided to buy
the property but sometimes a clover
meadow turns to sand and meadowlarks
vanish before the hawk—what makes
love or good earth barren?
She gave herself in trust
and you thought it was fee simple,
the promised land you hoped to settle.
She tried to tell you that love
can only be deserved but you
wanted to make a down payment
on a field you could never own.

Forecast

I hang a chart for prophecy
made by myself with signs of
my own zodiac. No use to warn
me of winds that blind my door
with rain, beat down flowers,
tear at the trees, not my day
to grieve. Your voice along
wired air opens my world to
different weather and I read
my own forecast that clears
the clouds when heart says
bright and fair.

The Gift for Love

Underbrush, grasses, weeds,
wildflowers, aspen trees
cluttered the glade
where the cottage stood.
Armed with an ax and scythe
I taught our slovenly acre
a few parklike manners.

I chopped and mowed,
sweat and swore,
a rabbit leaped away,
birds stopped singing,
a doe fled into shadows,
I shaped a neat estate
where paths ran to order
and domestic flowers
bloomed on schedule.

I made you a gift of the deed
but you turned back with a cry
and fled deep into your
heart's wilderness.

Important Question

I didn't come here
to tell you what to do,
wax the floors,
wash your windows,
paint the kitchen,
mow the lawn—
it's your house and if

it works for you what
business is it of mine?
I'll come in if you
invite me to have a drink,
I just came to ask you how
you keep your thoughts from
making a fool of you
on your private holidays.

Late for the News

Last week you said
it depresses me to look
ahead and see what
I'm doing now without end.

I tried to console you
with a new spring dress
to show you a brighter color
I hoped for you.

But you said, for God's sake
look at the clock, we'll be
late for the news.

Love Song

Deep in the woods I wake
under stars in night's lake.

I am without a guide
until a small flame
burns at my side.

Now the appointed place
comes to me clear,
and your beloved face.

So we will lie at peace
your breast on mine
in the pulse of release.

And while you sleep
I stroke your hair
in the watch stars keep.

An Older Language

Riding up on a southwest wind
in the wet March chill at sunset,
wild geese circled our farm and
dropped in to feed on a patch of corn
an early snow kept us from husking.
I can hear them now, talking softly
among themselves, a strange goose gabble,
strange as their long flight north.
Memory warns me as I listen,
goose talk starts goose flesh,
makes my blood drum with winged
savage pulses, wakes in my ear
a summons the old March wind
still carries.

Routine

Morning after morning you awake from sleep
and grope in the closet for clothes to wear,
groggy and blinded by the morning light,
owner of a heartbeat and a breath of air.

You wander from the bathroom still doubtful of the day
to button up your shirt and settle in your clothes,
you smell the toast and coffee that your wife prepares,
instinctively you find the hall and follow your nose.

A clock-instructed radio blares the morning news,
you fumble with the paper at the table as you eat,
but now you start to hurry, gulp your food and drink,
the clocktick in your mind is a loud drumbeat.

You find the street you travel to office, lab or shop,
the work you finished yesterday rides with you as you drive,
with never time to stretch and say, thank God I breathe,
or tell your heart, good work old man, we're still alive.

Note: See another version of "Routine," published in 1979.

Textual Matters

"Cross your legs," saith the preacher,
"and now that the gates to hell
are closed, let us judge by the text."
I was judged by the text and sentenced
to quarry stone until I become too
muscle-bound to dance. I turned vandal
among the tombstones where I buried
the gifts of a woman's promise, cleaned
the wreaths from a marker of an
old shame and wondered if a bed of
violets could grow where the roots
of the coarse thistles the preacher
planted never seem to die.

Try, Try Again

When I was young the girls were quick
to pleasure me with every trick
that Eve had taught them, Adam-wise
I played their victim in disguise.
Give me one more chance, Lord, one more chance.

In middle age a woman said,
to woo and win before you're dead
takes time, takes money, wait a year
and then I'll try your bed, my dear.
One more chance, Lord, give me one more chance.

Though age confesses what I lack,
my firm intent has not grown slack,
but girls alas seem deaf and blind
when I describe what's on my mind.
Lord, one more chance, give me one more chance.

Until the Storm Passes

The wheel-rounded wind races
across drifts, stirs a puff of snow
like the cloud of anger in your eyes
when my hasty breath shaped cold words.
Junco and chickadee snuggle
in dark-branched cedars, even the
crow shuns a dead limb for
a roost less forsaken. Aloft, deep
in the sky's vault a silver dot
wakes in the sun as it jets north.
Well, let us take shelter in
a mood of firelit warmth and be

abandoned only by cast-off chill
moments ago of frozen distress
and settle for the night in
a corner of our own windbreak
where no tear turns to silver ice
as the sun sets and we grow
strong as the roots of bare trees
where sap hides until the
storm of winter passes.

A Winter Review

The farm wraps itself for winter
and drowses off, a two-faced wind
shouts in the treetops and snoops
under barn doors. Snow leaps and
heaps over fences, a pheasant stalks
the cornfields, a crow coughs from a
bare branch. Around the house plastic
curtains shroud windows, straw
guards the foundation, cattle and hogs
line feed troughs, sparrows scramble
for spilled grain. Even the farmer
moves in a trance along paths of
accustomed chores. The farm draws in
to its center, leaves roots to bear
their burden of faith, waits in the
serenity of cold for the sun to rise
from its lowest arch and level
the drifts to water.

Judgment by Spring Rain

Some snarl-faced poet
in his weedy, unfenced youth
booted age into the winter season—
Would that age had the energy
of a blizzard or the bite of zero
or even the sculptured thoughts
lying in cold patterns on drifted snow.
Watch for the thirst for change
when a March sun gets a real foothold
in the sky and the drifts melt.
Patches of ground widen under trees,
see the debris that rides up,
a broken-backed board,
a double-faded newspaper with
who knows what headlines, junk from
the past—these show an aged mind
at its worst.
A spring rain will swell roots,
make them bulge with a sprout
or bloat in decay.

Revelation

Who ordained the flicker on my
metal ridgepole that he greets the
sunrise with such thunderous tattoo?
There he goes again, the hammer-voiced
prophet, rousing the neighborhood
to praise. Who wants to hear his
invocation at four o'clock in the

morning? The whole house shakes
with his fervor. Again and again
and again he calls us to witness.
Why can't he testify from a dead
branch for a mate and caterpillars?
And leave us to our own devotions
when we get our eyes open.

A Testament

That ant down there, dragging his leg,
pushes his crumb around stones,
cracks in earth, grass stems . . .
may not even see the sky.
No sign he asked for help,
his wife, the neighbors,
or complained that a good ant
now suffers, no Job of ants
on his dunghill to argue with God.
He seems to say,
you push your crumb and I'll push mine
with no questions asked.
I watch him drag that leg
around hills and down valleys
while he keeps the crumb moving
to push his luck home.

You Can't Plow Stone

The plow point starts the furrow,
keeps it turning, rolls it
off the moldboard, buries
stalks and grasses from last year's crop.
Now to begin again, earth worked over,

entered by new seeds, to risk weather,
bugs, weeds. Birds make a big to-do
in the furrows, flock behind the plow,
busy with worms.
The blade cuts through everything,
nothing is spared, a bed of violets,
some day lilies, thistle patches,
horse-radish roots, even a woodchuck den
is plowed under.
But wait . . .
that big rock there, it stands pat,
it has been bumped before,
see the scars, it won't give . . .
let's praise it for a show of resistance,
strength for endurance.

NINETEEN SEVENTY-FOUR

Auction

The house offers its private
life to the public eye with
fruit jars, china pitchers,
"Blue Boy" in a gilt frame,
mousetraps, a brass bedstead,
dress model, hot water bottle,
button box, old leather couch,
two sets of stereopticon views
of the Holy Land, a cradle,
steamer trunk, lace scarf—
strange hands claim them
who knows by what need, while
the auctioneer's hammer argues
the virtues of worn-out things.

Detention

The wilted flowers
drooping from a vase
memorialize the conflict.
The wounded classroom
bandaged with silence
still suffers from
twisted chairs and
blackboard indignities.
But piled on the teacher's
desk scrawled papers
confessing surrender
show what forces
once joined here.

It Happened

A rumpled bed,
stains on the carpet,
a dripping faucet,
daylight looks through
dirty windows.
Grease on the stove
smokes at breakfast
above sticky linoleum.
It is always the same,
like the front page of a newspaper
with a whore's boldness
the rooms expose their drabness—
it will never change.

But it does change, it will never be the same.
You brought affectionate hands
and words clean and bracing,

not a kiss, not even a touch,
just the fragrance of appearance
to fill the whole house.
It will never be the same,
it has all changed.

Last Day at the Swimming Hole

Two boys pick their way
barefoot down the rough sidewalk,
one bounces a ball,
they wear towels around their waists,
a bicycle pal weaves beside them.
The sun slides over brown skin,
bleached hair, dreaming faces,
a rock quarry with clear water.
They tiptoe half-naked bodies
down a path, gingerly as if
through nettles, toward
a waiting cage of desks
at the end of summer.

Listen

Clock in the bell tower
floods with morning light—
lake of bright water—
hears its tongue strike
wave of wavering tones,
the echoes surge after.

So a poem's freshness
fills the wakened ear
and E. L. Mayo,
pen raised, said, Listen,
tuned voices of words
in a chorus directed
create by strange magic
a music we know.

The Problem

The problem is to see the problem
to see the flawed face live with
its expression. An aspen tree curved
by a stone turns gold in autumn
like straight aspens, a rambler rose
caught under a foundation pushes out
and blossoms, a bluejay with a broken leg
fills his gullet, a hiker with a
hunchback admires the ruins.
A clutch of clouds is bitten by
lightning, a bruise of sky admits sunshine.
The inner eye stares through a cracked glass
without blinking, and reports its own view
of the signs presented.

Sight by Blindfold

I walked up the knoll
through the trees
to the cemetery and talked
with the dead.
They answered with names and dates,

I saw life ended on a name
and two dates.
I came to you to ask
if our faces marked with
shared tears, shared laughter
say nothing to us beyond
such simple history
and your hands over my eyes
gave me an answer
you never had to learn.

Virgin Prairie

This old squaw of a prairie
with no fence or furrow wrinkles
squats by a country cemetery
under the shelter of a lost deed.
She wraps herself in a blanket
of buffalo grass, beaded with
shooting stars, sweet alyssum,
fringed gentians, tiny yellow and
lavender petals, with wild roses
tangled in vines. She dreams
the memory of a wigwam empty now
save ashes whose breath rises
in ghost smoke of the past.

Yes, It Would

Wouldn't it be a gas some morning
to wake up loose as a goose
in the dew-spangled grass of dream
and not have to dress or fix

breakfast or answer the phone or run
for your life to meet a schedule,
but walked naked as a jay in the bright sun,
ignore newspapers
their headlines of wars and broken hearts,
eat what you want when you want it,
curl up your mind for a nap while
your hands and feet rest on featherbeds
of indolence, and the critic in you
lifts a leg to squirt on nice daisies
or sits on a branch to drop something
nasty on a passerby?

NINETEEN SEVENTY-FIVE

Chill Comfort

The sun rose, burned off the mist,
morning serene as a tranquilizer the dream,
busy traffic with its happy sound,
my stomach pleased with breakfast,
coffee aromatic, hot, waiting—
what more could I want?
An empty eggshell feeling
leaves me in a hollow of time,
pen heavy as a crowbar, paper blank
denies meaning to black marks.
All this because the damned telephone
said I couldn't see you today?
I look out the window,
even the bird feeder is empty.

Day after Day

The baby cries in its crib,
the young mother gives it
her startled glance to play with,
the father fingers his new moustaches,
packs anxieties in his briefcase,
holds up a finger for the wind,
sails to his office.
Beer in the icebox keeps better
than dollar bills, the rent wakes
and stares at the calendar,
a grocery list says the clock is fast,
why the hell wear out shoes
if no one smiles after the dance?
Who would die to be born again,
happiness stays in its mousehole,
the traps are all baited with despair—
a bottle of whiskey to take to church,
the sacred wafer to bribe the bar girls.

Each to Its Own Purpose

They said, don't use words
like epistemology in a poem,
use short, fat, beetle-browed
Anglo-Saxon words with
big butts, thick shoulders,
that clutch, hump, sweat, sleep,
that plant, grow, reap, store,
shake, fear, starve, haunt, die.
Epistemology, they said, in a poem
is like using a castrated bull
to settle your cows.
But I don't buy that, why castrate,

let him do what he was born to do.
It seems to me there's confusion here
between the use of a sieve and a bucket,
do you want to carry water or strain out pulp?
It's the joy of knowing that makes
the facts shine, or the Wise Men
would never have made their long trip,
nor any of us found our way
out of the dark wood where
we were lost.

The Groundhog

Scooped from his winter nest
by the icy fingers of the creek
(rampaging in a February thaw),
before his sleep ended, the groundhog
trundles across a field to our back door.
He does not beg, nor plead, nor—so far as
I know—pray, but waits expectantly
like a converted sinner for judgment.
Above him, from an open window,
I drop manna (kernels of corn) which
he collects and sits up like a teddy bear
to eat, then with no bow to providence
trundles off again.
He comes the next day and the next
accepting the crumbs of my benevolence
with never an upward look for the hand
that feeds him—he makes me wonder
if such a calamity would wake us
to accept unknown help on faith
without looking to heaven to see
if we are protected.

Hardened Arteries

When the office screwed a few bucks
out of you for the stenographer
who couldn't hack it after her surgery,
you bellyached to yourself all the way home.
You'd made it the hard way, you said.
Done without, cut corners, lived like a dog.
Even dumped Grandpa in the county home
after his dough ran out. Nobody ever gave you
anything. Let other people chew their
troubles, you had to swallow yours.
Over your steak and beer, you keep trying
to tune out that beggar's bell
calling up the ghosts of compassion.

High Winds and Low Pressures

The sun backs through a cloud,
points to rain spots on the
morning window, floods the table
and buttered toast while the coffeepot
chuckles and paper napkin hugs
knife-and-fork, the yellow gaze
of eggs stares from a plate and
salt-and-pepper shakers wear
stained faces.
It came with the morning paper,
still heavy with the storm that rocked
the house last night, glance through
the window at the oak tree's
broken branches, see the day's table
spread with domestic blessings and
turn to the headlines for
the world's unpleasant news.

Home Work

Today is cleaning day in the pens
hauling out rich ripe manure
to satisfy the hungry mouths,
the enormous appetite of growing plants.
Aw-w-w, who minds the muck,
it can be washed off and has a
sweeter flavor than the corrupt smell
of cities, the breath of greed, of men
knee-deep in servitude.
A servant to animals?
Well, they thrive, don't they,
the animals I feed, water, and bed down.
They don't shake my hand, or pat my back,
or plant a knife between my shoulders.
Labor with earth restores me, pavements
hurt my feet, the clout of the Pharisees,
bombs by Philistines make my eyes swim,
upset my balance, safe at home, free
among fields, I gaze at the moon
riding in the calm pond I was born with.

A Jog to Memory

The odor of wild honey
at this moment reminds me
of the bed from which we rose
without shame, without guilt,
and left the fragrance
of our discovery as real
as winds off the Spice Islands.

Happiness comes, happiness goes,
I do not expect perfume every day,

not in this world of ill winds.
We are what we are and the cry
we make to ourselves must be heard
somehow among our daily chores.
We hunt for signs to help us
remember the first garden
before we lost our way.

An Occasion

In the late afternoon
autumn's sun still warm,
in the eastern sky a hazy moon,
cornfields reaching from farm to farm,
at a picnic table among dry leaves
caught, you and I, in the net time weaves
day after day to enmesh all those
we know yet we stay more than friends
in this hamburger world with its paper rose
and struggle to cope with its odds and ends
and bear our capture without mocking to say
tomorrow today will be yesterday.

Outlived by Time

The empty hearse skimmed away
like a dead leaf chased by the wind,
pallbearers slipped off to their offices,
the church basement breathed
fresh coffee and stale odors,
he overlooked the grief masks of the
inheritors while he shook their hands.
He felt no worm of mortality webbing

his eighty-five-year-old face, only pain
from this latest wound.
His cane like a scythe whacked off
dandelion heads as he walked home,
the rewards of a walk home, home, home,
a shell to keep out strangers and the rain.
Pools of eyes under white-haired cliffs
reflected the shadows he shaped in words,
"Damn," he said softly, "every time
I see one of my friends, he's dead."

Plea for Persistence

Wait and begin again,
wait and begin again,
there is more to learn
than a hump for the spasm,
a pull for the bell,
a drink for salvation,
no church gives comfort
for the ransacked years
dumped in the ragbag of the past.
Trees bear blossoms each spring
even though the petals wither,
and who gathers the brown shreds
to keep memory green? Aw-w, memory,
grains of sand in an old shoe.
I tell you, strike home
no matter if the target blurs
or the gun wobbles. It is too late
when you doubt the strength
of your day's muscle. Take it,
take what comes, even windfalls,
even a blowsy romp in autumn lest
like Solomon, you got no heat.

Point of No Return

Grass in the cracks of the sidewalk,
cobwebs masking the door,
I toss the key from hand to hand,
this house where I lived before

shows me a rusted mailbox,
windows blinded by shades,
front steps tilted and broken,
the sense of my errand fades

as I think of the rooms' stale secrets,
is a wise man here or a clown
who would open a door he once padlocked—
why didn't he burn the place down!

Portrait of an Old Horse

I wonder what shaggy thoughts
lie back of the long bony face,
trimmed forelock between half-cocked ears,
eyes bugged out bright as brown-skinned glass,
sagging lip—mine droops in the mirror
when I neigh the hungry hope
fleshed behind bony brows.
He stands there switching flies,
shoulders worn, sunken collar sores
healed over with gray hairs
(my head full of gray hairs).
He pulled a plow, wagon, mower,
something, can't stop pulling,
he marches with a team as he
stands naked without his harness—
he'd go to meet a class even if

the classroom was empty,
what else could he do?
He never chased a butterfly
in his life or jumped a fence.
Now he's old, sway-backed,
scruffy-tailed, teeth smooth,
half-asleep, waits to be fed.

A Return to Facts

You check out the office
for the last time, lock the door,
turn in the key and you and your
battered briefcase, two old companions,
follow the stairs and down the hall
filled with years of your steps.
You bleed a little, feel empty days
open ahead, feel somehow betrayed
by the clock tick you never thought
to hear. Strange, how the future
shrinks to a row of yesterdays.
The hell with them let them mould
their way into history—old clothes
in a ragbag. The garden metaphor
seems foolish against real earth
when you work the seedbed with
your own hands. The hoe and rake
may be more enduring friends than
the ink-fed knives carving theses
into academic shape. Now on the camp stool
you reserve for holidays, sit and watch
the real thing, the actual sprouting seed
form green rows and climbing vines.
This is a way back to your beginnings,
cultivate a field of facts until
words fall away like dry pods.

Sad, the Way It Is

Stay, stay, pussy willow pussies,
stay, stay, bright daffodils,
little pigs grow into great big pigs,
sharp peaked mountains grind down to hills.

Sap bursts buds into leaves and petals,
leaves and petals cover the ground,
flocks of aunts admire new babies,
an old man in trouble, no one around.

Don't ring me the bells of winter,
chant in a chorus how staid stars seem,
just as well say a promise is forever
or that brooks and rivers run upstream.

Self-Portrait

The mirror lacks depth,
lacks the signature of mercy,
shows me a naked face, long, big ears,
narrow eyes, features unnoticed
by the inner eye. I am what I am
to the reflection. Break the glass
and behind it a bottle of aspirin.
Who said, "I have traveled widely
in Concord?" My tracks aren't meant
to be followed. I shadow the landscape
of mind with landmarks and forget them.
My roots don't show. Cut down a tree
to count the rings, my stump would be
different. A swollen seed, hatching egg,
a heifer dropping her first calf,
the pain of something broken, life draws

a first breath—I have seen it.
As I look into the glass, no vision
shines out, no stoic spirit, no halo
above gray hair, deep wrinkles,
scarred forehead, I cannot find myself here.
I lean toward tomorrow, a bricklayer
without bricks, a newsboy trying to collect,
an old farmer with empty pockets
impatient for a new year.

Stream and Tree

The stream's promise
of an easy bed could lull
a troubled man to sleep.
No dismay would alarm
the pastures nearby,
horses would still graze,
jays screech from a dying elm,
grasshoppers snap into
the depth of afternoon,
bluebottle flies attend
a dead rabbit.
But the young oak I lean against
grips earth firmly, reaches
toward the sun, grows into its future.
It makes my thoughts root deep
as I nod to the horses,
whistle at the jays,
drink from the stream and try
to think enough green signs
so I can go it alone.

Too Many Defeats Dull the Spirit

The worst was
too damn much rain,
the corn opening its first leaf,
the beans just breaking through—
you know a beanstalk
arches its back to open
the crust of ground and pulls
the leaves through after it.
Rain washed the earth down
like a silt glacier and
covered everything, smothered it,
killed it.
I had only a couple of low corners
but Henry Jensen lost all his bottom land.
He replanted twice, too late for corn
and still the beans could hardly
break through. It gave Henry
a kind of emotional seizure and
he stayed inside his house for a week.
His wife said he spent all his time
sitting in the bedroom under an umbrella,
but you have to allow for a woman
planting some ornamental borders
around the plain truth.

University

Morning light throws a wreath
over the buildings, wakes the clock tower,
mist lies on the grass, a butterfly
waits for the sun to dry its wings,
the sky's pages shine with color,
too high for a message from liberal arts.

The janitor shakes his mop
from a third-floor window, no one
hears the echoes of last night's music,
the silence rips like a silk cloth
when a cardinal by the graduate school
whistles and repeats.

A flag joins the top of the flagpole,
doors swing open, feet sound in the halls,
a student turns the key of his locker
and takes out a briefcase so lightweight
it might contain his future
and waits for the bell.

Outside summer dances with leaves,
midges swarm, balloons of dreams
rise unchecked to bump against the sky.

The Visitor

In the heat of the afternoon
I stopped for a drink and while
my sweat dried and hands relaxed
looked at my work. The corn showed
nary a weed, the plants dark green,
the third leaf showing, sun wakened,
a meadowlark bobbed on a fence post
and pumped out a trickle of song,
a morning glory climbed the gate post
I leaned against and barbed wire
ran shining along the field's edge
to protect my ownership.
A breath of air touched me softly
like a bird's wing across my face
and suddenly I felt like a stranger

who stayed here only by the sufferance
of growing things and I almost bowed
to the earth as a favored guest might
who was invited to stay out his visit.

Waiting

Waiting is not patience
it is a fisherman whose hook
caught in a sunken log
won't let go. He jerks the pole
this way and that while his shadow
jumps up and down the bank.
He gives his pole a yank but
the line does not break so he
climbs down the bank and gropes
for the log. His left wader fills
with water so he climbs back
with his heavy left leg and sits down
to empty out the water and stares
at his problem and pounds the bank
and talks excitedly to nobody there.

So when you wait for her to come
and an hour goes by and more
and you compose excited messages
for the telephone and curse
the empty door, remember the hook
in the sunken log.

A Woman and Her Wayward Garden

Maples and oaks turn scarlet,
grapes ripen, walnuts litter the ground,
the empty fields of October
fold their hands and grow quiet,
but the sun sheds warmth of another season
and signs of spring haunt my garden.
As if drowsy roots woke in their beds
an iris blooms, the syringa yields
one white flower, a forsythia branch
shows yellow stars, a lilac swells its buds,
and I am left, a wayward gardener
with green thoughts on an autumn day.

No one who lives here
knows how to tell the stranger
what it's like, the land I mean . . .
　ᖗ Landscape—Iowa

Abrasive Time

Just think how alert we would all need to be
some morning to catch the light just right
where it shines on the faces of things and see
the changes that happened during the night.

It's always the routine that day after day
we snatch at our breakfast and sweep the floors,
as if tired of our beds we hurry away
in the car, each one engaged with his chores.

So we do it over and over as children
over and over slide down a slope,
we crowd into aisles as cattle are driven,
tied by our nose-rings to destiny's rope.

We sew on buttons and mow the lawn,
lie in the sun and on Sundays nap,
and never notice how time soaks down
our cracks and crevices, dries our sap.

It happens at night, I think, when we sleep,
the ghosts of things worn-out share our beds.
Then slow as the slowest of creatures they creep,
the tarnish and rust from our feet to our heads.

As dust settles after the wind has died down
a flower wilts, a tree falls, gray on our faces
the webs form spun by spider unknown
if we search with our eyes only obvious places.

Can you notice the change overnight in the grass
how it turns pale and droops? How a deep well goes dry?
Though feet stumble, though eyes blur, they pass,
the long slow procession of things born to die.

At Least on the Surface

People who live in neighborhoods
learn how to tell "How are you?" from
"What do you want?" without a committee
report. This keeps us in good standing
with ourselves and with each other
at least on the surface where soft words
sometimes mask hard thoughts like,
"The son-of-a-bitch mows his lawn early
every Sunday morning!" We keep our hedges
trimmed, steps repaired, houses painted,
practice collective complaints over the
city's negligence in gathering dead leaves,
removing snow, fixing pavements, cracking down
on noisy cars and motorcycles. There is a
sprinkling of churchgoers, earnest souls,
a raft of parents hung up on the PTA.
The kids play both ends against the middle
by wearing Sunday School faces while they
sneak out to "learn about life." Eighth-grade
girls scamper out of sight, then stop and
light cigarettes, puffing and strutting with
the awkwardness known only by teenagers.
See? On the surface everything well-kept,
conscience-clean, paid-up, sunny-skies, all
respectable as a chrome-plated, plush-lined,
tinted-glass automobile, the kind we buy and drive.
But dark currents run underneath, rain keeps
the hay from being made, lightning strikes,
and blinds don't always cover windows.

Bluejay

Into the calm of morning as a stone breaks
the surface of a pond, where zinnias
uphold stiff colors and the air rises
in summer waves, a bluejay screeches.

In the oak's green house he cocks his head,
shuttered by leaves he strikes the view
with hungry eyes, alerted on his perch
by the sentinels of survival.

Look, deep in the corner of a pine tree,
a stir, tremble, a bequeath to his patience,
a robin leaves her nest of fledglings
and this appetite shaped in blue and white
closes its aim.

The mother wheels and cries, her ransacked home
bleeds in silence, the morning sighs on,
a cry harsh as metal triumphs, wings out
from the darkness of instinct on a bright day.

Born Again

He woke up when she died,
spread out life like a map,
noted historic markers,
ghost towns, campgrounds,
trails now paved, and
ownership, ownership everywhere—
too much tamed land.
He bucked like a bronco
in his thoughts but his hands
still watered the green valley.

The map showed roads like spokes
forking off to give him
a choice of horizons, a chance
to climb the high passes
for one more look.
Neighbors pretend to console him
but whisper behind their hands
as they watch him eat new fruit
from an old tree. He lets the grass
grow, explores a wilderness,
no one scolds him when he
rattles a key in the lock
at four in the morning.

Close Call

It was anger's shadow dimmed the room
as a shift of wind destroys the promise
of sun, where cold creeps in like treason,
snow bursts through the cloud's floor, air
in doorways whistles a harsh warning.
We disowned tears, joined hands, kept
the fire burning. While I swept out
the gray remnants of a quarrel, you stood
by a white sink in a blue apron, peeled
red apples under a yellow light and we
forced the storm outside where it
belonged.

Dirty Old Man's Poem

A dirty old man's poem
what shall I say.
I lust after girls.
I roll 'em in the hay?
A tomcat at night.
lie drunk in the gutter.
make witty remarks like,
"a girl's friend is her mutter?"
Too slow for a wolf.
a wild grape on a stem.
and girls who taste me
I'll squirt juice on them.

Evergreen Transformations

I. IN THE BEGINNING

"Who knocks on my door?" asks History.
"A bewildered confused student of yours
whose world asks more questions than it answers."
History asks, "Do you want facts or the truth?"
"You mean there is a difference?"
"My books record not what was said and done
but what men thought was said and done—
between the two truth sometimes leaks away."
In the beginning
one hundred years and more ago,
there was a building on a hill,
a shelter built for homeless children
made orphans by the storms of war.
This can be verified, some small research,
a spadeful or two dug from the past,
the bones are there, but the spirit?
What you call the truth lies elsewhere.

Ask the Phoenix that in deep Africa
flies to its secret tree and there in flames
consumes itself, then from the ash there rises
a brighter, more splendid vision of the bird.
There learn the truth of how the spirit lives.
When a date confronts us on the rock of ages
out of our human need we set a marker to say
we passed here. We lay stone on stone
to build a temple that keeps our testament
from oblivion's greedy hands, and by its altar
pray to be reborn.

II. IOWA STATE NORMAL SCHOOL

A temple of learning, let it stand
a marker to a noble aim, when claims
and counterclaims had burned away
something remained that shaped itself
inside the bricks and mortar, the empty rooms.
Wisdom teaches. Stronger than the tramp
of armed feet is an idea when its time
has come. Our country's frontier
maps more than Indian and the buffalo.
Listen to pages turned, lessons read,
the squeak of chalk on blackboards,
pencils on slates, the meager chime
of taxes from the General Fund won with
oak muscled will for the congregation
of the chosen few. This is what lived
after the campfires died, where they made
their stand, the pioneers who looked for
the promised land with its springs to quench
the thirst young men and women felt
as they blazed new paths to follow
away from the wheel rut road. Schools and
churches mark the trail of the pioneer,
and always the hope, ever the hope.

"New words for an old song," said History,
"that's mostly the way it is, or crack an egg
and release life, or plant a seed to spread
more seeds to rise from the decay of the
mother and wear her colors."

III. IOWA STATE TEACHERS COLLEGE

Begin, yes begin, urged the teacher, today's page
tomorrow will be yesterday's, who knows what star
the telescope will find and reveal its light,
what parasite confess its toxin to the microscope,
what flowers unfold after a strange fertility,
even the words we listen for will find a new voice
in the halls of learning to bring an answer
or a question for an answer to those who hear.
New walls must wait for ivy but cornerstones
contain the message they were built for.
The ghost of Gilchrist Hall remembers
the Bachelor of Didactics, but the new auditorium spoke firmly
for the new Bachelor of Arts, its voice still echoes down
our corridors. Laurel wreaths for the men and women
who tilled the fields of mind willing to wait
until a later season for the harvest. The way
of the pioneer is hard and often leads to an
unmarked grave. They who followed, tenured professors
of a later day, spoke in polished syllables
of their concern for the pitcher that goes too often
to the well and lies in broken shards, yet still
revered when the new pot names the potter from
an old design. "Now is the time . . . all brave men . . .
quick brown fox . . . the winter of our discontent . . ."
Signals from past spaces of learning strike the
antenna of a college listening in.
(Only when shadows fall as the light fades
does the bird transform itself.) Let a glimpse
of the way brighten eyes as young minds escape

the dark closet that has haunted men all their
lives. A student on one end of a log and a
professor on the other may make a university,
but buildings to house scholarship
have become the style. No matter, let life
be lived for its rewards—who dare say
it was wasted? The inspired dream lurks
in every corner.

Education, said History, is a two-edged knife
that cuts both ways and only he who knows
how to grasp the handle should test the blade.
One side may prune a dead branch from the
living tree, the other cut the tree down to
destroy the branch. Let each scholar wear a
placard saying, I am a dangerous person full
of signs and meanings, wielding the scalpel
of my trade to explore the body of culture,
until I prove my skill, you may not trust me.

History said, We live in the dark
not of caves only, we wear long shadows
cut to our measure by the shears of mind.
Cries of our prophets warn us as we plunge
down blind alleys to escape a future being
built from our playbox of thunderbolts.
A book may flash lightning, a page flare
with symbols, footnotes, engravings, words
that blaze to describe the fossils of
experience and we blink, wear dark glasses,
are dazzled. In flames the bird on its altar
reveals the miracle of resurrection that to us
seems not proven and like the sun blinds us
to its light.

IV. THE UNIVERSITY

The architecture of scholarship
survives, time may break stained-glass
windows and tumble stones, but the edifice
of faith and thought, poetry, art, harmony,
the probing sciences stands wherever men
have cherished it. Time, the vandal,
cannot tear it down, only men at war
with themselves in the heat of prejudice
can shake its walls. Scholarship walks
the corridors looking for open doors.
The petty politicians of the classrooms
squawk like parrots to repeat the thought
of wiser men, read coffee grounds as portents
and prove to students that a sow's ears
can be made from a silk purse. But the challenge
of the mountain streams out in its flag of snow
and hardy climbers roped together
spend their lives in the ascent. These are
the true masters who have worked their way
from the image in the rock to the star that
shaped it. All is not vanity, the skilled
workman from the past quarries the stones
to build today's chapel where students
begin their novitiate in the disciplines
of the humanities and sciences. Experience
is our dictionary. We learn its language
and meaning from our notebooks, words spoken
by the farmer, carpenter, priest and scholar.
We train our hands with thought, our minds
with the muscles of research, and with experiment.
Living is our aim, to learn to stand on
our own feet, speak our minds, find health
in the healing strength of our own character.
Now in the shelter of the University's
everlasting arms is the time to dream

of revolution, to hoist new banners over
old glories, to know the worth of bread
and cheese and wine. We are free to fly
the balloons of dreams, to trim the fat
from rich promises. The coming days,
shrouded in their anonymity, may wear
the scornful masks of the master of slaves
or the open faces of free men. The will
to choose lies with the mind and eye
of the beholder. Then shall we learn
that nature is ever reflected in the
spirit of ourselves where life, blood-warm,
may nourish itself on peace and wisdom.

Facts

I do not read portents,
bars of sunlight through a cloud,
a dog howling at night,
a bridge washed out,
a crow perched on a dead limb—
let some reader of oracles
interpret the signs.
I read on the day's work sheet
the facts of my existence,
corn to grind, pens to clean,
teach a calf to suck,
wrap roses for winter.
The wind rustles dead stalks,
says nothing I don't know,
my labor tongued hands assure me
that my sky is not falling
in spite of sickness, weather and age.

The Flower

The afternoon bent over
like a tired lily but you
spoke words shining as petals
just fresh from spring's root.
Though flowering trees, tulips,
the blue hyacinths, so bright
in their first array, fade in
the sun and shed pale ravellings
on the ground, today love blooms
in your eyes as if no flower
so whitely opened was ever spent.

Forked Road

It's hard to decide sometimes
whether to stay or go, to face
driving snow or stay by a warm fire.
But if you don't go, the little
sharp teeth of what you ought to do
will gnaw at your comfort until
you find fault with your dinner
and don't sleep well that night.
Even a small duty will give you
a hard time if you don't listen.
I know a farmer who turned his horses
out to pasture before he locked
the barn doors to prove he could
make up his mind without a nudge
from an old copybook. It's what
you learn from experience that teaches
you how to face a forked road.
I heard a forecast this morning that said,

"Showers and thunderstorms, otherwise
mostly clear."—Hard to beat that
for coming to grips with the weather
either inside or out.

Homecoming

So let's knock off for the day, I said,
The sun already had left the sky,
I picked up the last few bales of hay
And cooled my face till the sweat was dry.
We started the tractor and turned around
With a homeward pull in face and thought,
Two fields and a lane and at last the barn.
Someone was doing the chores, I caught
The sound of milking, I walked to the house
With nighthawks whistling above my head.
The door swung open to greet my step
And someone behind it still as a mouse,
Then lips saying all that the heart could say
To the farmer, home, at the close of day.

In a Country Cemetery in Iowa

Someone's been up here nights,
and in a hurry,
breaking the headstones.

And someone else,
with a little time to spare,
has mended them;

some farmer, I'd say,
who knows his welding.
He's stacked them up in

harnesses of iron,
old angle-iron and strap,
taking a little extra time

to file the welds down smooth.
Just passing through, you'd say
it looks like foolishness.

Instead of Honey

Let's get to work, time may be short with us,
clouds hang trembling from a lip of sky,
the wind waits behind the distant wood.
We lean on the arms of summer, and as bees
ruffle the clover blooms we search for a storm
of flavor to melt on eager tongues.

Dig for yourselves, turn the earth,
miraculous manna waits on your need
for last judgments when meadows lie down
in a tempest of frost, when the sun
runs south on wounded feet, when sap
dries in green veins. Who'll shovel your way
into heaven? Not I, my labor's too dear.

Come, spit on your hands,
those muscles tied to your head,
teach them. I tell you the day
crouches beside us watching,
and you are not saved.
Let the spade welcome the hand
that builds on rock.

Keep the Storm Outside

Rain patters on my roof
with the paws of a small animal
and the wind whisks its tail
down my fireplace chimney.
Snug in my solitude of blankets
under shelter of a roof I watch
leaves twist on their stems while
branches toss and rise like waves.
I comfort myself with this
moment of right action when I
keep the storm outside and lie here
in the calm of inner weather.

Lying in bed, listening to the rain,
secure under the arched hands of the
roof, in an embrace of blankets,
I squat in the cave of my mind before
a small fire and unpack the secret
comfort wrapped in thoughts and feelings.
Snug in my cave I inspect these
treasures while the feet of the rain
dance to the wind's tune on the roof.

Not artifacts and shards and fossils
of my past, no plaster-of-Paris replicas
on exhibit in public places, but precious
ore mining from the heart's mountains,
nuggets from its living streams, here are
mementos laid out on the blanket we
weave together, my dear, not yet finished,
its black border shot through with streaks
of despair and grief, but now brighter
colors of trust begin the pattern we
designed. Snug in my cave, hidden from

view, I think of you and warm myself
with the fire built from moments a man
gathers for his own sake for comfort
on a stormy day, under the shelter of
a stout roof aching to be discovered
by your need to share his fire.

Landscape—Iowa

No one who lives here
knows how to tell the stranger
what it's like, the land I mean,
farms all gently rolling,
squared off by roads and fences,
creased by streams, stubbled with groves,
a land not known by mountain's height
or tides of either ocean,
a land in its working clothes,
sweaty with dew, thick-skinned loam,
a match for the men who work it,
breathes dust and pollen, wears furrows
and meadows, endures drought and flood.
Muscles swell and bulge in horizons
of corn, lakes of purple alfalfa,
a land drunk on spring promises,
half-crazed with growth—I can no more
tell the secrets of its dark depths
than I can count the banners in a
farmer's eye at spring planting.

The Maid Who Served an Ogre

She washed the dishes, cleaned the sink,
mopped heel marks from the kitchen floor,
put out the garbage and made the beds
and walked to the grocery store.

But these chores did not fill her day
and she slipped out, a small brown mouse,
and breathless hid behind a hedge
because a man was in the house.

He spoke to her with kindness, still
she thought his glance stripped her for bed,
his lips swelled open buds, she sweat
with fear no matter what he said.

She cringed when she hung up his coat
as if strange hands played on her skin,
under her apron she hid a knife
at night when she brought his dinner in.

Mother

The photograph fades, turns yellow,
but the woman still sits erect
on a velvet chair, her piled hair
adorned with combs, her bodice tight and smooth,
sleeves in folds, her skirt billows,
one child at her feet, one beside her—
she is beautiful.
If time shadowed her proud smile
with work-worn hands, tremulous mouth,
the fierce hawks in her eyes
sent him howling like a beaten dog.
Her children remember the odor

of home-baked bread, a table bright
with silver, white with linen
where the farm rubbed its elbows,
numb fingers hanging out sheets
in freezing weather, young and hungry minds
fed with books and magazines from
her saved chicken money. She bent
like a tree in the wind, scarred by
wounds of love and labor.
But now in the picture she lifts
her beautiful proud head, innocent
of praise, of tears, or storm clouds
threatening the sky at sunset.

Muskrats in the Cornfield

Persuasion of rain and sun
makes stalks thicken, stretch up,
bulge with green sap, bathe in
chlorophyll, confirm my faith
in miracles.

In a pool by the tile's mouth
near the road, humped-up houses
like bubbles of straw belong to
invaders with sharp animal teeth.
Brown furry night sneakers
whoop it up among the cornstalks,
soft, luscious, green, juicy,
cut a swath in a widening arc
and leave a desert of stumps
like a cut over forest.

Instincts on four feet run with luck,
my tame daytime two-footed wits
limp snarling at any appetite
that makes a shambles of my seedwork.

Neighborhood in the Suburbs

Take our garbage cans, a man may be known
by what he throws away, a woman too.
The trash collects in bags and cans and waits
on the curb and the garbage smell almost hides
the smell of fear, of hate and despair,
of broken promises, stale toast of old quarrels.
If God were the garbageman—or the Devil—
these witnesses for judgment might speak too plainly
for His mercy to droppeth as a gentle dew,
or keep the bonfires of exposure from burning.
What shall we say of the cancelled checks
with forged signatures by the son in college,
the wrapping from a dress shoplifted at the
department store, long distance phone bills
to a lady of leisure in our convention city,
whiskey bottles from a childless couple,
whiskey bottles from a family of twelve,
a foetus wrapped in a towel where a daughter
is ill, decayed dressings from an old wound
where the miracle did not occur, pages from a
hymn book, "Rock of Ages" around a poison bottle,
a love letter marked *shit* in angry strokes?
We shall say nothing, the neighborhood knows
how to keep its secrets, we all know
the neighborhood mind and speak the
neighborhood tongue, we keep the order
that defends our ways—the rich have estates
and the poor have alleys but we own front doors
and the keys that lock them.

No News Is Good News

Having read the same names in the paper
day after day, having found after six months
of non-reading that the paper looks the same
as when I left off, having found that most
interviews leak top-secret inanities, I wonder
at the drab life the rest of us must lead.
We must feel passed over, neglected, when
we hear of the exciting lives of people who
make or break the laws. I thought it was a
marvellous adventure—truly a miracle—
when our cow had a calf, a small replica
of herself that comes out of her and is
on its feet and sucking in fifteen minutes—
but no news story. When the neighbors gave
a party (really farewell) to Selmer Stout
because he was dying of cancer—no headlines.
(Don't go away, I've almost finished.)
And when the kids in our block taught one
of the cops to jump rope—no headlines.
According to the news life just serves
us ordinary folk one empty plate after another.
And to keep from starving all I've got left
is the chance to call a massage parlor
that answers "outcalls only."

Praise

When I forced the flat land with seed
I hovered mother-like over the green uprising,
and routed smartweed, thwarted nettles,
mounded each folded shoot with earth,
nursed anxiety at my muscled breast.

When the harvest tide arose
I rode the waves of ripe grain
and filled my granaries—
now I can let the fields go.

Now I am free to close the gate
and turn and embrace my wayward acre
where willows wet their feet in a pool
at the tile's mouth, and flourish there
cattails, gentian, alder berries;
there the fence upholds the goldenrod
and black-eyed susans, the rank bull thistle
brooms his purple across the air,
Michaelmas daisies and yellow asters
and blue vervain win me with color—
these few wild moments of life
to stand dumb before, then praise
with naming.

The Snapshot

There we four sit, quick perched as sparrows on a wire,
no rheumy eyes, no trembling hands, no wheezing cough,
warm as lovers, snug in the moment's cloak,
the present like this and the future
a long way off.

It's the Holidays, cake, candles, hot punch drinks,
parties, dances, evenings around the fire,
the family all at home, guests, girls for the boys,
the snow outside smoothed by a fuzzy moon,
inside warm with desire.

A tree in the corner winked its colored lights,
we sang and mixed the steaming drinks with a laugh,
no misery of sickness and age dared enter the house,
my brother and I with our girls sat on the couch
for this photograph.

Still Heard but Faintly

What chime struck from the iron air
will warm us when a view from the window
shows the shrunken days
wrapped in clouds and shawls of snow.
Bitter winds remind us
of the glimpse of a sinking sun
on its far horizon.
We long for the glory
of a vision thrice betrayed
on this dark day when green shoots
are folded in roots asleep.
A distant chant reminds us
of an apocalypse in a stable
and we strain to hear a faint note
of peace and good will.

Take This Guy

Now take this guy next door,
always on the prod, kind of a preacher
about stuff like love instead of hate.
I say, shut up and keep your nose clean.
But not him, hell no, hit him and
he'd turn the other cheek. I ask him,

ever been in the army? Yes, he says,
even won a sharpshooter's medal.
Then how come, I says, you're so against
the military? He says, murder's wrong.
You're full of poopnagel, I says,
ever meet a payroll? Yes, he says,
I ran a small factory once.
What can you do with a guy like that?
He had polio, you know, limps a little.
Now he teaches music, gives programs,
sings in the choir—I got to hand
it to him. His relatives? Hell, they
never go near him, like to tuck him away
someplace, a nursing home or something.
They'd send flowers on his birthday
and quit feeling small the way they do
because they never had his guts.
He don't say so but it's like he sees
us weaned on plastic milk, I guess
he plants a different garden than we do.

That Kind of a Day

A kitten plays with a mouse,
the wind plays with the leaves.
(I see the sparrow's mate
rumpling her nest in the eaves.)

The cock on the weathervane
in the brisk air checks and swings.
(It was on this kind of day
she gave up the world of things.)

The grass lies stiff in frost
(her mouth lay soft on mine).
I answer a neighbor's salute,
I travel my boundary line.

(As dry as a locust's shell
and empty the heart that grieves.)
A kitten plays with a mouse,
the wind plays with the leaves.

Two Men

The stiff man scrubs his hands,
finds time to vote, respects money,
supports causes, hates guitar music,
suspects new neighbors, goes to church,
points out immorality in movies, TV,
books, schools, fears radicals, advises
children to work hard, save money,
marry a nice girl (boy), buy a home,
pay bills promptly, don't be late at night.

The supple man neglects dirty hands,
scoffs at voting, piles up debts,
sneers at posters, enjoys rock music,
skimps his work, swears at taxes,
enjoys women, gives money to radicals,
feels burdened by property, stretches
vacations, confides in children, aches
for their sorrows, prowls at night.

These two men share my table, bed,
office, home and sign their letters
with my name.

Veteran's Day

How thankful they should be,
the young men I know,
playing their games, excited by girls,
muscle in their language,
voices uneven as their beards.
Thunder on the horizon
breeds no fear in them, hand curved
to catch and throw, to clasp
books, shoulders, breasts,
never the chill steel of bayonet,
nor slimy vines, nor ooze of jungles,
beds in mud, blankets of snow.
How thankful, ears tuned to bellowing
transistors, shrieks and laughter,
teachers' assignments, coaches' bark,
not captain's command, nor sergeant's shout,
nor machine guns' clatter, nor the
stealthy step in the dark.
How thankful, their names scribbled
on papers, letters, walls, sign-ups,
not written in stone on a statue
in the town square where pigeons roost
and no one reads them. How thankful,
November 11 is just another day off
when bells and whistles sound at eleven A.M.

They died, goddam it, they died,
the young men for whom the bells toll,
never to have homes or wives or children,
or the comfort of a warm bed.

Winter Mood

Warm in mackinaw and boots I read
the morning's message on my land,
on frosty vines dead leaves post
news of the sap's descent, a mouse
scribbles in snow on the stump
of a fallen elm, a mile away a phrase
of smoke invokes a house, my breath
repeats itself in adjectives, and
flashing wings refute the stare
of vacant places, rabbit tracks define
the fencerow where a crow
in three sharp jeers mocks
my signature on the field's page.

Wonder of Hummingbirds

Glass cells of red syrup hang
from the eaves, glisten in sunlight,
colored needles trail threads of flight,
spin a web where my eyes struggle
helplessly. I am enthralled by this
moment to share my pulse with wingbeat,
the gray bench teeters under my shifting,
threads of color startle my eyes as if
a cloud of geranium petals drifted down
to excite the air.

I shall sit on a bench outside this morning
and watch the hummingbirds color the air
from feeder to feeder where red syrup glistens,
they weave in their flight an invisible snare

where I fall the victim by my own volition,
amazed to be part of a moment which binds
us together, they spin their threads of flight,
I am bound in such wonder a man seldom finds.

It fascinates me to share
the morning landscape with hummingbirds,
those arrow-gifted flights of color,
to think we spilled from the same pool
where life began in a greenscum
lit by sunlight. I sit in the shade
of an aspen while they thread the
branches and snap their wings at me
(as if this chance meeting did not
meet with their approval). I sit in
wonder how it feels to be shaped so,
while they seek flowers with bells
oozing honey, they stand off each other
in mid-air, fiercely as eagles.
Their rapid wingbeat finds no
comparison to my slow pulse but here
we are together, each a part of the
day's handful of space and neither of us
matched to the slow breath of the mountain
which grew from the same darkness into light.

Note: See a variant of this poem published in 1979.

Wren Logic

The stump braces its roots,
bumps off ax and spade,
shows no sign of giving up
before I do. I stop for breath,

watch two wrens build a nest in a
box hung in a tree. They poke sticks
through its round door and after
each success they flutter their wings
and sing their heads off. Plainly
all's well until they hoist a forked
twig too wide for the door. They turn
it over and over and end for end
as if a change in circumstances would
alter the situation. I smile in spite
of my blisters, knowing well the law
of facts, when suddenly the stick
goes in and I am left without a leg
to stand on before the miracle of
wren logic.

And I see, with limited view,
how a man on his threshold
feels betrayed by mischief
in his calendar.

      ✒ Calendar's Mischief

Alive and Well

Don't fill the kitchen pot
with husks and nutshells,
nor wear the gunny sack of
poverty of spirit, nor cut
paper dolls from the daily press
to prove you are upset.
Cold and snow may bury the yard
with sleeping drifts but this
won't starve the cocky sparrows.
Days tick off on the season's
slow clock but we tell time by
an evening's fire and the door
we opened for a starving kitten
on a naked afternoon. There may be
a lesson in the endurance of roots
but let us be thankful
their long sleep is not our habit.

Born Each Morning

What a shocking way to enter the world,
whacked on the back by a stranger,
held up naked by the heels
in front of strange women,
inspected like some plucked chicken.
But each morning I feel the exposure
when I slide from the warm and cozy
amniotic atmosphere of the bed
where all night I floated in a

suspension of sleep. Now like a yell
of beginning, the sharp glare of light,
the demand on arms and legs after night's
languor, groping through morning chores
when all still seems obscure in
the cloudy terminals of night. What carrot
leads the poor donkey from his stall
each morning, the dim image in the mirror
that brays his protest for his rebirth each day.

Calendar's Mischief

A day of shock,
sharp sense of loss
in the withered berry,
shrunken vine and grass
stiff with frost.
Now fireweed blooms,
pebbles gleam in creeks,
the trees astound me,
I have not worn such color
even in my thoughts.
The slant sun blazes
on a window, green bleeds
from the garden stems,
clouds peer from the horizon
as wind wraps the house
and moans down the chimney.
And I see, with limited view,
how a man on his threshold
feels betrayed by mischief
in his calendar.

Celebration of Losers

This morning the roadway lacks friends,
the bench by the garden side is empty.
A bicycle nestled against the arbor
seems remote and no dog enters to smell
the trees, hollow, air boasts no birds,
children stay hidden behind their echoes,
and, poor in spirit, I dredge up my
failures in recollection.

Shall I wear a black armband?
weep in my beer? Not me, boy,
I can still flap my wings.
Tonight I shall throw a dinner for
the mayor of Detroit, a boy soprano,
a major in shining boots, a priest,
and we shall eat crow together
and carve our habits into tombstones
and mark the New Year.

Cleaning the Barn

We put it off, not having to prove
we were Hercules, but the day came
(as it always does with work not done)
when we took our forks, spit on our hands,
hung our coats on a nail and started.
All winter the calves tramped straw bedding
to hard-packed manure with a yellow smell,
tied in with straw and two feet thick,
every forkful strained our shoulders,
with every forkful we grew thick grass
on meadows where we spread this waste
from the farm's gut, remains of corn and hay

back to the fields again. It was a place
of odors, incense to bless the land,
we tugged, pulled, swore, joked,
strained with sweat and our slippery loads,
dregs of harvest for another harvest.
A spring day on the wheel of seasons,
when the pen was clean we smelled to high heaven,
lame in our muscles, weary beyond rest,
we picked up our coats, banged the forks
into their racks, made our bed on a
bale of hay, heard for applause
a banging barn door.

Daydream

Warmed to drowsiness by the
autumn sun I stopped the tractor
at the end of the field, closed
my eyes against the black furrows
in the spell of another autumn day,
years ago.

A young woman in a red suit,
tousled hair shining, frolicking
with her dog under the trees.
Branches above her trickled leaves,
a red maple dropped one in her hair,
the dog raced in a circle.

No one I knew, still I could see her
alive with color and motion,
long legs flying, arms outstretched
as if to embrace the day, all warm,
young, happy as if no grief or age
or loneliness could spoil this joy.

Each Day Alive

The desk calendar
where I turn a page each morning
reveals no secrets between
yesterday and tomorrow. I try
to focus on its use and write
notes on the pages, addresses,
telephone numbers and memos
that assume the future will
be true. I know that somewhere
a plow turns earth, a seed sprouts,
a stalk rises—a resurrection
by faith the earth has always kept.
And somewhere a man grows
one day older as he turns his
calendar. But it keeps secret
the day . . . yet I don't pry
or guess, and refuse to wish back
my want to hear a mermaid sing
or see the rose of sharon bloom.
A gray-haired man digs out
dandelions and shares the interest
of a robin on nest duty that sings
and chirps about the miracle
of eggs.

Eighty Birthdays

This cake, a snow-topped hill,
bare, not eighty candles to march
with flaming banners as a victory
over time. No, the decorator
with his spurting artery stained
a red 80 against the white.

If I could blow out eighty candles
and make a wish, I would wish
for a new body, strong as a tree trunk,
hungry for love as a stallion
searching the meadow for thighs
hidden in the grass.
I ride this old donkey,
a trembling beast, lame-footed,
worn teeth, blind to directions . . .
He still haunts me, my stranger,
the sturdy-footed memory
with the ape still in his heart
who strayed through the country
gathering grapes and girl's cries,
kin to the dawn man who gnawed bones
and painted trophies
on his cave's wall.

Emeritus

He cleans out the file and crams
the wastebasket with dog-eared hopes
stale as lecture notes and grade books.
He walks, from his desk to the door,
a path worn deep in time, turns the key—
a gardener at the end of his season.
He has worn his degrees like medals,
let them tarnish in the box of age.
He waves a brief hand at a bushy-tailed
young scholar busting his gut to find words
that will startle his first faculty meeting.

The Enemy

That girl who now switches
her tail, juts her breasts,
struts her wares, is scared in
her blood as a rabbit that knows
the hawk waits. All that flesh
in bloom for the summer, the
withering touch of her calendar
still hidden. Silently she begs
in her need for the lustful eye
to seize her in its talons, for
the gardener's hand to pluck her
while her perfume lasts. She denies
the grinning skull behind her cheeks,
a skeleton's bones in those long
brown, lascivious legs, those soft
embracing arms. Yet she knows
the ambush where her enemy lurks,
and her lips open in a laugh
shaped like a shriek of terror.

Escape Artist

Well, well, so this is the way
he answers the call to come out,
sulks in his study with his thumb
up his ass waiting for a gush of
warm pity from his wife's eyes. He plays
the role from memory, slumped in a chair,
eyes staring, fingering his chin
as if he could read signs there, signs
of the tragic hero who has been wounded
by a sword of words his wife used to
slit his disguise and reveal the man,

the husband and father with work to do,
decisions to make, a home to support.
But now he takes it on the lam,
tries to make a dramatic exit to this room
where he slumps, peeking between
his spread fingers for just one clue
that the audience appreciates the act
enough for the show to go on.

Flight and Return

The locked house next door
now shows signs of life,
people have moved in,
a man and his wife.

Don't let the word spread,
please keep the kids quiet,
don't question the mailman,
folks might start a riot

if a few of them knew
they had come back again
to a place no one thought
would be occupied when

the owners moved out,
sold the place for a song,
pulled shades down for grief,
for right turned to wrong,

as the floors of a heart
cave in under the weight
of stone words piled up
by the white hands of hate.

Growing Up

It is time to leave the grove,
the warm dark secret embrace of trees,
the wigwam of horse blankets and
maple poles, the campfires where we ate
half-baked potatoes and charred sweet corn.
The years have straddled our backs
and spurred us into the open sky beyond
the forest paths we traveled
to a field alive with its sowing.
This is the temple of work marked by
the stations of sweat and callouses.
Now the dung loader and tractor's voice
will send anniversary greetings
to our knees and shoulders, and a
mouldy saddle and rusty bit offer
proof of our fleet-footed pony.
Come out of the woods, the snakes
chuckle in the gardens, long windows
of the mind look out on auction sales
flying their pennants along the tired
main street of property.

Hostility to Order

Today the sun's eye
curls green leaves,
stares me down, earth
under my steps cracks
in dry protest. What?
A conspiracy? I am no
outcast, leper, pariah
knocking at the gates.
I own my homestead and

work it to impose discipline,
straight rows, weedless fields.
I take my stand here and now
to ripen seeds into harvest.
I do not cringe from the sun's
glare nor earth's apostasy.
But the still room's empty
doorway, the loneliness
(after you left on your long journey)
persuades me again of the hostility
to order in my world.

I Set My Chair

I set my chair on the driveway
and try to feel my way
into the evening solitude
as the sun and wind both call
it a day and walk over the hill.
I want a drink from the well
of silence, I want to feel
the green hand of twilight
full of its own quiet
touch my face.
Just merge, I said to myself,
into this country of stillness
as if you were a tree or wave of grass
where no one shouts or starts machines.
But the mood did not come at my call
and all I did was to strike at a swarm
of gnats around my head and swear
at a kid on a motorcycle
who had left its muffler at home.
I watch as the twilight without
a murmur frees the sky of light,

I shed a coat of hot summer sun
and shawl myself in silence.
Not quite, the motorcycle spurts
a smoke ring of obscenities—
the vulgarity of the young
is beyond apology—so I lean back
and rest my head on the stillness,
absorbed by the holy calm
as the day dries its seat and
shuts the door. Here, so still
the air seems to hold its breath,
is a transcendence of natural things
I cannot imitate. Wrapped in the folds
of my efforts, held in the hollow
of a tree's shadow, my head buzzes
with a swarm of thoughts like gnats
as if a hole had been torn in
my screen of meditation.

It Never Went Away

In daytime the cellar seemed safe,
whatever hid there, slept, or rested
or changed shape. The jars sat primly
on shelves, potato bin and apple barrel
breathed their odors, a mousetrap
guarded a corner, a smoked ham hung
from a beam, all friendly, at your service.
But at night it came out. Even armed
with a lantern you could hear it, a sigh,
scrape of claws, sudden shadow on the wall,
a slight hiss through bared teeth.
You climbed the stairs backward, lantern
held in front, daring it to come, afraid
to turn your back. Upstairs you were thankful

to be rescued. It still lay in wait, even when
you grew up and were ashamed to tell it.
You, late night comer, braced your foot
against the garage and fled for your life
to the back door, thankful for Carlo's bark,
a chance to dry your sweat.

A man woke from a troubled dream, got up,
turned on all the lights, searched the house.
Stepped outside, fired his shotgun twice
into the darkness to say who is master here.

Lock the Door

Now you have burned the letters—
did you save one? No, no, let them all go.
The afternoon drifts into twilight,
the peace of evening shadows the silence
of an empty house where emptiness
drains your eyes of tears,
if you could still weep.
You are no priest with holy water
to wash the past from your hands,
revive the dead plant in its dry earth
hanging by the window, nor wipe
the dust from the tables once altars
for fresh flowers.
Do you sweat to restore your pictures,
or do you sweat here to prove the owner
will not let his books mold,
the dresses hang for strangers to discard?
You walk the floor to make a sound
to keep you company, wipe down spiderwebs
as if the years lay in wait to trap you
in the snare of your own spinning.

Flies lie here that have forgotten flight,
the fireplace sits in its ashes,
no scouring powder under the sink
to scrub the stains from the linoleum
you lock the door when you go out
burdened by the calendar.
There is no sorrow as desperate
as the memory of happy days
when you are sick, old and alone.

Not Born Again

This land partly from me,
given back all the years
of my slow death where I
discarded skin after skin,
layers of growth sloughed off
to make earth sloughed off
to make earth, I shed myself here.

Here fingernails I pared,
there an old jacket in shreds,
a rubber boot left in a tile ditch,
a notebook on calving time
dissolving in manure, a straw hat
blown off in a field, and everywhere
drops of sweat, pee beside the
corner post—all part of me
going back to make land and grow
whatever will grow. Immortality?
Who said Immortality?
Nothing like me in the morning glory bell,
thistles resemble nothing in me,
foxtail and smartweeds sport no features
of mine—my crops? They grow

the way I plant them.
Something of me goes back to earth
in a stream of ashes burned
from my life until I blow away
like a dried leaf yet with no features
for a wild rose to copy.

One Way for an Answer

No way, just no way,
to question a mountain
unless you climb a rock face
and learn its features.
Your hands and feet hunt for
steps and holds, your eyes watch
for a crumbling ledge, loose bush,
trees with tired roots and decayed.
Mountains weather,
you must be alert for change,
last year's solid shelf
is this year's danger. My uncle says
if mountains weren't the way they are
they wouldn't exist—he has climbed them all
from a comfortable chair in his study.
I think differently, I think you must
come to grips with the mountain,
scrape your knees, bruise your hands,
admire with wonder trees and flowers,
how they stand up straight on steep slopes,
crawl on your belly, suck in thin air,
risk the fall that awaits you,
roped, shod, gloved, you think with muscles
to reach the top. There in the lonely peace
above clouds, in the roar of the wind,

you ask your questions knowing
you have earned the answer.
Truth comes slow from mountain silence,
you can hear it only after
the trial has proved you—
otherwise there is no way,
no way, no way . . .

The Promise Seems True

Snow wastes away, icicles rot,
tax receipts describe the land
you walk in rubber boots.
The gate rips your sleeve with a
loose wire, an arch of cornstalks
snares your foot, the waterway
up which you walk trips you with
a mat of weeds, a hen pheasant soars
from underfoot, the sun squints
in your eyes. Have you read this page
plain in the mud, or its legend
about the mustard seed or the fool
with green eyes who gave thanks for manure?
You trudge past rows of stalks, broken
by iron teeth, a half-shelled ear
of corn, rabbit signs, fringes of
dead grass, a crevice where a gulley
starts—do you remember when this land
was the land of hope? You breathe hard,
damp March air, slush in your path,
the year marks you older, but still,
in your cells, lit caves ago, spring's fire,
stir, warmth, makes the promise seem true.

The Road

It opened the way
from our farm to town,
a road between two fences.
People weave paths in a net
to catch distances and tie
them together, a way to
the outside and make us
travelers with a pocketful
of errands.
Like a hunchback with a limp
and a hitch we troubled our way
home in axle-deep mud, horse-high
drifts, a smother of dust,
in wagons and sleighs with logs,
coal, flour, sugar, salt
(barrels of salt, 100 pounds of flour),
with the tramp of cattle and hogs
on the way to the butcher, eggs
for the grocer, the road heard
the doctor's wild team at midnight
and the pad pad of children's feet
indentured in the country school
to teachers with more will than knowledge.

Now the road threads the country
with a carpet of asphalt and the
snowplow grunts a wide track, blind
to the ghosts of straining men and horses.
One winter each evening I ran
the distance from high school
to warm-lighted supper table.
Tracks and trails lie mixed, my fold,
neighbors, horse buyers, cattle traders,
lightning rod salesmen and the

icicle-covered, heat-wrapped,
dust-blind mailman and his load.
Wagons, buggies, sleighs entombed
in museums of memory along with
drained sloughs, sprayed pussy willows,
and no wild flag decorates the tile's mouth.

No, the husking pegs are hung up
and the lanterns blown out.
A man with years in his eyes wonders
if life is only the wearing out
of boot soles.

Same Thing but Different

The paperboy slammed the screen door
as he always does two jumps ahead
of my alarm clock and gets me up to
wash my face, shave and dress. Then
the mailman banged the lid of the
mailbox as he does each day, and the
garbage men tossed the lids of the
cans on the ground the way they do,
and the meter man whistled his way
down the basement steps always
off-key. And I prodded with surprise
into the belly of my thoughts
to ask how this routine could replay
itself so casually as if your absence
didn't matter and damned if I didn't
burn the toast and let the coffeepot
boil over explaining this rip-off
to my conscience.

Shaped by Names

You must exist somewhere
back of the trellis of the names
I give you. I keep flinging
words like blossoms over the
lattice to fill the emptiness
if you are not there.

My tongue spells out syllables
like nets to catch you where
you drift on time's stream
that flows away from me. I search
for sounds that form a name
to bring you into the light.

I chant a rune that should
return you to the human shape
I knew, I ask you to appear.
If you are not my names for you
I am not who I was, I have
no place to go, my tongue knotted with silence.

Song

In *now* time beg the sun hold still
the sundial's shadow, on your hair
petals like apple blossom words
describe the light crown shining there.

But *then* time, oh, oh, wish it away,
or it will catch us unaware,
and breath that warmed our words as slow
as winter's crystals fill the air.

Surprise

Some friends of ours decided to
make a little money on the side
and grow mushrooms. They covered
the garage floor with dirt, sprinkled
the spore over it, wet it down and
hoped for the best. But nothing,
absolutely nothing happened. After
a few months they shoveled out
the earth, spread it on the lawn,
cleaned the garage. After the first
warm June rain the lawn mushroomed
with mushrooms.

Note: See also "Surprise," an entirely different poem, published in 1957.

Susanna and the Elders

Let us put thought aside
and imagine a pool
clear, water smooth as the
cheek of a still moment.
Hide it in a nest of fern fronds
above the grass, beneath the trees.
What balance, delicate,
quiet as a caught breath,
sustains interlaced images
grown used to each other.

Now stir the depths and produce
the shape of a girl, she wears
the air of innocent youth,
nude of course (please do not
escape into fantasy, we have

more work to do), she worships
the secret soul of the place,
the tension tightens but her nakedness
keeps the harmony unbroken.
She smiles at herself, then
shatters the mirror with her foot,
joins the pool up to her breasts.
Shadows hold their breath,
trees, flowers, ferns and water
wait for the spirit to speak
and with its silence become a
garland in the ritual of the unexplored.
(Now comes the bad part.) Like trumpets
of triumph the brassy eyes of the Elders
tumble the walls of privacy and a
startled gasp erects no shelter.
Communion bread molds, wine sours,
innocence finds no wilderness
safe from barbarians' hands.

There Must Be Somewhere to Go

Wait for me, wait for me,
the small bird chirruped,
but her face turned into
a cracked mirror that reflected
only half of the way
she had to go.
She had learned the song
by heart but now the direction
was new, her feet felt lost
where all the signposts
spoke a different language.
She bowed to the flowers
she remembered, and one old oak

her father had planted,
and took a chance the way
led somewhere.
Now only a stranger would open
the door she closed and he would be
surprised that the dust
had settled, as for a bed,
he would have to make his own.

Ute Cemetery

Gravestones lean every which way,
some, uprooted, lie flat. Grass
contests with weeds, the fence of
split rails unmakes itself
where the posts rot. A clump of
fireweed blazes beside stalks of
lupine as if neglect could not
erase all memorials. One wooden slab
says, "Soldier, 25th Infantry,
Illinois." Death does not need
his name. All the Indians lie heaped
under a long mound, not even marked
"Warrior." Here passion sleeps
in the graves. The yells and cries,
the hot bullets of Meeker Flats
awake no echoes, rouse no memories,
speak only from yellow pages
of an old newspaper. Life became
death with no meaning for today's
tourist. No one remembers the bitter
struggle, the lost cause, the bravery
in victory and defeat. No one even
remembers the cemetery.

Vacation in Colorado

The street's hullabaloo tramps
through the morning with an armful
of tradition faded by motel signs.
He hoisted a backpack and fled
to the mountain. The stream ran clear,
a Stellar's jay jeered, aspen leaves
whirled, rocks gripped his shoes,
the sun burned off the fog—too
burned off clouds back of his eyes.

His glance circled, wilderness paths
offered directions but a flag of smoke
led him like a compass needle.
When he broke through the underbrush
he stared at the town dump, burning trash,
old mattresses, piles of papers, tin cans.
His eyes closed over the bright image
of a solitary campfire on a rock ledge
blanketed with pink columbine.

The Wall

A door builds a strange wall
with two sides,
one to let you out,
one to let you in.
A 4′8″ piece of wood
separates two worlds
we explore at our own risk.
Sometimes the worlds mingle
in summer when the door swings wide,
maybe a good thing, maybe not,

I do not want street's traffic
in my living room nor
the privacy of my bathroom
exposed on the front lawn.
The threat of the outside
to invade the inside
keeps me awake
when I should be sleeping,
but a rasp-voiced key
sounds an ALL'S WELL
to protect my sanctuary.

The Way It Is

Prepare the ground, I told her,
channel a straight row, select
the seeds, drop them in the
open furrow, and cover them.
Observe these facts, I said, to keep
a garden from being helter skelter.
A radish seed won't become a turnip
because it's in a turnip row.
Seeds carry instructions,
even know the season, look how corn
sweats and heats at planting time.
(Lectures in her ears,
a mosquito buzz in bed.)

Why tug nature's skirts, she asked?
Let things grow their own way,
all this digging and raking and
pulling a string tight just to make
a straight row—does a radish care?
Why not crooked rows, room for more

seeds? Look at you pulling weeds,
don't weeds have rights, aren't they
alive with a will to grow?

I chopped angrily, hoed out
a young cabbage plant, left
a thistle standing.

Wedding Anniversary

A frightening day
for a celebration,
Abel Jones mucked up his mind
on corncob thoughts
when a screech owl hooted
churning his guts.
He saw his hopes
stunted, twisted, bare
from too much rain in April,
too much sun in July,
and the harvest in sackcloth and ashes
reminded him of the owl's warning.
But when a dry leaf
from a dying tree
dropped in his shirt
just out of reach
he beat his wife because it all
had to be somebody's fault.
"He ain't mean," she told the judge,
"he just ain't thoughtful."

Whatever Happened

When I was young I discovered
a new country inhabited by folk
who lived for my fear and pleasure
in an acorn cup or castle of cloud
or asleep behind a wall of roses.
I walked the paths of Sherwood Forest
or sank underground where a gnomelike smith
forged a sword and I killed the dragon.
I became a prince, then a giant,
I snatched Excalibur from the white hand
of the Lady of the Lake, sat at the
Round Table, rescued my mother from
a witch's spell, put her in charge
of the King and his men and lived in
the whoop and glory of my own world.

Now on a street of dying elms I puzzle
over the dull prose style of work and worry.
Where did the magic go, the wonder
that armed me with my power each morning,
let me revenge my tears and punishments.
What flip of calendar leaves brought me
to this bow-legged street, this boxlike house,
this mirror where I see an endless stretch
of suburbs, lawns, houses, meetings,
parties, PTA, Rotary Club, golf at four,
bridge at eight, who knows the time.

I let the princess die, the giant win,
the wizard destroy the castle, the witch
survive to eat the children, I forgot the way
to Sherwood Forest, have never kept my vow
to kill the wolf, find the foot to fit
the slipper. I am charged by myself
with murder, wear dark glasses, wear gloves,

false teeth, paid off with a sports car,
swimming pool, tax exempts, stylish wife,
a butt for statistics, gelded by habits,
indicted and condemned by the voice
of facts.

Who? Who?

Do you ever stop to wonder—
say, right now, this morning—
what you'd see in the mirror
with your mask off?
Oh, I don't mean casual glimpses
when you are shaving,
or combing your hair,
or cleaning out blackheads,
when you hardly see anybody at all.
Nor when you play a role,
a time when you are jealous
and thoughts about the girl
cut like fine wires and your face snarls,
or maybe at a party you took
one drink too many and made
an ass of yourself and you can see
the shamed look in the eyes all right.
No, I mean eyeball to eyeball,
you look that guy in the mirror
right in the face without any cover-up
and, my god, he's a stranger,
someone you never saw before.
A face drowned in a pool of glass
floats gently on the surface
caught in the drifting weeds of time,
mute in the shadow of my question,
Who, who are you?

The Will to Possess

Shoemaker had some Bokhara seed to sell,
the neighbors hurried to buy, filled with hope.
You'd think the seed had been blessed by the Pope,
how the word got out, none of us would tell.

Rumor whispered, here was a special seed.
I guess it's natural we keep looking for
a bigger crop than we've ever had before.
Rain lurks in every cloud when you're in need.

But still we didn't know what the seed would grow,
the hint and secrecy just tempted us that day.
What we could count on Shoemaker wouldn't say;
here was his price and here was the seed to sow.

In spite of this we felt the urge to buy
this gold-husked seed, strange, with a foreign name
(knowing that hope and harvest are not the same)
we couldn't resist the gamble. We had to buy.

Words That Smell Bad

Neighbor, your "friendly" note arrived
via the mailman and I wondered if we
weren't speaking or if you had bronchitis.
I am with you in keeping trim yards
and a clean alley. I will prune the
tree limb that overhangs your line,
pick up the beer cans from the picnic table,
level the pile of dirt where I dug out
the elm stump. If you will clean your
Sunday papers out of my hedge, shore up
your wall spilling on my lawn, collect

the turds from the hound you loose
after dark to run through my backyard.
Let us define our views on cleanliness
and order, we Americans have a knack for
instructing our neighbors. We who live
with polluted water, smog, junkyards and
the detritus from a people who litter
streets with their crap and all the poop
that squirts from our bottles of amusement.
Sure, we say, clean, clean up, clean up the
blacks, the colleges, the u.n., Cuba, the
whole caboodle, the world needs our deodorant.
Once a game warden sniffed around my father
for pheasant shot out of season and my father
said, "Take your nose out of my ass."
Neighbor, I wish I had thought of that.

NINETEEN SEVENTY-EIGHT

At Least Once a Problem Solved

Sometimes I feel like a shadow
searching for its body but today
I rubbed out the copy and found the
original man. This young heifer,
she couldn't birth her calf, and the
straining, struggle, bawling had
gone on long enough, she called for help.
The veterinarian wasn't in, the girl said,
but she would leave a message. And let
the heifer die? I washed my hands,
soaped my arm and went in. As if he
had rejected the outside the calf lay

wrong way to. "Breach presentation,"
the textbooks say. I couldn't budge him,
and the suction sapped my strength until
the arm seemed useless. Have you ever
thrust an arm into a cow's vagina to
turn the foetus? You know the problem.
But I rode to the rescue on desperate
measures. Clipped the hair on her right side,
honed the edge of a butcher knife, slit
her side and pulled out the calf. A little
bull, stood on quivering feet. I sewed her
up with a darning needle, the calf sucked,
she licked it, chewed her cud. Now I want
to wear a big grin and sit in the front yard
under a flashing sign that says, "Here a man
once rose to the occasion."

Bereaved

Granted, a meeting with her,
on the steps, in the hall, or a
room, granted too, an occasion,
return of a book, a business talk,
casual invitation, what occurred
seemed on the surface scarcely
worth mentioning. She made up
a smile, offhand greeting, an eddy
in the day's tide. But out of her words
welled tears, grief of eyes overflowing,
cheeks caught in the grimace of the
lonely of heart.
I told her there is the sudden break
called death, and the long suffering
called death, and we are not free
to choose, the end is the same.

Only you can speak for your lonely bed.
You cannot depend on us, the day comes
when you make your wailing wall private,
not to be seen by family or friends,
you keep your passion to yourself,
let the wound heal slowly.

But she was not comforted.

Birth Pains

I do not remember birth pains
nor the indignity of being slapped on
the back by masked men, held naked
by the ankles before strange women,
inspected like an archeological specimen,
no, I do not remember.
But to be born again each morning,
to leave the warm, cozy, amniotic
safety of the bed where all night long
I floated in a suspension of sleep,
this is where the agony starts,
the pain of beginning. The sharp glare
of light on helpless eyes, cruel demand
on arms and legs to move, the torment
of flexing a muscle still paralyzed
by night's languor, or make a sound,
some gesture of hope, when all seems
obscured in the cloudy terminals of
darkness. What carrot, honey, flower
can lead the donkey, the poor ass,
to morning's duties? Still stained with
birthmarks I face the mirror and the
rubble of my face reminds me of an
abandoned movie set, the façade crumbling.

Change in Appetites

We had a hired man whose remarks
seemed comical because he had a
different outlook than we did. In the
spring the farm bulges with birth,
generation and gestation, the boar
having the sows, the stud the mares,
the bull the cows, birds hopping it
wherever you looked, even the shelled
corn in the bin moist and heating.
This is the farm's business and we
go about our work as a matter of fact,
and jot down dates in a soiled notebook,
and work up the fields with an eye
on the weather. One day when rain
drove us into the barn we leaned on
a door waiting for the sun to come out.
Worms lay on top of the ground, birds
had a thanksgiving, this barred rock
rooster took out after a hen and just
as he caught her he saw a worm beside
her and stopped to eat it. Our hired man
nodded and said, "I wasn't never that hungry."

The Cure

The bush at the corner of the house
explodes softly in sprays of yellow stars.
My last step ended a pilgrimage
I should never have begun, but how lucky
I am to see this forsythia
prompted by roots to its spring duty.
The time spent trudging up and down
in strange cities picked my pockets

of a promised future and led me into
blind alleys filled
with garbage cans.
Let a bellyful of journeys teach you
homesickness; trains run late though
each station chalks up timetables
and you flip a coin
whether you go or stay.
I want to say something for
cultivating the ground you stand on
before you lie in it—and when
did you see anything as lovely and familiar
as this forsythia in full bloom.

A Disowner

Not my world today
I find ghouls
in the graves of my ancestors,
jackals yapping over a lion's skin.
I live where the two-faced man,
the split tongue, mocking applause,
hiss of envy, poison smile,
owns the time.
It takes courage
to stand by your name when somewhere
a computer records your missteps,
spies on your bathroom recess.

The land keeps its promises
where even a barren field
brings a crop of weeds to harvest.
I find no duplicity in an ear of corn,
no moral decay in a brood sow,
I belong to furrows and fencerows.

I was not born to wear out my boots
chasing down a paved street
calling for a policeman.

A Hawk Is Not a Rabbit

He got the message!
A birthday gift from his son
(and daughter-in-law) who
kept his house, a certificate
for a corner room in
Retirement Manor.

He tramped out to the garden,
whacked off a few dry heads
with his cane, sat on his campstool
and stared at the landscape.
It stared back. He tore the
certificate to shreds and poked
the pieces into the dirt.

His wispy white hair stood up
in a challenging crest,
his hands trembled as anger
stiffened to pride, never a hawk
to be trapped like a rabbit.

The Inevitable Words Like Signposts

This morning's paper carried a story
that stabbed me in the soft underbelly
of memory where I am most vulnerable.
Another old friend had left the field
and closed the gate behind him.

I walk back along the road until
those nights appear when we played
poker, drank prohibition booze and
harangued like pitchmen at a county fair.
Mac Kantor Don Murphy Cliff Millen
Stuffy Walters Viggo Justesen
names from the great days.

Now in my thoughts I hold a quiet
service with the candles and altar
we knelt before hoping our prayers
reached the Surveyor who drew
the maps of our future. But in these days
only the inevitable words like signposts
mark the way to the autumn woods
where leaves fall.

It Could Be Worse, Maybe

My god, such a night!
A charley horse in my leg,
muscle spasms in my mind
a desert of sleeplessness
filled with thorny reminders
to prick a tender conscience.
A parade of gulped-down pills,
a rumpled bed, what provokes this
shabby treatment the night gives me?
Morning breaks my shoulders
with the load of another day.
The sun shines brightly, birds
chant hymns of their own worship,
leaves glitter with their usual
jewels of dew, enough wind to make
the flowers nod approval.

And here I am stale as an ashtray
of cigar butts waiting, just daring
someone to smile and say Good Morning.

Learning

Sometimes you must break in
a new neighbor as you would
a young colt. This youngster,
just married, first time on his
own place spooked easily at my
casual suggestions. He'd tend
to his business, you tend to yours.
A little shaggy there, Buster,
I thought, you need to be curried
and have your mane trimmed.
His cows broke into my cornfield,
I drove them out, pieced the wire
enough to hold for the moment and
drove around and told him.
Too bad, he said, hope my cows don't bloat.
What about my corn I asked.
Keep up your fence, he answered.
Fences are shared where properties join,
I told him, half yours, half mine.
What? he asked.
Look, I said, you walk around your farm
counterclockwise, the first half
of the fence on the right-hand side is yours.
We have eighty rods of fence
between us, forty rods is yours
and that is where your cows broke through.
He shook his head, I never knew it,
never knew it, he said.
I'll help you fix it, I said,

won't take long.
He kept shaking his head and muttering
an old farmer's saying,
I don't know enough to plant two to a hill,
not even two to a hill.

Modern Design

How can you clean up the place
and have any kind of order if you
let all this stuff grow the way
it wants to? That rambler rose
by the kitchen window, dig it out.
Saw down that maple so we can make
the gate wider, and that ivy on a
trellis and the honeysuckle hedge,
grub 'em out and pile them for burning.
Spread some crushed rock in the
dooryard, we don't need all that grass.
make the place slick and neat like
a new car, give it style. Oh, look,
there's the playhouse the kids built,
it looks crummy, tear it down too.

On Guard

The sun protects my back
as I step into the morning
anxious for its promise.
Last night I saw blood
on the moon and howled
myself to sleep. Even in
daylight I stay alert for

any danger lurking in the
thickets of night's warning.
I sniff the wind, knowing a
keen nose scents the quarry.
If I could find my fear
I would jump on its back
and tear out its throat
to keep another moon from
casting portents for the body
that claims my shadow.

Our Country

The lady in the harbor
who holds up the torch
pointed the way for my ancestors—
like the outstretched arm of Moses—
to the promised land.
Now smoke clouds the sky
around the light and exhaust fumes
wither the leaves around
Independence Hall where the
great names are rooted.
Sometimes I walk cement paths
with the furtive air of a man
who forged his father's signature.

Penalty for Anger

The walls of heart shook
under the blasts of mind,
in an upstairs bedroom
plaster fell on the empty bed
and a door slammed its protest.

Silence rolled back on
velvet wheels, a robin's egg
hatched with a crackling shell,
a bee stirred in a flower,
a vacant window danced naked
in the sun.

Whisper of a timid key
roused the lock, the door swung
in a welcome arc,
a stained traveler washed
in the waters of home.

Mind knelt in disgrace,
heart bowed to an audience
of empty chairs.

The Professor Enrolls

I decided to major in leisure
after years of heavy classloads.
A few naps brought good grades in indolence
and I filed in the wastebasket
all appeals from the mailbox.
I won my degree with a thesis of daydreaming
and after I awarded myself a diploma,
I cast out solemn grade books
for the wind to collect.

Relief from Pressure

The forecast said rain,
hot muggy air confirmed it,
we still had almost thirty acres
of alfalfa mowed and ready to bale.
The minute the dew dried off
we went to it. The baler plunger
shoving in there 45 strokes per minute,
the needles slipping through and
the knotters tying, a bale kicked out
every ten strokes, four a minute,
we couldn't do better than that.
Dust rose and the sweat poured down,
sticky, hot, half a sun showing,
the temperature boosting up and up.
Twenty minutes for lunch and
start again.
Then they began to loom out of the west,
high, snow-topped thunderheads
with a row of windclouds below.
They towered up there and kept coming.
Streaks of lightning cut through them,
the air stood still, thunder rumbled.
As we scooped up the last windrow
the rain began with a rush of wind ahead.
We hit for the barn in high gear,
drove in under cover when the deluge came.
But we had finished and after a bath
and supper I saw a rainbow arched
in the east and I was courteous
though firm with two men at the front door
who tried to sell me cemetery lots.

Sauce for the Gander

The last person to bed starts the
dishwasher, locks the front door,
pulls the screen across the fireplace,
makes sure the basement lights are out
and checks the thermostat.
It's the devil in me but on a cold
winter night, snuggled warm in bed,
the window open and register closed,
I say to my wife, "I don't believe you
started the dishwasher," and she groans
but goes to see. But her mind works too
and a few nights later she asks me, "Did
you lock the front door?" And being too
unsure to argue, in the cold dark,
I make the barefooted pilgrimage.

They Never Came

Our town prepared for invasion
by admonishing the taxpayers to
invest in two huge sirens erected
at strategic places. And to keep
in voice these metal-throated robots
practice their warning at eleven o'clock
on the fifteenth of each month.
We grow used to it knowing the
barbarians are not at the gates.
But still we regret the money spent
and it irritates us to be reminded
at eleven o'clock on the fifteenth
of each month that the Russians never came—
and we find it hard to forgive them.

Virtue of Logic

He believed in the generation
of opposites by the compulsion
and necessity of their own logic.
He whetted his mind to a fine edge
on the grindstone of science and
argued that a south pole assumed
a north pole, summer matched winter,
a friend for an enemy, systole
and diastole, left hand and right,
high and low tides, a web and a fly,
an invisible wind that washes away
man's granite monuments.
But when he stood on a stream's bank,
a dill pickle in one hand and a
sandwich in the other and a hummingbird
twice (not once but twice) plunged its beak
into the pickle, he took off his shoes
and pressed bare feet against sharp rocks
to prove the virtue of his logic.

A Way by Water

In the basement this morning
a water drop squeezed through
a pipe joint and fell. The basement
smelled, it was musty, in two minutes
another drop formed. Not much of a
leak, a wrench and dab of white
lead would stop it.
Down in the field where I went
to check on a crazy sow who rammed
through the fence to have her pigs,

in the rain,
I noticed the creek.
The water ran freely, bounced over
rocks, divided around a sunken log,
slid under the fence, not tamed
by obstacles. Something welled up
in me that felt kin to water and
before I thought I rode bareback
on a whale, rubber boots and all,
down the creek, into a river and on
to the ocean. When they surface,
these deep-mind beasts scare the
hell out of me—the sow had eight pigs,
laid on one, seemed content in the mud.
I went back to the workshop for a
wrench and dab of white lead.

In the attic of my mind
sits a trunk packed with the
clothes of old ideas . . .
   ᠅ A Secret to Live By

An Account of Failures

I woke this morning and felt
the day ask me before it started
how to endure facts without some
pious or optimistic butter to
spread on my bread.
I live easily with overcast or
sunny skies, the sweat from work,
the jar and jolt of traffic.
I count dollars, balance a checkbook.
But this morning my conscience bled
from the jibes and stabs of memory.
I would take back words sharp enough
to wound my friends, sweep up
tacks spread for the feet of women
who needed my hand, post a danger sign
by the quicksand where my family
struggled for solid ground.
I wish back the stone that broke
the window of my house when I
pretended to be a stranger.

Alien

The winter trees replied
when the wind questioned them
but no words I understood nor
did they speak to me.
The barn humped its back
against the low sun and

threw a shadow across my path.
Melting snow trickled past
a manure pile, stained
the edge of drifts and a rat
busy in corn spilled from
the broken side of a crib
made the solitude bearable
as if to say the lesson learned
from hard facts should teach me
the consolation of hunger.

Apparition in the Afternoon

The telephone lies in its incubator.
Voiceless.
Waiting for a wrong number.
Shadows crawl like roaches on the wall.
The disemboweled refrigerator groans,
the radiator gurgling
as if its throat has been cut.
Dust is disinterred with the furniture.
This room does not bury its dead.
I crochet cobwebs
and hang them from the ceiling.
Every day is a desert,
a vacuum sucking in my brains.
Time passes like a parade,
a soap opera reversing itself.
Time is yesterday.
I will live, haunting myself.

Arrogance of Things

The growth of the cornfield today
answers yesterday's question,
but tomorrow? No guarantees beyond
the moment. A dark cloud with a
blast of hail tells me destruction
waits for no man. A touch of frost
will wither oak trees, cornfields,
living flesh. It is the stones,
bricks, machines that go on and on
in the arrogance of existence.
Even this typewriter and desk will prove
more durable than my nerves and muscle.
Dishes, for god's sake, outlive the hand
that cleans them. No wonder kings filled
their graves with possessions. Who wants
things (bought, stolen or given), to squat
like idols before the future's greedy eyes?
It may be the junkyard will get us all,
people, crops, tools, machines, but now
my fountain pen which I could snap in two,
mocks me with no signs of age. Swear or weep,
the shadow of the sundial haunts the human face.

The Backward Flow

A man bent with the burden
of too many birthdays walks his dog,
shuffles through dry leaves piled
ankle deep along the sidewalk.
Everywhere the retreat goes on,
flames die in the sumac and maples
unseen, unheard, the roots draw in
the sap for growth when the call comes.

The man, fortified with morning prayers,
watches with his cane for snares
a tilted sidewalk square sets for him.
He neglects the view around him
for a narrow focus on his path as
each foot seeks a firm step before
abandoning an old position. Naked
trees wait in the confidence of
resurrection. The man plods to the
end of the block, turns and faces
the interminable journey of return.
The small white dog burrows in leaves,
dances on hind legs, catches a mouthful
of torn paper, makes the morning alive
with its ignorance of the backward flow
in tree and man.

But the Earth Abides

The windmill squeaks, flaps broken vanes,
The barn needs paint, gates sag, weeds grow,
A manure pile leans against a shed,
Everywhere seeds that decay's hands sow.

But good news, good news, a new owner comes
With his bride, paint cans, new-fangled machines,
Where the old man gave up the ghost and left
Once more clover learns what the sickle means.

Day of the Cornfield

The day of the cornfield all right,
hanging ears kernelled by pollen
pulsing down hollow silks in the

slow ejaculation of creation.
In the book of earth the farmer
throws a giant shadow, his eyes
greedy, hands gnarled like roots.
Now he leans on the gate, strokes his dog,
tired with spent passion. He notes a
rabbit nibbling a fallen ear, a cock pheasant
slips between the rows, he quiets his dog,
his voice stuffed with yellow sounds of corn,
the heavy ears wrapped in their message
of the season.

Death of a Marriage

They reached home,
she went in and locked the door,
he drove away . . . all these years
and they did not even say,
"Good night."
A house is only a statistic
when the hearth fire dies
in a bed of stale ashes,
stale as past promises.
Lares and penates will not stay
where the clenched hand,
bitter words, angry tears
insult their benevolence.
A package of letters tied
with a ribbon keeps company
with a diary whose pages curl
in the morning mist as they wait
on the curb for the garbage man.

Do People Care for People?

Appetites in the barnyard bawled
for more feed than the grain bins
offered, so we looked for corn
to buy. Sure, one of the neighbors
said, I'll sell you this round crib.
So we measured the corncrib. Now what,
I said. Figure the number of bushels,
he said, multiply by the price . . .
You ever go to school? Yeah, I said,
but in arithmetic class we papered
rooms with doors and windows. His pencil
flickered, area times height and
divide by 2.5 equals 850 bushels.
Multiply by $2.20—you can do that?
I nodded. He wasn't through.
Two-and-a-half cubic feet for
each bushel . . . how many cubic feet
in the world for each person?
What do you mean, I asked. People,
goddamit, people, how much room
for people, not factories or
four-lane highways, or shopping centers,
but people. Room for a guy to
have a garden, a yard, a place for
trees, hammock, croquet set.
Man, I said, you live in the past.
But not in a condominium, he said.
You know what's the trouble? People
don't care for people, nobody gives
a damn for people, not even people.
Nations stand with their britches
bristling with six-shooters, glaring
at each other, daring each other,
who's the Bill Hickok to make the

fastest draw. I wrote him a check.
Glad they taught you to multiply,
he said. People multiply, where can they go
when mother earth finds herself layered
and cross-layered with all the damn junk
that takes up room? No wilderness left,
not even shady backyards . . . pipelines,
high tension towers, blasted developers
with their shoebox houses . . . We will
come and get corn next week,
I told him. Probably be a new airfield
here by then, he muttered. I drove away.
You'll see, he yelled, you'll see
how much people care for people.

Dragon Lesson

This country needs live dragons,
real fire-breathing, tail-swishing,
scaly, gold-guarding, maiden-snatching,
nasty-tempered beasts. The real McCoy,
that would terrorize the countryside,
eat a few defiant people, burn down
churches that don't believe in dragons,
not fake scenes on a stupid TV screen.
Think how we would huddle together,
crying out for another St. George, and
longing for peace. Think of us longing for,
pleading for, praying for peace, just
imagine it. And think of the lesson our
brave young men would learn, that if they
win the gold they have to keep the girl.

End of the Game

FOR MY BROTHER ROBERT RUSSELL HEARST

Two little boys dusty with pollen
would need clean faces to come
to the supper table. In the
cornfield we hid from each other,
racing up and down the rows like
rabbits, you always gave yourself
away with a snort of laughter.

It is your turn to hide while
I cover my eyes. I hear the rustle
and murmur of leaves drying in
the warm October sun. But now you
are quiet and I cannot find you.
Come out, brother, come out,
I am afraid. Soon it will be dark
and mother will scold us if
we are late for supper.

Fact

I knew a man once who gave up the ghost
When he no longer cared what happened next,
He had less curiosity than most—
I wonder if his present state is fixed.

I like to look ahead to another season
And expect a bigger crop in the coming year.
I do not think the plan is out of reason,
I have my way to make while I am here.

The Fact Is . . .

A duck ate the worm
and I ate the duck,
so without stretch or squirm
worm lifts from the muck
as the tree of life shows
how branch after branch
from sea slime we rose
in a chromosome dance
to climb where we are.
So now worm ascends
as it follows my star
to limitless ends
if my soul proves its name.
But earth's hunger for man
will make me worm's game
when I follow time's plan,
so I eat what I can.

Father

Nailheads broke off with the sound
of rifle shots, blizzard winds
shook the house, snug as squirrels
we burrowed in our quilts
until morning came.

The upstairs an Arctic cave,
a floor of ice, but Father
braved it and we heard him downstairs
shake the hard-coal stove
until all its isinglass eyes
glowed red, the low roar
of a bucket of coal poured
in its mouth.

When he called, "You can come now,"
we scuttled downstairs to dress
in the lovely warmth.

But no one ever said, thank you,
or praised him, or simply,
we love you.

Grandfather and the Evangelist

A tent with a platform and with folding chairs,
a different church than the one where we belonged,
Grandfather held my hand, said I would hear
a deep-voiced man climb up the golden stairs.

Grandfather said I ought to hear a preacher
who sanctified himself with anecdotes
of Me and God and sold religion to all
like a medicine man, not like a prophet and teacher.

Grandfather said it was time I saw how sinners
can be relieved of guilt and dollars too.
"Woe unto you" was the fare Grandfather said
the saved sheep ate before their Sunday dinners.

I blushed and trembled when the big voice thundered,
"The devil lifts the skirt and fills the glass,
show him no mercy and reap your reward in Heaven."
(And would they lift skirts there and drink, I wondered.)

He had me all mixed up. I couldn't find
the reason to be saintly here on earth
and take your pleasure when you got to Heaven;
it seemed to me he had this on his mind.

Grandfather said as he took me by the hand,
"Experience is the way you understand."

Hang On to the Grab Bar

Caught in the revolving door
of the walking world, he must
calculate each maneuver inch by
inch lest a goddam miss flip him
flat on his face. So measure with
the eye, test with the hand every
move to hold on, no sure thing for
a man who cannot stand squarely
on his own feet. The girls pass
around him as on safe ground where
no adventure pops from the jungle
of their explorations.
He wishes for a refuge in the
mountains where he could live
in a cave, give love to the birds
and shove curious glances and
muttered excuses over a precipice.
He makes a family of himself
to comfort him and wonders at
bedtime if he can face the threat
of another day ahead.

Hard Way to Learn

A trickle of water from
a rotting snowbank tells me
the time has come to haul

one more load of manure to
the field before the frost
goes out and lets the muddy
ground suck the tractor wheels
down to the axle. The earth
will let me know when it is
ready to take the plow, as a
heifer in heat lets the bull
know when she is ready. Think of it,
forty years I farmed this place
and I still wait on it for
the time to plant. My wisdom
seems a little shaky compared
to what the land knows and makes
me suspicious of what I think
I've learned. I read signs and
add seed, ground, work, weather,
and luck and hope for the best.
Strange, at my age, to be so
unsettled in my mind about crops,
weather and women but no one gave me
a diploma when I was born.

Here and There

It's true the days are longer,
the sun didn't get caught under
December's dark horizon after all.
Buds in the maple seem swollen, signs
of an early spring lie out for all
to read, today breaks open with
sunlight, it makes no sense at all
to blunder in ravines or swear at
barred gates.
No fires burn in the streets, food
cascades from the market shelves,

water flows from faucets . . .
The old man, homeless, naked, hand
broken by torture, eyes sunk deep
in sockets, wanders in a season
where the sun contends with clouds
alive with bloody beaks and
extended claws.

The Insatiable Demand

He chopped his work
into little pieces so he could
fill the pockets of his awareness
and carry it with him on his trips
to everywhere as he hurried to catch
the tail feathers of his errands.
His office door kept swinging
and his car never cooled as he tried
to be elsewhere at the same time
he was here. The letter to mail,
the contract to sign, the man to see,
led him to such haste that the
telephone never stopped ringing
in ears tuned to calls he could not
find time to answer. It is said
he slept with one eye open lest
a knock on the door catch him napping.

Land of Beginnings

The door you once closed lets you slip through
back on the way from where you have come
to feel the soft earth of the land you plowed
(kneel, old believer) between finger and thumb.

Here corner posts marked the farm's boundary lines.
I push one and feel it move, loose with decay
like a worn rotten tooth, the fence wires stripped off,
to merge field into field, the fashion today.

Scarcely a foot of this ground hasn't been
under your foot and your team and machines,
where you ended the days of labor and sweat
and learned the hard lessons a harvest means.

You find your hand shakes as it pulls up a weed,
in your land of beginnings. When all's done and said
if it still seems like home you may as well stay,
so plow yourself a furrow and plow yourself a bed.

Let It Come Down

Glad that at last the litter and waste of winter,
Drift ends of dirty snow and the icy splinter
Of eaves-trough decoration, dissolve again,
I stand at the window watching the first spring rain.

Let it come down, let it come down in torrents,
I signal the clouds, so great is my abhorrence
For the sooty lives of houses, for the unkept
Complexions of fields dulled by the months they have slept.

Strike to the bone, let the earth again be clean
That willows and lilacs can line the air with green
And hold their color, that the least bird throat
Can point to the sun and form no tarnished note.

It would spare nothing the fresh birth of grass
If rain by touch can make this come to pass
I will deploy my roots nor hold aloft
This body of one who is sheltered under a roof.

A Misery Bleeds

A misery bleeds inside of me
today and will not let me be,
it is a day like any day,
subtract or add a small degree.

There must be something ails a man
to plague himself on this bright day
when what he wants is what he has
but what he has will not say.

Morning Song

I often think of night as a wave lifting me into the morning
where the light pours as softly as snow through the clear glass
and birds raise sleepy offbeat notes like birds learning
their first songs and mist blows white across the grass.

No time of day is so full of hope as the new morning
when green stalks are crisp with life and the clover shines
under its sheet of cool dew like a lake and lifting
clouds of fog from a world refreshed and renewed in its signs.

The lover and the loved find strength and peace in the morning
as they seem to hold time motionless, a fruit without decay,
and remember the swift pulse of desire in the love warning,
the passion of a cock pheasant crying in the day.

Need for Magic

After a lonely night and an empty day
while neighbors talk of politics and weather
you finally admit she's left you and you seek
a spell that will bring a man and his wife together.

You try to make up a recipe for magic,
of remembered things, her hands like folded wings,
hair curling from under her scarf on rainy days,
her awkward pose while she reads what the mailman brings.

And her words, her words, oh, any common phrase,
letters she wrote you starting with Dear Love,
notes to herself she often scribbled down
on a calendar that hangs beside the stove.

It might add enchantment to touch what she has touched,
straighten a picture, empty a vase, the door
to her closet to shut, her gloves on the davenport
tucked in the cushions, attempt a household chore

the way she did, for ingredients of the charm,
clean out the fireplace, polish the kitchen chrome,
wash a few windows and act as if you are sure
this spell shaped like a prayer will bring her home.

No More Chores

The old farmer nurses rheumatic joints
in a wheelchair beside the window.
He watches spring come
with all the fullness thereof,
his eyes dim with the smoke of the past.

Memory plows the years
where he planted his future,
he feels between thumb and finger
the earth's soft body, his inward eye
shines with banners of leaves
waving from cornstalks.
Each morning he wakes
from dreams of past harvests
roused by the cry of a cock pheasant
in a nearby field.

He stares as if the days ran backward
through a mirror, in the corner
a spider waits in her web.
He tastes dust in the wind,
feels stems grow in his fingers,
the distant yammer of a tractor
reminds him of hard-calloused hands,
he smiles as he nods off to sleep.

No Nightingales, No Nymphs

The imperatives of spring
snap their fingers and we jump
to obey. We prune the apple tree
and grapevines, haul away
the brush, sweep out the granary
and sack up seed oats, shell
the last crib of corn. We
separate the boar from the sows,
scrub the hoghouse with lye
and hot water to kill the germs
before the baby pigs are born.
We plow the garden, as we

promised Mother, as soon as
the ground is dry. We clean
the stinking calf pen and spend
a day among plows and tractors.
The farmer keeps his nose to
the grindstone when spring comes—
no pastoral shepherd to dance
in the moonlight, crowned with
vine leaves, singing to nymphs—
he plows himself to bed, tired
beyond dreaming, snores his way
toward daylight.

No Symbols

The barn's warm breath
smelled of pigs, straw, dust,
fresh manure. The night wind
rattled doors, poked fingers
under sills. The sow heaved and
grunted. He waited for an end
to waiting, the sow stretched
at his feet, her swollen belly
heaving. He reached into her
with two clumsy fingers, felt
tiny sharp toes not yet in this
world, tried to grasp them but
they slipped back. He shrugged off
his gunny sack shawl, ready to help.
He burned a match along a wire
with a loop and sharp hook.
Gently, tenderly, slowly he
inserted the hook and locked it
into the jaw of the unborn pig.
His finger in the loop he pulled

in time with the sow's labor,
brought the first pig through the
door to the outside. He watched
six more come kicking out
of their shells. A ray of light
shaped the window, shadows are born old.
The pigs rooted the sow's nipples,
if there was more meaning than that
he was too tired to care.

No Word for the Wise

We can tell the year's close
by its harsh zeros and by a
drifting mood of scattered leaves
and withered stems warning us
the woods are empty. We expect
short days and long nights but
not this stumble in the pulse
as age races to match the season.
Let this news ride the wind,
there is no one we want to tell.
I split wood for the fireplace,
blanket the foundation with straw,
mulch the garden, stand at the
window with you in a house we built
with lumber from trees in our
own grove. But I cannot tell you
how to account for the roots'
advantage as they store the sap.
Wisdom never knocked on my door.
If I were wise I would know how
to dig a burrow and sleep there
with you until spring.

Not to Be Overlooked

We had a bull calf born premature,
never amounted to much, we kept him
in a small pen, remembered to feed him
and bed him down. Sort of a runt, he came
to be a fixture like forks and baskets.
Oh, we rubbed his head when we went by,
and checked on feed and water. But one day
when he was about six months old,
he backed off in his pen, took a run for it,
smashed the gate, hightailed it
through the barn knocking forks from
the racks, upset a basket of oats,
found an open basket of oats,
found an open door and ran wild around
the barnyard. It took four of us
to corral him and herd him back to his pen.
There he lay, quiet and serene as if
nothing had happened.
And I thought, I know folk like that
who have to show off just to prove,
I guess, that they are here.

November

The sun dripped honey-colored days
into the valley of November. I watched
trees glisten in pale amber, bare twigs
pricked against the sky, felt blood and
sap pulse with the memory of spring as
the wind kept truce on the horizon,
and the valley opened its heart under
the Indian summer sky.

And so I filled your hands with
apples, ripe beyond their time but
still sweet in the mellow flavor of
desire. I beg you accept my harvest
while gold light blinds us both to
the withered aftermath of frost.

Note: See "Indian Summer," a poem with similar lines, published in 1965.

Off Limits

He burned the grass
to kill weed seeds (so he said)
along the roadside. Thick mats
of grass from winter's bed
exploded softly in flames
that reach out to skim earth
cleaner than a flock of goats
would do it. Leaning on a
rake handle he watched his beast
lick up its prey. Grass grows
greener after fire, a proverb says
(country proverb, not Solomon's).
But fence posts began to smoke,
an arm of flame reached for the grove,
cat's paws of fire bounded outside
the fencerow, he struck at the
sudden leaps, stamped, beat wisps
of blaze with his jacket.
His pant legs smoked, wind blew
toward the house, he smothered
a runner of flame with a wet sack.
At last the fire died with a smokey sigh.
He counted four burned fence posts,

a scorched tree, a blistered leg,
a charred patch on the lawn.
He started the fire to kill weeds,
not to run loose on its own account.

Outsider

The field stretches from morning
to evening, passes no verdict on
work done. The tractor shouts,
smoke pours from the exhaust, the plow
turns black ridges where I hold a
straight line until the fence turns me.
A spring sun warms the air, I see
a flock of ducks waver north,
a wild plum, gnarled and stunted,
along the fencerow bursts into bloom.
I should cut it down, I farm to grow
the seeds I plant, not those from
some wandering hand that sows
god knows what tares and thistles.
A rabbit hides in the grass, a cock
pheasant calls to his hen, tenants
of a wilderness I destroyed to cut
land into furrows for my own sake.
Like them, I am an alien here for
the sun, wind, sky, earth do not care
if I can shoulder my way into Canaan.

Pause between Clock Ticks

Like a caught breath
the pendulum stays,

a dewdrop hinges
to a leaf's edge,
an ant spies a crumb,
a ray of sun meets
its reflection, a bird's
wing arches to beat
a glance begun, pulse
on tiptoe, a wave crest
hovers, a sigh breaks,
all held at zero motion
while "yes" trembles on lips,
"no" waits to be said.

A Prejudiced Witness

This morning my wife and I
found two bluejays
making a rumpus in a tree
down by the creek;
they squawked and scolded
with the eyeball fury
of two people trying to
outshout each other
in a kitchen quarrel.

A weather warning broke out
so often in the conversation
that we felt our survival
depended on shingle shelter.

No two people are the same
except look-a-like twins
and a man and wife who
for fifty years have grown
into each other's faces.

Retirement Blues

Neither anger nor reproach will
change the date on our time slips,
nor restore the keys to doors now
opened by other hands. We stand
outside the gates but the sun rises
and sets as it always does, and dogs
and cats go about their affairs, weeds
thrive, the temperature goes up
and down and we wear the same clothes
we wore yesterday. The mirror of
time's lake reflects our wrinkles and
gray hair. We think of paths never
followed but dreamed of and forgot
how once it mattered if skirts were
short or if life existed on Mars.
I nearly fell off the back porch
yesterday when an oak tree bowed
(it may have been the wind), but even
accidental courtesies must be taken
personally to keep me from feeling
forsaken.

Retirement Time Is the Time to Retire

About twilight, swallows stitched
the air, whine of insects almost too
high pitched to hear, cornfields breathed
moisture into an Iowa sky where
thunderheads caught the last rays
of sunset. He balanced on the hind legs
of an old chair he kept by the garden
for thinking and resting. Tonight the
slaughter of weeds around the tomatoes

gave him more sweat than comfort.
He lay back to squint at the first star
and tell himself to shape up, other men
had plowed their last furrow, left the field
and closed the gate. But he felt pushed aside,
worn out, not needed by love and labor.
Once he had joked about this day when
it lay far ahead in some misty future.
Suddenly it faced him, here, now.
He bent over to tie his shoe and the words
of an old farmer came to his mind:
The time to plant corn is at
cornplanting time.

Routine

The boy drowning under waves
of sleep felt his father's voice
pull him to the surface again
and again until he crawled up
the beach toward morning chores.
He fumbled with both feet in one
overall leg, shirttail dragging.
The morning sang with sunshine,
with birds, with pigs squealing,
with a neighbor's dog, clear but
distant. Winking mirrors of dew
scattered the light, vanes on the
windmill wheel blazed as it turned.
The cows to milk, cows, cows, where
were the cows? He rode the long-legged
pony with her halter, too bleary-eyed
to find the bridle. The cowpath
threaded its way through the pasture,
he galloped, a few cows ambled toward

the barn, others stood or lay apart.
Sullen with sleep he cursed them, his
shrill words whipping the air. It rose up
in him, the indignity of forced waking,
his anger hurt him with Father's voice.
Sullen with sleep he beat the pony over the ears and she
promptly threw him. He walked
behind the cows in his bare feet,
warm cowflops squishing between his toes.

Note: See also a different poem with the same title published in 1972.

Sap's Rise

The creek retreats from flood rage
to its summer voice, trees
shake out leaves, turn the page
from dark and cold to seize
on green directions, now
blackbirds float from bough to bough.

Sap's rise wakes an old tune.
Almost persuaded now I hear
rustle, whisper, sight and soon
flowers burst from bud, eager
to return again to this new start
where violence detonates and bursts the heart.

A Secret to Live By

In the attic of my mind
sits a trunk packed with the
clothes of old ideas, also

age-yellowed snapshots of friends,
relatives, sweethearts taken in
fair and cloudy weather. The baggage
memory keeps, a broken birdcage
of a canary whose neck I wrung
in some childish rage, the usual litter,
dust, mouse droppings, a dead bat,
a basket of broken toys. But hid
under the eaves, hidden away,
lies a sealed envelope that holds
a secret I wrote to bolster my faith
in the traffic and market we live in.
Once I had a revelation of an
instinct for order in things great and small
that rang a bell for meaning I still try
to hear above the jostle of the street.

A Shabby Day

Out of doors, office-bound,
I breathe the exhaust of
trucks and buses, listen
to sirens, search for my
direction on a one-way street,
and the morning begins to
pucker my mouth as if I had
eaten sour grapes.

My work sheet lags behind the clock,
a tick-tock joke at my slow feet.

My reflection in a store window
reminds me of a stranger, I grimace
to consider my indenture to the
day's facts.

I choose to think of libraries,
schools, playgrounds, parks with
flowers, the homes of friends,
and reject the presence of neon signs,
junkyards, dead elms, vacant lots
filled with tin cans. I stop at a
drinking fountain to rinse my mouth.

Shove It, Brother, Shove It

From bedroom to bathroom to
breakfast table you break your
knuckles to shove the wheelchair
toward the smell of coffee.
For you to face the morning,
dressed, cleaned, fed gives you
a day's work before the day
is under way. Read the paper,
the news "out there" seems so
much blackmail to be paid in daily
installments by a draft on the
good things you want to believe in.
You discard the map of rough roads
where your indigent legs can't
beg their way.

Small Thorns

The odor from garbage my neighbor
burns in a trash barrel corrupts
the fresh breath of morning and
I find the curtain of silence easily
torn at night by a barking dog, and

my taste runs to birdsong early
Sunday morning rather than the blasts
from a neighbor's lawn mower and
I have never subscribed to the steel
fences built to keep kids from
homesteading vacant lots. But we
neighbors know we must bear with
each other for it is the small thorns
that prick tempers and lame the feet
of good will. Yet no one, I repeat,
no one gives us directions of how
to change things as they are.

Something Not Tamed in Us

Early this winter morning
I saw two cock pheasants stroll
out of our patch of woods to feed
on corn my wife had scattered under
pine trees for the squirrels.
They moved with leisurely step
and pecked at the corn in such
a regal manner you would think
it was a favor to us for them
to eat our corn.
The little birds, the juncos,
chickadees, nuthatches, sparrows,
even cardinals and bluejays crowded
the porch feeder, squirrels rummaged
in the snow for buried nuts,
a rabbit stretched up to gnaw
the bark on a young apple tree.
But these are old acquaintances,
pensioners we've cared for four years;
they know where their welfare lies.

But the pheasants, newcomers,
majestic in bronze and purple vestments,
made us feel alive in ways hidden
beneath daily banalities as if we
tapped some spring in a wilderness
hidden in our lives and out gushed
the waters of our beginnings.

Statistics and Waterfalls

The textbook lies on the
reading table in the fiction room,
its statistics, diagrams and graphs
as factual as a cement walk or
lightbulb. Dropped by some
absent-minded hand near the shelves
that offer journey to the
rock candy mountain and haunted
waterfalls (return not guaranteed)
where unknown countries wait to be
explored by curious travellers.
The textbook knows the number
of board feet in a forest tree,
but not the shudder stirred by
a stealthy movement in the leaves,
the glimpse of a black paw
poised to strike.

The Tarnish

The afternoon failed of its promise and the sun
Hid in a thicket of clouds on its downward climb,
The bright day's petals tattered and fell apart
Lost as a tower clock's voice asleep at its chime.

I rocked on my heels and saw sleet's rowdy hands
Rumple the tulip bed, a cold wind goaded
A child at play till she cried, I turned to stare
At a shallow hill where the topsoil had eroded.

The small mean faults of the day like blisters broken,
Rubbed raw, were slow to heal, I felt time's wedge
Split need from the order of things, like a farm run down
By shabby intentions, a plow with a rusty edge.

I carry my doctor's degree on such occasions
And speak at length on the tarnish of small losses.

To Build a Fence

We stretch a barbed wire from corner post
to corner post, 160 rods, half a mile.
It's a line to go by, even so we step back
a few rods and sight over the tops of the
posts already set to line up the new post.
Who wants a crooked fence and wouldn't
the neighbors chuckle. We turn the auger and dig
a hole two and a half feet deep and hope
for no rocks or tree roots to block the
twisting blade (tree roots are the devil,
you need an ax for them). We sweat and
place a post in the hole (creosoted post
that won't rot—we hope), line it up and
tamp the dirt in as if we planted it.
The corner post takes the most care,
it has to stand the strain of the tight
stretched wire all the way. We set it in
concrete, brace it against another post,
tie them together with strands of wire
twisted so tight it sings. One post has my

initials and date scratched in the cement.
We hung a gate on that one too. We staple
to the posts a thirty-six-inch woven wire
with three barbed wires on top. That's what
holds the outside out and the inside in.
Simple, as if the farm insists on order.

Wheelchair Blues

Two raised steps deny him
the door though it stands
wide open. No prisoner in
leg irons has less chance
of passing through the door
than this poor cuss sitting
waiting . . . for what? Help?
The last day? A miracle? He
tells himself it could be worse,
there could be three steps.
So he waits, waits in dreams,
waits days and nights as if
barriers would dissolve or faith
lift him to his white useless feet.
Love goes by in a busload of
laughter with the doors shut,
he waves but it never stops.
Oh, the poor bastard sits there
day after day dreaming of valentines
and the days before the war.

Women Shearing Men

The wind whistles a bawdy tune,
ears fill with spring's rapture,
men gnaw on the bones of their jobs
and hide their sly hunger behind their long hair.
Clouds soft as marshmallows soaked with rain
sink in the vast wallows of the sky.

Women lugging big shears
roam the streets driving the men
before them. Soon the men find themselves
penned in on every side and the shearing begins.
The women squat and hold the men's necks
between their knees, the men cry out
when the shears nick their ears and tender scalps.

All the while flocks of blackbirds swing
free above new leaves, dogs flash back
and forth through alleys, a squirrel
leaps to a tree in sudden frenzy,
a tricycle pushed by the wind falls
off a porch.

The women take a coffee break, heat
their coffee with a blowtorch from a
plumber's van, beef it up with a dollop
of bourbon, run fingers through the
men's hair, jostle them to the ground,
while the men huddle in small groups,
hands over their crotches.

The men with naked heads stray about
like strangers who have lost their way,
miserable as sheep without a shepherd.

Wonder of Hummingbirds

I shall sit on a bench outside this morning
and watch the hummingbirds color the air
from feeder to feeder where red syrup glistens,
they weave in their flight an invisible snare

where I fall the victim by my own volition,
amazed to be part of a moment which binds
us together, they spin their threads of flight,
I am bound in such wonder a man seldom finds.

Note: See variant of this poem published in 1976.

Time cuts down the years
and lays them in swaths
like the grass of a new-mown field.
  ᴁ Melancholy at Night

Banish Morning Fear

When he woke at dawn, it was his habit to think
each new day offered another adventure for him;
he smiled at himself, at his age to be concerned
with such thoughts, but still he liked the wonder of them.

But today, as he lay half-roused, a finger of fear
troubled his mind as if the morning's surprise
might point out a sorrow born ahead of its time—
just then his wife stirred, opened her comfortable eyes.

Castrating the Pigs

It always seemed to be a rainy day
when we *cut* the little boar pigs.
The warm humid June air soaked up
the smells of hogs, manure, sour breath
of the slop barrel, it all stunk.
Father used a special knife shaped
like a half moon, honed on a whetstone
until it would shave the fine hairs
on his arm. The pigs, two or three
weeks old still penned with their mothers,
squealed when we boys grabbed them
and leaped out of the pen just ahead
of the chomping jaws of the mother sow.
The hired man held them by their hind legs,
spread them apart, Father squeezed the
scrotum to make the skin tight, made
two quick slits with the knife and out
popped the testicles like small eyeballs.

He tossed them over the gate into the
alleyway where our collie dog feasted.
Once in awhile, not often, Father
cut into a ruptured pig and its small
guts boiled up. Father gently pushed
them back and carefully sewed up the
wound with Mother's darning needle
and stout black thread. They always
healed, I never knew one to be infected.
It was a day to get past, hot, stinking,
clouds of dust where the sows barked and
churned up their bedding, pigs squealing,
men shouting, blood-stained overalls.
We boys kept our heads down, ashamed
to be so ruthless in cheating nature.
It wasn't funny to us when the hired man
winked and said, "They'll never know
what they missed." We felt our own
manhood threatened as if strong hands
reached out to rob us.

Cerebral Palsy

Each morning the wild, random
conduct of muscles tests his strategy,
almost ambushes the effort to
pull on a sock. But he struggles
and tames them to permit his
journey from bathroom to breakfast.
But he must plan campaigns his
partners never know. He could
hoist a white flag and surrender
to an institution far from the office
where he devises wills, conveyances,
contracts for his clients. Other men

shoulder who knows what burdens of
anxiety, worry, despair that curl
the edges of the spirit, but not
this daily rebellion of nerves, this
denial of the flesh to come to order.

Consider a Poem

If I speak to explain myself
and you do not understand,
it is not that I mumble in tongues
but that my syllables sometimes invest
the common meaning with a strange humor.

Nothing I say will take the IRS
off your back, nor stop construction
of four-lane highways, nor vote down
the next shopping center, nor win you
a divorce (if you want one). Sounds
I call words are sometimes so deep
in my throat I must wait to hear them.

But let us work shoulder to shoulder
and you listen and you may be able
to say honestly, I share poetry for the
same reason I drink a glass of water.

Espaliered on a Wailing Wall

Farmland lacks immunity to the
toxin spread by the creeping edges
of the town. A fungus of junkyards,
beer joints, car washes, food stands,

neon flashes. A four-lane highway
spreads the contagion and no matter
how fast I run, my feet move
too slowly to rescue me from the
corrupt breath of car and truck exhaust.
In this hamburger world decorated
with plastic roses I dream of
clean clear streams and wooded hills,
and secret parks of nature where
a man could stand alone. I look
at a leaf, plastered to my driveway,
and see the perfect veins, the
serrated edges, proof of a pattern
shaped by an order of things with
no action by the city council.
I look at myself, honed by the
abrasive facts of progress instead
of growing out of my beginning
into the man I hoped for.

Housebroken

The year has turned,
light begins to stretch the day,
snow ages under its crust, hope
feels its sap rising.
Wide fields glitter, pages signed
by rabbits and foxes, tree branches
sparkle with ice, I stand at the
window and appraise the view.
In my thoughts I wear thick fur,
slink on padded paws, my long
tongue slides over teeth hungry
for the kill. I smell blood.
But I stand inside the window

housebroken by phone and desk.
Loping across the snow
my neighbor's dog finds a trail,
my excitement runs with him.
He knows what he is meant for.
My instincts raise a leg at the
signs at every crossroad.

An In-Between Time

He hasn't quite left her,
she hasn't quite given up.
The children have grown and gone,
echoes from empty rooms
make the house seem larger.
He baits a hook for a mermaid
but has not yet made a cast,
she dreams of a journey's promise
but has not yet packed her bag.
It's an in-between time of life
after the garden is harvested
but not cleaned up for next year.

Lack of Seed Power

He drooped like a wilted flower
this bright bay stallion too weak
in his flesh to breed the mare
who stood dripping in her heat.
He walked around her, nosed her
and hung his head. My grandfather
said, "Too many trips to the well."
But I scorned the argument, I wanted

the stallion to rise on his hind feet,
grip the mare with forelegs and teeth,
and squeeze into her with strokes
of his muscled rump. I felt
shamed by his failure, this insult to
potency. Beyond the yard I ran to
a clover field where bobolinks
nested and the child in me asked
the future man, how many chances
have we missed, even for stars,
seeds we lack that might have grown
into marvels we never dreamed of?

Melancholy at Night

Each evening at bedtime
I go out of doors, winter or
summer for a breath of fresh air
and to look at the sky. I always
look up, is the sky star-filled
or cloud-covered, or does the moon
waxing or waning slip through
misty veils like a bride's face
on her wedding day? Some nights
an almost intolerable melancholy
overwhelms me and I wish I were
an old Jew who could free his
tears against a wailing wall.
My sadness seems to grow from the loss
of relatives, friends, neighbors who
in leaving took part of my life
with them. Time cuts down the years
and lays them in swaths
like the grass of a new-mown field.
I mourn for their sweat and work,

their anger and love and anxiety,
for the rambler rose by the porch,
the oatfield ready to harvest,
fallen trees, the hard elbows of
their need for a place in
the sun, for their busy hands
and minds, for the spirit of
their day, all lost in a vacancy
called the past. And let me wail
like an old Jew for the boy I thought
I was and go to bed comforted.

Something Is Given

Something is given
as if to a poet,
a piece of land perhaps
to plant his words in.

I plow the sod,
disc it smooth.
In this lap of earth
spill my seeds.

By the waterway where
once a gully flourished,
tall grass hides rabbits
and pheasants, shy as
my thoughts.

I cultivate the land,
keep the weeds cut,
pray for rain in a dry
season. I hope for mature
stalks and ripe corn

before frost.
This, my land, far from the sea
and its empty words repeated
wave after wave.

Sooner or Later

My roots search for water
in the land that feeds me.
It's like sorrow itself
when the grass dries, a hot wind
blows its breath through
shriveled leaves, grasshoppers
suck green stalks, willow roots
reach deeper, heat waves soak up
the stench from barnyards.
The sun burns corn tassels
until they turn white and sterile,
I hear the dry whisper of leaves,
dust rises in spirals of
twisted wind, air smokes from a
plowed field. I chew the stem
of a wilted flower in the shadow
of *what happens* aloof from
city folk who tread their mills
untouched by weather. But my trouble
seems so small I laugh it
to sleep knowing some mother,
some child somewhere die of theirs
every day. I blow my breath against
the sky to form clouds: sooner
or later the rain will fall.

Stepchild of Nature

Open morning's door and listen
to a medley of sounds . . .
wind caught in a bush,
grass bent to whisper,
earthworms in their tunnels
(a sharper ear than mine for that!),
birds everywhere from the robin
in the cherry tree to the cardinal
whipping his call from the top
of a maple. To all this chorus of
the day's voices, add the gnats'
high singing, even the green shine
of leaves seems to change color to sound.
And I sit on the back steps
inarticulate; I lack the tune,
the family ties, the pitch
to join this summer's discourse.

There Are Still Some Mysteries

My young neighbor attended an
agricultural college and came
home with a diploma and a major
in genetics. He bred the son
of a prize bull to a cow whose
pedigree made her the queen of
the country. Then he bled anxiety
for nine months to pass.
He invited me over when the cow
reached her term. And one day
when the weather let me finish
morning chores before I had to

start the chores at night, I went
to see. His face wore the look
of a man who explored a new land
with the wrong map. He showed
the calf, the cutest little whiteface
you ever saw, lively as a cricket—
but a dwarf! He shook his head,
there are some things, he said,
I do not understand.

The Way the Light Shines

The shrill singing of cicada
reminds me that last spring
I found the shell of a cicada
perfect in detail but without
the living body. Tonight we four
friends, old in affection, sit
around a candlelit table
and smile and joke as the soft
light dims our features. When
the shrill doorbell announced
the paperboy collecting his pay,
someone snapped on the light
and I saw as shadows vanished
how the greedy years had sucked
the honey of youth from us.
But I noted how the outlines
of our faces kept familiar the
portrait of the person we remembered.

Weather Words

The garden waited to be covered,
the outside faucets shut off
when I came home on an evening
with weather words speaking of frost.
A man stooped with the day's work
shakes hands with easy decisions.
In the warm basement I shut off
the valves to the outside faucets
and told the garden not to worry.
In the morning the geranium leaves
stiff as metal reminded me of
last night's excuse, nagged at my
conscience when they drooped in the
midday sun. Oh, I will have other gardens
but I learned again what I already knew
about the sudden attack by frost
and the mortal blow that can be
struck by any season.

NINETEEN EIGHTY-ONE

Anyone Can See

Anyone with half wit can see
how his land yields to its people.
Farms flaunt their fecundity
as fields turn fact into miracle.
Here the spring sun stirs seeds
in farmers and plants, breeds crops
and dreams. Trees embrace farmsteads,
shoulder off rough weather,

furnish green rooms for birds,
blossom in huge bouquets when frost
sets its teeth on morning's edge.
Winter slows time in this country
when we speak through cracked lips,
keep barn doors tight, finish chores
after dark. The land provides for
those who endure it, the home lovers,
the deep rooted, who can stand
against the wind.

Bound to Happen

At the haybarn's peak where
rafters lock, a brace loosened,
probably from a push of wind. He
climbed the extension ladder rung
by rung for forty feet. I'm a bit
too old, he thought, to breathe
this air in comfort. Don't look
down, he told himself, hammer in
the spikes. Praying for balance to
let his hands go free, he held one
spike and drove it in. Was it the
reverberations that made the ladder
tremble? He felt it shake again and
looking down, saw a nemesis formed in
a big black brood sow rubbing her back
against the ladder's legs. He held
his breath and squinted, could he
drop the hammer straight enough to
hit her on the snout? The ladder
shook, he clutched the brace. Then
through a half-closed door he saw

his collie enter, spy the sow, start
creeping forward. Sweat blessed him
and his Angel said, At least now
something is bound to happen.

An Evasive Fellow

Lust worries the
good people, he's a
devil of a fellow,
a worm i' the bud.
They call him snake
and poke him out of
hiding places. They
think they beat him
to death with laws
and ordinances only
to find it was last year's
skin they nailed to the
barn door.

A Few Good Licks

So you said I would be the
light of your life and the comfort
of your old age. Well, before we
reach the finish line how about
a New Year's Eve party every week
we'll buzz Times Square in your
little old airplane and make out
in a gondola on a Venice canal.

If we are going to build that
stairway to Paradise we better
get in shape for stair climbing,
it's a long way up they tell me.
And how would you like a bed of furs
in an igloo on an Arctic shelf
for a change of pace? We gotta
make a few fast trips before comfort
wraps us in its warm wooly folds.

Let's light the candles on a huge
birthday cake, the kind you can't
blow out and let 'em burn until
the frosting runs. I'll throw one
slipper over my shoulder and you
drink champagne from the other.
Mrs. O'Leary's cow burned up Chicago
don't let us be cowed from burning up
a few streets toward the future.
If I'm to be your Light and Comfort,
let's get in a few good licks before
the teakettle boils.

Gift for All

The miracles of creation
are not honored by us. Unbelievers,
we lord it over our domestic servants,
cat, dog, horse with the brass
knuckles of authority, an arrogance
swollen by the servility
of its captives. Given time
we will mark for destruction
the polar bear, the whale, seals,
eagles, provide a hemlock cup

for rabbits and mice and coyotes,
breathe with a deadly breath on
the little household dwellers,
spiders, ants, moths, all beloved of God
since He made them . . . then . . . then . . .
we nations can send lethal toys
to each other.

How Good Is Good Enough

He must have read whatever signs
tramps leave on gateposts, a hot
June morning, muggy, mud from
last night's rain on his shoes,
he knocked at the back door.
Mother promised him food—she always
did. Younger than most, whiskers,
ragged coat but solid shoes
laced with twine, he lounged
against the platform where three cans
waited for the milk hauler.
We circled him like puppies around
a strange dog. Mother called,
I took the tray, bacon, scrambled eggs,
coffee with cream and sugar, toast,
even a napkin. He looked, shrugged,
"If I ain't good enough to come
in the house, I ain't good enough
to eat your food." Pushed away
from the platform, took strong steps
to the road. Scared, confused,
I gave the tray to Mother. With tight lips
and angry eyes she told me
to scrape it in the dog dish.
But I found enough good in
myself to share it with Carlo.

Improve the View

Why don't you decorate
that plot in your mind
with lawn grass, ornamental
shrubs around a flowerbed,
it would improve the view
of the plot where your
hopes lie buried.
Dig a grave too, for
self-pity and you will be
free to ignore the hubbub
of expectations and read
Proverbs where the Preacher
saith, A merry heart
drives away care but a sad face
drieth the bones.

Liberated by Generosity

Today was a turning point
in my life and at my age
the day should merit at least
honorable mention. My strictness
in money matters received a shock
which cracked and shook
my basic principles. Brought up
on a tight string, I grew into
the habit of denial, resisted
the seductions of credit,
I paid or went without. To owe
money came next in the book
of sins to coveting your
neighbor's wife. But today
in a hardware store I bought

a saw and was a dollar short
in payment. A stranger tossed
a dollar beside mine and said,
That will do it. When I asked
his name he smiled and said,
Pass on a good deed, walked out.
Here I am the owner of a saw
on which I owe money I cannot pay
and I feel liberated beyond redemption.
I wish you all such generosity,
may it fall like rain into your lives.

Love Is Not Earned

A display of my skills
slapped up on a billboard
would need more than neon
lights to catch the public eye.
Father always made his hay
before it rained; Grandfather
said his say with an orchard
and beehives, Winesaps and
comb honey. My talent for
indolence keeps me from being
an Orville Wright or an
Isaac Stern or a Pinter (Harold),
and I make any Sunday morning
speak softly that calls me
to examine my conscience.
But you set a halo on my head,
a crown of love and I know
(even if it slips on occasion)
I never earned it but like
grace it was freely given.

Mr. Norris and the Civet Cat

We four boys liked to fish
and sometimes after chores
we'd jump on our horses and ride
four miles to the river where
if we let him know old Mr. Norris
would unlock the gate to the
stretch of water beyond Norris's
siding. We were predator-triggered
in those days because of Mother's
chickens, baby ducks and all
young things a farm shelters.
So when we saw this tiny civet cat,
wet, muddy, mewing like a kitten,
our impulse was to stamp out its
life. We circled it cautiously
because civet cats and skunks are
born ready to shoot. But Mr. Norris
picked it up and stowed it inside his
shirt, mud, wet and all. Poor thing,
he said, even wild mothers sometimes
abandon children, it ain't always humans.
We tried to cover bloodthirsty
thoughts with a show of concern.
What will you do with it? we asked.
He said, warm it, dry it, feed it,
let it suck cloth soaked in milk
for its mother's tit. Turn it loose
when it's old enough. All babies have
a right to live. We're here to protect them.

Now in this violent, indecent, ruthless
weapon-driven world, I find relief in
thinking of Mr. Norris and his baby.

Nag, Nag, Nag All Day

The buzzing sound in my ears
is not from flies, mosquitoes, gnats,
but from the nagging voices of errands
born with the day in trivial detail
that clamor for attention. The phone
intrudes, doorbell insists, mail lies
waiting to be answered, an eaves trough
leaks, the hose won't reach the
flowerbed. My tolerance of demands
barely equals my sense of responsibility.
Who knows how long I can hold a pen
or the windows of my mind stay
clear enough to see more than the day's facts?
I look forward to just one time when
no bells ring, no letters beg,
no thistles grow in the garden.

Responsibility of Being Young

All I knew concerned my
errand and I felt proud
to be entrusted with that.
My breathless haste prompted
bare legs and feet. Father
needed Andrew to help with
the work, and I knocked at
his mother's door. The woman
who opened it had long sad eyes.
"He can't come," she explained,
"he drownded Sunday, they was
all swimming and he drownded."
Her words flew over my head,
their sense out of my reach.

"But Papa wants him," I insisted,
"to help with the work."
"He drownded yesterday," she said
and gently closed the door.
I stood outside, hands full
of my unfinished errand, wondering
if Father would be cross with me.

The Short Run and the Long Pull

Our fields lay side by side,
we farmed as best we knew,
my neighbor and I, and took
what the land gave. Both fields
sloped south with the topsoil
flowing downhill. Land moves
faster and farther than you
would suppose. We fed the
hungry land, he with manure,
I with nitrogen. He prophesied,
"Don't stuff mother earth with
chemicals, I'll have good land
after yours is poisoned."
And, you know, on nights
when I can't sleep, I wonder
if he is right.

Shy Breeder

The heifer is in heat but
she won't take the bull.
He lumbers after her, dark,
heavy, old but alive to his work.

He rubs against her, licks her
to persuade her to stand. But
she feels muscles contract as
he gathers to mount her and
runs away. Across the pasture
through the herd she shies from him
burning with her need. He is wet
with the sweat of pursuit but
bound to his calling. She stands
at station after station but
is nimble in escape. He crowds her
in a corner where two fences meet,
licks her, rubs her, lays his
heavy head on her back to weigh her
down. She squats, open in her torment.
His sheath drips, suddenly charged
with fury he mounts on his hind legs,
reaches with forelegs to clasp her,
foam flies from his muzzle but
she whips from the corner and he sinks
empty-handed and stands alone.

A Small Matter

The farmer knows he's no match
for storms. We drove the steers
out of the pasture into the yard,
shut cows and calves in the big barn,
locked the hoghouse doors and windows,
let the horses into their stalls.
The horses were waiting, they have
their own storm warnings, the radio
is ours. We drained the radiators
of truck and tractors, wedged shut
the machine shed doors. I piled wood

for the fireplace in the hall and
cautioned my wife to let her errands
wait. And then it came, a bellyful
of wind blasting out of the Arctic,
pellets of snow driven in lines
to rattle on roof and windows.
I watched the temperature fall
then sat by the fire and thought,
it's something to have done the best
you can and not feel guilty in the
comfort of your own shelter.

Subscription to Salvation

What do you know,
this fellow who just knocked
on my door has a magazine
full of recipes for salvation.
I never knew if I was saved
or not and it's a little late
for me to start worrying now.
He said I should be reborn
but I don't know, we're
getting along pretty well,
paid the property taxes last week,
had the old bus tuned up for winter.
Just the Missus and me, the kids
have all flown the coop. We have
a highball before dinner, eat at
the Club on Friday nights, watch
football on Sunday P.M. —I don't know
what I want to be reborn as.
I tried to make a little joke and said
I'd probably be reborn as a garter snake
and chase the girls out of
the strawberry patch. But he

gave me a sour look and walked away.
I'm sorry now I wasn't more polite
and let him finish saving me.

Survival

Lightning hit the poplar tree
and blasted it to smithereens.
We cut the stump close to the
ground. It had volunteered
its way into the yard and
survived despite the mower's
nudges and our disapproval.
But now it was gone and we
piled the logs for burning
as if a victim of the aristocracy
of oaks and maples. But we
were not done with it yet.
Shoots sprouted from the stump
and thin treelets from the roots
pushed up through the grass
around it. And we wondered
if our own instinct would give us
as many chances for survival.

There Is Time to Be Cheerful

On the back steps
in the dawn light
you put on your shoes
while the collie nuzzles you
ready to be sent for the cows.
You yawn, watch the pigeons
circle the barnyard as if tied

to a string. You hear voices,
familiar as dew, deep hog grunts,
a calf crying for its mother,
across the fields a neighbor's jackass
honks for mares. You breathe the spirit
of space, sound, feel the fresh stretch
of earth's body. Beyond the
honeysuckle hedge where the ducks sleep
head folded under wing, sun reflects
from barn windows, the children's pony
rubs its rump on a post. Fertile fields
could make this morning talk in symbols
but the fact of chores stirs your mind
while in the kitchen a voice hums
a breakfast tune. The odor of coffee,
bacon frying, rouses you to feed
the farm's hunger. When you come
from the barn the morning wears
a flower face. You kiss your wife
good morning.
The children in place at the table
catch the contagion and laugh at your
good morning, good morning festival.
You count the hour as a new start
untouched yet by the day's anguish.
Outside the window the hollyhocks nod
and each moment seems about to bloom.

Time to Cross Over

A black man with his family
moved in across the street and
he started to clean up his yard
and wash down the steps.
I like neighbors who take care
of their place and waved to him.

He didn't wave back. Why, I told
my wife, the sonofabitch won't wave.

But his kid batted a ball
into our yard and I yelled for
him to come and get it and
my wife gave the kid enough
fresh cookies she just baked
for the family. And now the guy
waves like crazy and I must
cross over and meet him someday.

We Ought to Burst into Bloom

This morning my wife brought me
a scilla blossom in a little
toby jug. It made an oasis
in the desert of my desktop.
It isn't so much that it is
our first spring flower though
that is cheerful in itself
as it is that such a small stem
could hoist such a bloom and
color it such a deep blue.
There are marvels everywhere you look.
I wish people when touched by
the fingers of spring, the sun,
birdsong, warm rain, instead of
folding the morning in a briefcase
with the calloused fingers of habit,
would burst into flower with green hair
and petals opening at every joint,
and perhaps a leaf or two to remind us
of the clothes our forebears wore
in the Garden.

The Windmill

Time I greased the windmill,
Father said—he did not know
my urge to be a man. Before he
left the dinner table I was gone.
Oilcan in my back pocket I faced
a wooden tower seventy feet into
the sky that tapered to a point
where the wheel turned and pivoted
on its bearings. (I shut it down
before I climbed, turned in the
vanes out of the wind.) My Mount
Everest calling me, I climbed.
Wood rungs to clutch with hands
and feet, no squirrel to scamper,
I gripped hard. Up, up and up,
the tower grew narrow, like a leech
I clung. I poked my head through
the platform, then rose to stand.
My god, the wheel looked big,
its counterbalance huge, wind gave it
a push for half a turn, I groped
for safety. I squirted oil, I greased the axle
as far as I could reach.
Then seized by mania I climbed
to the top of the housing
and carefully stood up and balanced
there with nothing for my hands
to grasp, and stared into the sky.
Clouds moving made the tower
lean to fall. In a vortex of
madness I felt the falling tower.
Whirlpools of vertigo, clouds,
tower, boy and a forming arc.
(It is easy to die when you are young.)
I stood on the iron housing,

slippery with oil, gripped my balance,
arms outstretched like a tightrope
walker, dizzy with clouds on a
swaying tower. My monkey hands clung
when I stooped, feet felt for the
platform then the ladder's rungs . . .
to tremble until I reached the ground.

Winter Morning

I enter a winter morning
under furrows of cloud plowed
by the wind, and watch fingers
of light pick out trees, the
silhouette of the chimney,
touch panes of a farmhouse window.
A refugee from the daily news
where love in exile, bombs of
anger, a forecast of blood
on the moon shame us for our ways,
I listen while the country speaks
with the bark of a dog, the whisper
of still grass under the foot,
a crow announcing a new day.

NINETEEN EIGHTY-TWO

After Snowfall

Sky smooth as a country
untouched by the plow,
earth as unmarked as the sky
under its thick snowfall.

Morning soundless, muted
now marred by my tracks
to the field where a monster
of snow becomes a corn picker
I have come to grease.
Grease nipples emerge after
brushed by my mittened hand.
I check the outlets, ends
of the fluted snapping rolls,
gathering chains, drive shaft,
elevator sprockets. No sound
but the lever working on the
grease gun, the soft squelch
as bearings fill and grease squirts
from the safety hole. The morning
gleams white as apple's flesh,
silent as an empty church.
Only my gnomelike figure and
busy arms disturb its peace.
The time seems breathless.
Then a rabbit leaps from
beneath the machine and leaves
a trail, a dog barks, a plane
scratches the sky, cows bawl,
sounds that break the silence.
I note a snowcap fall from
a fence post, I wipe my nose
on my mitten, the day begins.

Alms to the Giver

The mail this morning made me
wonder if the plethora of "worthy causes"
divides us into givers and takers.
The begging letters half-fill the

waste basket—money, money, as if
we owned a goose that laid a golden egg.
Someone is eager for our answer,
one envelope marked "Urgent," two
marked "Important" and one "Your
Greatest Opportunity." Such concern
should puff me up until I notice
an enclosed envelope to make it
easy for my reply.
My vision is limited. Instead of a
multitude waiting to divide my
scant loaves and fishes, I imagine
a marvellous creature who stops
polishing her nails to open my letter
and when the check spills out she calls,
"Hey, Bert, another sucker bit the dust."

A Balance Sheet

From my father's family I inherit
this long face and a need for facts,
on my mother's side a delight in
tales where the hero slays the dragon.
The mirror repeats my age and shows
the wrinkles of my discontent.
I am tangled in webs of habit.
I eat an apple each day, dress up
on Sunday, make love at full moon,
share as much as I borrow, brush
my teeth before I read the headlines,
drink my coffee black with toast.
My files bulge with notes from
committee meetings, I keep a
running account of my expenses.
This stencil for living stamps my work

but I move with purpose. No one
on either side of the family
ever made a journey just to see
the sights.

Double Talk

The exercises we schedule
for our extinction face the
bared teeth of instinct.
One side of our mouths
begs for thunderbolts,
the other side coos like a dove
for peace treaties. But deep
beneath polite plans for
mass slaughter live a hibernating
bear, fanged serpent, cunning fox,
eagle in flight to teach us
survival in this goddam world
of double talk.

Let It Shine

The guy who hides his light
under a bushel ought to be told
to let it shine. He won't push
back the edge of darkness if
he waits to be noticed. Let it shine,
for god's sake, we need all the light
we can get.

You know damn well the guy
without a light nor even a bushel,
would give his eyeteeth for just
a tiny candle. Then he might brag
about it until you thought it was
a torch. No objections from me,
at least he'd have something
worth a shout. And anyway,
as the Master said to his Ass,
It's all right to make the big noise
if you have no close neighbors.

Missed Fortune

Late for our dates,
the stubbornness of chores
(and girls don't like to wait),
my brother and I barreled
out of the yard toward town.
A shabby overloaded car
sagged on the road's shoulder,
two women struggled to change
a tire. We braked, backed up,
jumped out. I maneuvered
the jack, Bob twirled off
the nuts, we mounted the spare.
Suddenly aware of the women—
heavy gold earrings, fancy scarves,
full skirts, crazy-colored
blouses, black hair, swarthy skins,
our eyes popped, gypsies!
The older woman opened her purse,
Bob gently closed it.

In a soft voice the younger woman
said, hold out your palms
and I will read your fortunes.
But we were late, I tell you,
and we tore off down the road
to keep still hidden in our hands
the dark roads she might see ahead.
And anyway it was enough for us
just to know the girls would
still be waiting.

No Advice Today, Thank You

Why, the presumptuous bastard
peddling his stock of conjugal doctrines,
trying to sneak a feel into
the warm tangle of our affairs.
Who asked him to butt in with
sawdust words stuffed with pretensions?
Let his pious nose sniff elsewhere
for gamey odors—I'd like to rub it
in the carcass of past rumors that decayed
before they died. I have more advice
now than I can use. Let him open
a roadside stand and offer real food,
potatoes, apples, carrots, instead of
the sacred wafer to hungry people.
Let him earn humility by good works.
We live as we must live and things
happen as they happen and no
cock-a-doodle-doo ever hatched out
the chickens we counted on.
We try to accept the thorns in our
flesh as if we deserved them.

Not Really a Quarrel

Granted we slept well and
ate breakfast together,
the sky has not lost color
nor the sun its light,
birds seem busy at their
feeding and indoors the rooms
keep order, no failure
of light or heat, faucets
do not leak and no real quarrel
worked up a storm. But some
insistence on your side
made you scrub the sink
with sudden vigor and I
skimmed the paper without
reading the news. Trapped in
a disagreement we could not
define, we simmered in a
half-angry, half-apologetic mood.
After all these years together
it is still hard for one of
us to say, I was mistaken.

Not the Last Goodbye

Hat askew, coat open,
purse on one arm, car keys
in hand, she scans the
grocery list and bumps
into the door. She backs up,
kicks it open, steams into
the garage. I hear the car
grumble, cough, then roar.
The hand of the kitchen

clock zip zips from second
to second, and the morning
grows. I retreat to my study,
open and shut drawers, hear
the house empty itself of
voices and rush and stir.
Be careful, I told her,
there are bastards abroad
witless in cars, mind the
cross streets. I did not
say goodbye. But what if
it was goodbye? The thought
so skewered me I did not turn
a page until she returned.

Now Hear This

Your Honor, she cried, I need help.
My old man is drunk on salvation.
He spouts the Gospel like a pot
overflowing, chants Psalms in the
bathroom, intones the Ten Commandments
before breakfast. I am smothered
in Proverbs, if I could put them
in vases I would have Parables
blooming all over the house. I am
dizzy from kneeling, I suffer sinus
complaints from frequent baptism.
I am called to bear witness and each
night in the bedroom with hosannas
the shepherd seeks his lost lamb.
I throw my self on the mercy of the
Court to save me from these Days
of Judgment.

Only Flowers Seem Not to Die

On our May Day anniversary
I went to the garden we planted
and filled a basket with daisies
and delphiniums. Though choked
with weeds and guarded by a
rusty hoe the garden still sends
petaled tokens and the morning
offered me this memory with
blossoms from our haunted wildwood.
Their fragile colors reminded me
how you opened your arms in delight
each spring when they returned
and knew in them the roots of survival . . .
Then the hard hammers of fact
began to pound in my head.

Photograph

A photograph taken from
my best side assumes
a stance with a cigarette
held between nonchalant
fingers. I don't ride a
horse, wear a western hat,
or with empty hair and open
shirt hug a flat tire.
Impossible to tousle me
into a place in the great
open spaces. I don't even smoke.
How about a bookcase for
a backdrop or fireplace
cheerful with its burning?
No, no, place an arrogant

cigarette leaking a stream
of smoke between my fingers.
I want to add a half-smile
showing my sophisticated
incisor at the ready.

Resolution

Strokes took off the big tree's top
          out back; pressed soot into
white wood the length of the split;
          tore wires like webs, cracked
conductors as if they were
          glass nuts, where now flat snow
kicks back light scoured
          of impurities, tensing waves
straight, bundles brittle as twigs
          all lying in the same direction.

Shelter under Glass

The seventh grade came to visit
my greenhouse. The teacher said
they are studying flowers. They
arrived in a school bus—I could
not deny the request—and filed
in past the teacher who stood
at the door and spoke tight words
out of a fixed smile. The boys
dropped their jackets, the girls
carried theirs as better mannered.
They all kicked boxes on the floor,

complained of the dirty sink,
joked about broken pots. They left
like a trampling herd, praised
everything, thanked me to death,
moved as from a plague. Flattery
did not warm me nor was I soured
with exasperation. I watered
the African violets, moved some
begonias out of the sun, wondered
about Plato's ideal greenhouse.
Beyond my lair far out in the distance
I knew men hurried to keep step
with the sun while children
dawdled on the way to age.

Sign-Directed

I was born under the sign
of the threshing machine
and lived by its portent.
The meaning of the hot August
day when I entered this world
stays with me even in
coldest January. I move
in the sweat and dust of the work,
hearing the engine whirl
the cylinder, shake the sieves,
turn the auger as belts slap
and clack and pulleys spin.
I haul in my crop to
separate wheat from the chaff,
closed in the zodiac of
a hot August morning while
Leo roars among the stars.

Taking the Bull to Water

The herd bull leaves his stall
to do his duty by his wives
(as some men do not) and goes
with me twice a day to the
tank for water. Tight curls
of hair pack the wide space
between his eyes which seem
to regard me with an amiable
but stupid stare. But his
polished horns warn me to
have the beast in him respect
the beast in me. I crowd his neck
behind the horns to untie
his halter rope, then snap
the leading stick to the ring
in his nose. He accepts my gestures
without protest and follows me
with heavy steps. I walk backward
all the way, facing him, the
halter rope over my shoulder,
the leading stick in both hands.
If he would hook at me I have him
where it hurts, the ring he wears
in a tender nose. At the tank
I climb up on a post,
unsnap the stick while he sucks up water. He looks up
drops dripping from his muzzle.
I throw a half hitch around
the gate post until I snap
the stick in his ring. We
return, paired as before, he advances,
I retreat one step at a time.
Our moment comes when I must
lift my foot high enough to
clear the barn door sill and

not trip and fall. I can't read
his shaggy thought but he knows
as well as I this movement counts.
I feel his muscles gather and
a push from his bowed neck.
I jerk the stick to let him know
I feel him. (We lost a neighbor
once who missed this step.)
We enter, I stand aside not to be
caught between him and the manger.
I tie the rope, unsnap the stick,
pat his back. He's relaxed now too
and munches hay. I play the game
my way, he gets a drink, I keep my skin,
to date we have not changed the rules,
he waits the day of an exception.

Walls

My terrace wall dropped
a few stones. I lift them
back, use a dab of mortar
to lock them in. Rough on
hands but I like their hard
skins and sudden weight.
Frost, chipmunks, roots
niggle stones from my wall
and leave pockmarks on its face.
Men like to build walls,
always have. The Great Wall
of China, Roman walls, and
walled cities fill history.
Walls mark boundaries, protect
territory. My wall holds earth
firm, keeps in place some
ground to stand on.

The Weed Cutter

Earth soaked by a thunderstorm
excused us from fieldwork on a
hot muggy June morning. Time
to cut weeds in the fencerows.
"Son of a bitch," I said, weary
with sixteen years. Corn taller
than my head kept off the breeze,
gnats swarmed over my sweaty
face. I hung my shirt on a
fence post, whetstone in my
hip pocket to sharpen the scythe,
a jug of drinking water hidden
under grass to keep it cool.
Large hemp stalks tough as leather
I named for people I disliked
and whacked away. The neighbor's
stupid cows stared at me across
the fence where the blade of
my scythe caught and nearly tore
my arms loose. Who would want
to be a farmer and work his ass off
on a day like this? Resentment
poured into my muscle but a nap
in the shadowy cornfield never
tempted me. As in a game
to win I swung the scythe and
conscience heavy with Father's
orders kept the score.

What's Time to a Hog?

Today a man asked me
for the time, I told him
what my watch said but I had
a funny feeling about asking
for time. Could a beggar
on a street corner ask passersby
for a quarter or half an hour?
Might they say, We haven't time
to give you time, or some real
smartass would say, I wouldn't
give you the time of day.
A banker might say, Time is money,
and if the beggar said, I'll trade—
what would the banker say?
When I was a boy in school
one of my teachers scolded me,
You mustn't waste time looking out
the window. I wasted paper, broke
my pencil, scuffed my books,
but no one gave me time.
How could I waste it?
I could understand "tide" in
"there is a tide in the affairs
of men," but how could I
"take time by the forelock"?
I know we had days and nights,
seasons and years but I measure
life by what I do. Though I'll bet
my tombstone will be marked with time.

Wither Away, Friend

An ill-matched pair,
I'd hate to drive them as a team,
she with a big full-bosomed voice
full of muscle, and he squeaks
through the debris of his replies.
She sentenced him to her kind of order
and prophesied dire moments
if he did not keep his backyard tools
picked up and stored out of sight.
As it comes to some men,
a revelation came to him and
his toolshed became a safe house
where an old rocking chair
and floor lamp made a cozy refuge
from the harsh weather of her tongue.
Now a file of girlie magazines
makes the sap rise and he smiles
to think of the whole house,
with room after room empty of him
for her to holler through.

Witnesses

The orchard basks in
the mellow light of autumn,
leaves drift along the hedge,
a late mouse scurries for its burrow.
Three pheasants, a cock
and two hens stroll with
arrogant steps through
frosted grass and dry leaves.
Their bronze and purple splendor
witnesses as wilderness

beyond the tame acre
of my study. They burn in the sun
and wake a vision of barbaric wonder
against the windows of my
safe retreat.

NINETEEN EIGHTY-THREE

A Believer

A dirty carpet of March snow
underfoot, the sky a black iron bowl
welded into place by stars. The lantern
drew a circle of light around my feet,
invaded by my shadow. I was sixteen,
moved in the dim light to the barn,
alone except for the collie dog,
a rolling ball of shadows in yellow light.
My chore brought me from bed to the box stall
where our purebred Belgian mare
should have her colt tonight.
Mares like to have their colts in privacy.
Last year she lay too near the wall,
forced out her colt and broke its neck.
Tonight I am the guardian of unborn colts.
The mare stands as if she was carved from wood.
I speak calmly to her and she hears me
but other business concerns her!
I shove hay bales together for a bed,
pull a horse blanket over me. The lantern
stinks of kerosene but burns steadily.
No one to speak to, my life ages while
I wait. Sleep tempts me, perhaps I doze.

Hay tickles my face, the blanket smells
of horse sweat. Suddenly I rouse, the lantern
burned out, pale morning light gropes
at the window. The mare nurses
her colt. I stand and stretch
a stiff body, a believer in life
as birth and death and struggle for
existence.

Cleaning Lady

Her coat is vague as fog but she herself
ever at odds with plump and lazy houses
walks with pride and vigor and respects
only the gleaming dish in its proper place.

She rips a sullen cobweb from the wall
that seems to challenge her authority,
then straightens slouching rooms and disciplines
the sloven manners of the yawning beds.

Her mop and broom hunt shadows until floors
mirror the order of the furniture,
as if in guilty blush the color comes
back to the carpet's washed and patterned face.

She patiently instructs the willful house
in lessons that will save its character,
then turns it back to us as to a child
who takes for granted what he hasn't earned.

Lord, let her have in heaven a shining home
who on this earth has borne upon her hands
the stains of labor, let windowpanes
open like eyes on the white floors of her soul.

Fallen Sign

There comes a time when
everything seems to repeat itself
as a calf or colt resembles its mother.
Thirty years ago I entered this gate
and planted the seeds I wanted to grow.
Any comfort at my age came from
the confidence that each seed contained
its own architecture for the plant
it would build. I could see the fertile
fields and rolling hills as far as my eyes
could travel as they lay under the sun.
I heard the crows making a racket in the grove.
Meadowlarks perched on fence posts,
corn borer moths like winged snowflakes
settled on the stalks. I watched it all
with an owner's eye as if a man owns
what he sees. The sun took its time to cross
the sky, rain clouds drew their curtains
to darken the day. But I stood there
with a mind counting what I had done
or did not do, moments passed slowly.
Each one marked off the length of life.
I picked up a fallen sign hidden in the grass
where once a young man had spelled
his name with hope.

Moments of Being Away

Today I walked through the house
to touch things I once knew.
It wasn't as a stranger I came
but more an uncertainty of where
I belonged. I mowed the backyard

as if hired to care for the property
and gave myself permission to pick
a panful of string beans. I found
a rabbit's nest with four little
white cottontails, a pair of brown
thrashers searched under an oak tree,
my neighbor's dog sniffed the hedge,
all as much at home as if they owned
the place. A few clouds dipped
past a sun which has slowed down
two-thousandths of a second in
one hundred years, a southwest wind
brought up moisture from the Gulf,
nothing out of the ordinary,
a usual summer day. Then two boys
asked to cross the backyard to fish
in Dry Run and a neighbor stopped
with a petition for me to sign and I
felt earth, mine, firm under my feet.

The Shelled Pea News

To shell peas on a hot
morning in a pan with a wide
bottom takes all the character
she possesses and her temper
climbs with the thermometer.

She shucks them because she
won't eat pods, cows chew cuds,
she has only one stomach,
sometimes more than enough.

She keeps a week-old newspaper
in her lap to catch the pods,

and reads that there are
one hundred million solar systems
in our galaxy. That takes
her mind off the Russians.

One hundred million solar systems
in our galaxy, how many other
women are shelling peas?

At the bottom of the page
it says, never run from a bear
but don't threaten it. And she
shells peas in a pan with a wide
bottom on a hot morning, citizen
of one hundred million solar systems.

So Much Change

Remember how the book would not
stay open when we studied together
and the prim-faced man at the end
of the table gave us the eye until
we hushed our fooling. I met him
lately with his full bag of books
coming down the library steps and he
asked about you. I could not answer him,
I can't account for so much change
nor understand it. We did not plan it
this way, perhaps what we counted on
was never ours to keep. I remember
how you jumped out of bed naked
and ran to the kitchen to plug in
the coffeepot. I thought you looked
beautiful without a stitch on like a
Greek statue come to life. Oh,

in those days love lived forever
and would bless all the days of my life.
I thought our flowers would never wither.
Now I worry, half a year ahead,
about New Year's Eve, about who will hum
Auld Lang Syne in my ear as we dance
and kiss me when the clocks strike twelve.
Now as I look around lilacs
are not anything but lilacs,
the oriole is just another bird.
Everything is just itself and not
a transformation into something new
and lovely as once I saw it.

There Are Those Who Say This

I lit the bonfire,
a pile of dry weeds,
dead vines from the garden,
dead twigs from the willow tree,
boxes of yesterday's trash,
heaped residues of autumn,
let them burn.
Encouraged by the wind,
fed by its own hunger,
the fire got out of hand.
It lunged toward
my neighbor's house,
crept through dry grass
to threaten mine,
as if to say in tongues of wrath
that destruction will have
the last word.

Time to Go In

You poke the fire in the fireplace,
the burned-out logs release two
tiny flames then crumble to ash.
Not enough flame left to send sparks
up the chimney and startle some bird
in the belief the stars are falling.
The night seems quiet, you mark
your place and close the book
and stretch, the last word has been read.
Did you ever feel the wet tongue
of a dog ready to go out? You scratch
the soft ears, head for the back door.
The cold air takes your breath away,
not winter yet but a winter sky
forming its constellations, you
try to identify them while the dog
chases a shadow under the lilac bush.
His warm footprints leave dark marks
on the frosty grass. You let him run,
shiver slightly, the fireplace seems
far away. Why does a man study the sky,
coatless, hatless, in this weather?
To orient himself, mark his place,
to let him know where he lives? But he owns
a zodiac and sorts out the stars
as a stranger might the signs
in a foreign country. It is growing late,
call the dog, time we both went in.

Within Limits

One afternoon in early spring
I collected debris from the
backyard, the deposit from
winter's glacier. The hedge
offered me an armful of stale
newspapers, faded as the
news they carried, a broken
box, three mittens, a basket of
twigs shed by the weeping
willow, a broken-backed kite
and a gnawed bone. I heap them up,
these discards of a season and
the yard can now boast of its
clean features. My kind of order
craves a match to burn this pile
of trash, but time's order, with a
patience older than grass, waits
on the burning hunger of decay.
And you, my dear, watch me with
fire and rake and keep within
limits my forward look.

This is my time today
and I better make the most of it,
there may not be many more.

   ᔄ Today Is Now

Abandoned Orchard

These weathered trees
like fierce old men
endure and endure.
Fungus, neglect and
age do not chasten them.
They lean toward falling.
Shoved by the wind
on brittle roots
with thin sap they pump
each spring the roots'
stores into leaf and
blossom. They bear
wizened apples
shrivelled by frost.
Winter storms shake them,
branches rub and rattle,
and break as if too frail
to bear their burdens.

Away with Boards

The last storm shook
the forsaken barn until it
wobbled on its foundation
fragile enough for one more
wind push to crush it down.
We looked at it in silence,
she and I, without words.
She owned the barn, I did
the work. She made her

decision when she said
to herself, "Those gray barn
boards would bring a fortune
in New York." Like a caress
she said again, "old barn boards."
I shrugged peasant's shoulders.
After she had gone I would
set a match to it—let the city
find its own boards.

Claim for Damages

"The man recovered from the bite,
the dog it was that died." This
may be the end of the ballad but
it is not the end of the story.
The dog's owner sued the man
bitten on the grounds that the dog
had the right to assume it was biting
healthy flesh and not a leg tainted
beyond a normal dog's immunity.
The jury found for the plaintiff
and awarded him a million and a half
dollars in damages. The award broke down
into these items, $150.00 veterinary fee
and body disposal; $500,000.00 for
lack of companionship and protection;
$500,000.00 for mental anguish, worry
and loss of affection; $400,000.00
for libelous and defamatory remarks
by the defendant about both dog and
master and for accusing them of a
relationship which did not in fact
exist; $99,350.00 for the neglect
of the defendant to make

friendly overtures to the dog
and attempt to persuade him
not to bite. The defendant
appealed the verdict on the grounds
that in running away from the dog
he had no breath left to speak
kindly to it; that his pants and
sock were torn; that he was so upset
he could not resume conjugal relations
with his wife until the wound
healed; and the dog knowingly was
allowed to break the leash law.
The judge took the appeal under advisement.

Crop Inspector

The farmer opened the gate,
tramped the line between
his cornfield and the alfalfa
to see if the stand of corn
measured up to the amount
of seed he had planted.
He granted a few hills to
gophers and pheasants but
depended on the rows of green
shoots to grow into the crop
he expected. He checked for
bare spots in the alfalfa
where frost may have shrivelled
a few crowns as it sank cold fingers
into the earth. Still thick enough,
he thought, to smother weeds,
as for the corn, let the cultivator
shovels keep order. His firm steps
on eighty-year-old feet carried him

to the far fence and back.
He poked the ground with his cane
and thought, how many roots
have I favored, how many destroyed.
He felt them underground groping,
searching, reaching out with
hungry mouths, sucking in food
as they hoisted green stalks into
sunlight. He whacked a thistle
with his stick and said, not yet,
old boy, not yet, you will wait
a while before I lie down
as ransom for what I've taken.

Hope Goes Whoosh!

We just could not believe our luck.
A For Sale sign on the house next door.
It's like seeing buds on the tulips
after a hard winter, I could hear
birds sing when I drove home through
traffic. What a day of jubilation.
For months we shaped our faces
into friendly beacons, smiled if it
killed us. All the while their kids
left junk all over our backyard,
he never touched the lawn mower
and let dandelion seeds spread
over the whole township, and God,
their damn radio blasting away
day and night. Will we celebrate!
When I met the guy coming home
I said (I hope) in a neighborly tone,
"We will be glad to help you move."
"Oh," he answered, "you didn't notice?

We've changed our minds, took down the sign."
Did you ever wonder how a balloon feels
when it bursts? That's our sky-high
hopes stuck full of pins.

Never Too Late

He grunted, jammed
his foot on the spade.
Eighty years old, he found
earth more solid than
it used to be. He sharpened
the spade, let the hose run
where he dug. His leg
trembled when he pushed
with all his might.
But he had a rosebush
to plant and come time
or tide he would have it
near the window where he
could watch it grow.
He told himself, it may be
a bit late to forgive me
my transgressions but it is
never too late to plant
a rosebush.

Reason to Get Up in the Morning

All this chatter about
each morning a fresh start,
new day full of surprises and
unknown promise, a return

to life from sleep like death,
all turns me a little sour.
Maybe some truth in it like
"full of surprises" rings a bell
(mostly unpleasant like interest
due or taxes or discovery the roof
leaks). It all seems so routine,
the alarm clock shrills, you yawn,
wish for forty winks more, decide
against it, dress, wash, shave,
brush your teeth, find a clean shirt,
take a gander at the headlines,
eat the same cereal that tastes
like sawdust, hope three cups
of coffee will get you in gear.
It's a pattern of repeating repetition.
True, the weather changes, thank god,
any variety is welcome. Well maybe
the car won't start or the stupid
garage door won't open—not the variety
I'd choose. But at least I don't ask
myself what's it all for. The work
is there to be done and if I didn't do it
I wouldn't have anything to do.

Strange Things Happen

I found a ball in the yard
and tossed it as high as I could
and waited to catch it.
Not mine, it probably belonged
to the neighbor kids—
weird in appearance, stripes
around it like Saturn's rings,
stars and a moon on the sides.

It may belong to a game
where the pattern fits the play.
It lay in my yard, fresh shiny cover—
I never saw one like it.
It's been years since I played
catch. We never had a ball
marked like this, just an old
faded red one with a chunk
knocked out by a bat or dog's teeth.
This ball looked different,
not ordinary, not play-worn.
I tossed it into the air
(that was years ago).
I remember it never came back.

The Tide

Today is our anniversary
and resurrects my belief
that time runs out like a tide
and no moon brings it back.
I study my wife's face.
Where once it bloomed with
the soft skin of a petal
it now hardens in the wrinkles
and paleness of her age.
I take her for a mirror
of us all with our scars
of failure, bruises of grief.
I do not ask to change her
for the girl she was but
my thoughts would trouble her
if she heard them. I add
a hope of her forgiveness
to what speaks to my eye.

The Trimmed Bush

Grouchy, she said, you are
grouchy this morning. Your face
looks like leftovers from
yesterday's casserole.
He thought, she comes to
breakfast with her hair in
curlers, wrapped in a sloppy gown,
bare feet in flapping slippers.
She used to bloom in the
mornings with a fresh dress
and neatly combed hair. Perhaps
I ought to trim her a little,
shape her clean and neat.
She asked, what are you grinning about?
He answered, I was thinking of the
spirea bush I cut back last fall,
the one that burst out all white
with blossoms this spring.

Today Is Now

It doesn't need headlines,
I see it, my age stamped on
the mirror each morning. So
that's the way it is and I go
to bed so I can get up or
get up so I can go to bed
with a day wedged between or
a night, habits I've acquired
through use and I don't ask why.
Deep, back in the mirror stare
the eyes of the young man

I used to be, who did other
things than I do now. All right,
let him, I am not going back
in memory and pick up after him.
Let him pay his own debts,
the girl he borrowed love from,
the parents he never paid back,
the friends he forgot to settle
with—the hell with him, he had
his chance. This is my time today
and I better make the most of it,
there may not be many more.

What Matters

It rose high enough
to float the clouds,
this fountain of leaves,
this cottonwood tree
alone in the field's center.
A shade on hot days, a sundial
at noon, a landmark in any weather,
its roots dug for moisture,
it stunted the corn under it,
its trunk shoved machines aside.
It owned its ground by roothold,
dominated the field. My father
sawed it down, soaked the stump
with kerosene and burned it
even to the roots. Now furrows
run straight, make a slight hump
over the tree's grave, give the corn
its sky without shade. Meadowlarks
and bobolinks did not mourn

where they nested in meadow grass.
My father fitted the new pattern
to his work, only the passing birds
if they stopped would have to perch
on air and who knows what matters
to them, if they grieved or not.

What Time Is It Anyway?

You can't win 'em all,
he said when he lost his job
as manager of a small factory
that made sleds and coaster wagons.
He said, Our product does not seem
to be in demand and no one can
think of anything else we're
good for. Like the rest of us
he had bills to pay and a family
to support and at his age the
big companies weren't anxious
to interview him for a job.
He found work with the Park
Commission mowing grass in the
city parks. If he felt a put-down
he kept it to himself and paid
his taxes and renewed his credit
at the bank. But he asked himself,
Have I outlived my time? Am I
at fifty an anachronism?
It's hard to accept defeat
of sleds and coaster wagons
by a day of snack bars and
the instant replay.

The Hurt of Pleasure

Once a week she comes to share
time with me. Today I spread
manure on the garden and she watches.
I have a wooden paddle to clean
the spade, Iowa loam absorbs
moisture and is sticky to work
as I turn it over. She holds
tulip bulbs in her lap and does not
say much but I know she feels queer
about the muscle in her roots—
plants that grow underground
like carrots, potatoes, beets:
she knows the tulip bulbs
won't explode but she handles
them carefully. We think our own
thoughts on a day like this
and say them to each other
without words. Beneath the topsoil
of memory our human rootedness
in each other stays alive and she
comes on a spring day to watch me
plant the tulip bulbs she held
in her lap as if she felt the hurt
of pleasure in sprouting seed.

Not the Day to Listen

This nifty gent with a spry tongue
sells shares in a cemetery association
with radical options strange to us.

No ceremony, he said, prompt and efficient
disposal of the body, no church services,
no gathering of relatives and friends,
no reception afterward with food and drink.
On a morning like this, lilacs in bloom
all over town, he couldn't sell flies
to a spider. A fresh carpet of grass
edges the garden where seeds just broke through,
weeds lifting their heads, dandelions
in the front row, the kids off swimming
after their chores, Mama with a tub
full of dirty clothes—who has got time
to die on a day like this?
I leaned on my hoe long enough to tell him
we weren't ready yet and besides
we had made plans for tomorrow.

Winter Reverie

Winter grips the farm
with an iron hand, ruptures
foundation, freezes water pipes,
seals furrows in ice. The yard
paved with frost rustles with drifts
of straw, paper, husks,
gathered and spread by the wind.
We have the endurance for survival,
we read in the plowed expression
of fields, harvests to come,
pastures alive with calves,
the shouting strength of tractors,
tips of green pushing, pushing
into the light. And we, with the sun
on our backs, follow our footsteps

of years past, indifferent to eyes
from the road staring at us
as they pass, our steady gaze
aloof from passersby who have no stake
in the furrows we turn.

NINETEEN NINETY-THREE

Benchmark of Plunder

We needed an onion, the row
in our garden used up so I
slipped over to the garden
my neighbors keep—they were
out of town for the weekend.
Their onions packed in two
long rows gave me one, and while
I was there I snipped off a head
of cauliflower, beautiful firm
white flesh untouched by spots
or worms, and picked a small pan
of green beans which I hope
they won't miss. Their garden
is loaded for harvest.
I have been reading about the
Romans, what a grabby lot they were,
no wonder the barbarians clobbered
them. But you have to hand it to
them, wherever they plundered
they left something, roads, walls,
aqueducts, some say they lined
the baths in Bath, England, with lead.

After all they owed something to
the people whose country they robbed.
Now where did I leave my good paring knife?
I had it when I cut the cauliflower . . .

Best Not to Hope for Miracles

He had heard that water
could be changed to wine.
His hands trembled, dropped
a plate, scooped up the pieces
in the dustpan. He could not
scoop up his anxiety. The morning
seemed cheerful enough.
The sun rose at sunrise,
dew shimmered on the grass.
A bluejay squawked at the empty
feeder, a squirrel climbed
an oak tree, children tramped
off to school, minutes fell
from the clock as the second hand
jerked around, curtains stirred
in a light wind—the calendar
said it was summer. Mustn't forget
to put away the cream and rinse out
the sink. His hands remembered
the clutch of frail fingers,
but eyes helpless before her
mute appeal. The hospital whispered
past on rubber-soled shoes.

Better a Bonfire

Hitch up the mule,
I said to myself,
and haul this stuff
to the garbage dump,
all these boxes, bundles
of remembered deceit, anger,
violence, enough scandal
here to blow the neighborhood
wide open. I wonder why
I hoarded these items?
A lie here, a cheat there,
a battered wife, abused child,
whiskey bottles by the case,
a boy who stole a car,
a girl who needs a husband,
all decayed fruit from
the neighborhood tree.
Let me come with clean hands,
come on you jackass, lean into it,
for god's sake take it away.

Choreman

I am a born choreman.
In the book of records
I will be named "My brother's
sweeper." I follow instructions
on a daily work sheet and never
dream of a legacy from a rich aunt,
a winning lottery ticket,
the long shot at the races.
I sweat for my bread, debt

would leave me a hunchback
if I borrowed my supper. I even
haul away trash on my day off.
But I eat well, sleep soundly,
know a plain girl beds
as lively as a beauty.
I save my wages to build a house
large enough for a choreman
within call of folk whose unkempt lives
resemble their cluttered yards
and stables.

The Comfort of a Friend

We have wandered as we wished
through groves and meadows of our choice,
and all the streams in which we fished,
the meetings where we raised a voice
roll up in a map of time when finished
the years when we were girls and boys.

Now that we've spent our hoard of years
in careful or in careless measure,
what have we left of hopes and fears
we boasted we enjoyed the leisure
to waltz until our star appears
to lead us to our rightful treasure.

But when at last we march our road
we find the ending seems abrupt
at tables either home, abroad
where sins are gilded as we supped,
unconscious of the rich man's load
where worms creep in and moths corrupt.

When we no longer can defend
the shrunken yields left in our keeping,
the spirit that we had for friend
through bursts of joy and gusts of weeping
will be our comfort at the end
of days of sowing and of reaping.

Dulled Appetite

Your letter today
came after such long absence
I had forgotten I worried
about not hearing from you.
It's a dull appetite I have
for opening your letter.
Of course I hope you are well,
have a job you deserve,
receive good news from your folks.
I wish you luck when you need it.
But too much time, like water
under the bridge, has flowed past
for me to be aware of you
as once I was, and I opened your letter
in turn among bills and advertisements.
I did not tremble to reach for it
as I did once and fumble
with eagerness to open it,
every word a precious sigh.
I glanced at it with the same
attention I give to a letter
from a business firm I no longer
do business with.

Echoes of Memory

A birthday card from you today
wakes the pain of an old wound,
like a stitch in my side,
of a day in midsummer
on an abandoned road arched
with leaves, hugged by a stream,
where we lay in the shade,
mocked by birds for our lack of song,
as they eyed us from nearby bushes.
We embraced and spoke in whispers
meant to keep us true forever.

Today the woods are bare,
crystal points edge the stream,
the birds have flown save for a bluejay
in a bush of shriveled berries.
If the past speaks to us, the words
sound like echoes of memory
where no rain like tears
falls to revive the wildflowers
where they shared our shelter
in one day of summer.

Expression of a Homeplace

If I close one eye
and don't turn my head
I can see with clarity
what's on one side of my nose.
A familiar country exposes
itself, phlox blossoms,
half a cement drive,

half a car, a whole swath
of lawn, and farther up
the street, houses of neighbors,
trees on the parking,
a satisfying view of where I live,
enough to give me the expression
of a homeplace.

The robin left her mud-glued
nest of sticks and said
to the woodpecker, "Who
would live shut up in
a hole in a dead tree?"
The woodpecker replied,
"Who would live anywhere else?"

Fear of Play for Keeps

It's just for the program,
the teacher pleaded, and
it would be real cute, you
and Astrid. The boy shook
his head, set lips in a stubborn
line. The schoolroom gave him
no support, blackboards stared
blankly, the map offered no
route of escape, the big
dictionary just squatted on its
table with closed covers.
He couldn't do it, he just
couldn't do it. Oh, he could
sing the tune and liked the song
until he realized what the teacher
wanted. "Come now, won't you

play house, won't you play
house with me? You shall be
pappa, I will be mamma, won't
you play house with me?"
It made him sick to his stomach.
He didn't mind Astrid, she was
all right for a girl . . .
What was play and what was real?
He couldn't have Astrid
hanging around his neck
for the rest of his life.
He scraped his shoe. "No, ma'am,
I won't do it. I don't want
to play house."

Flowers Would Be Better

My wife calls me to see her garden.
Forty blooms of iris in purple, white,
gold, lavender, the falls one color,
the standards another, such delicacy
of structure, such perfume, such magnificence
of color and bloom. It eases my mind
that a woman at work on her knees
in earth with patience and rain and sun
can will up such an extraordinary vision,
as if our stay here could be celebrated
with flowers, not by young men,
asleep forever because swords rattle
in the hands of old men.

Goodbye, Mrs. O'Flynn

I am not carrying on with Mrs. O'Flynn
who was my housekeeper till yesterday.
A good cook she was and neat as a pin,
but a loose tongue told her I happened to say
at a parish meeting where I smothered a yawn
when the talk dragged on over some simple task,
"You're not sleeping well, are you, Father John?"
I said, "Mrs. O'Flynn is the one to ask."

I only meant that she always knew
from my morning face how I spent the night,
whether at peace with myself and you
and your parish affairs. Imagine my plight
when our gossipy member tilted my words.
She has packed and gone, who will tend my house
and cook my dinner, like Elijah, the birds?
May your consciences itch like the bite of a louse.

Man with a Shovel

The man with a shovel on his shoulder
wears a faded red-and-white plaid mackinaw
unfastened, a red stocking cap on the back
of his head. His hands are bare but his
overshoes neatly buckled. He strides past
the houses across from my window, slushes
through melting snow in the alley,
gently boots a sled off the sidewalk.
He doesn't smoke or whistle or twist
the shovel handle but marches one-two,
one-two, brisk without hurrying.
He glances at the sun, swings his

empty arm in time with his steps.
He walks with vigor, a man confident
who knows his way. He does not stop
a stranger to ask the time or for a match,
or where the street runs to. It would take
a smart guess to know if he is coming from
or going to work. He isn't in view from
my study window long enough for me to make up
my mind. I doubt if it would make the slightest
difference to him if I knew or not as he
heads in the direction to where he wants to go.

Memorial Day 1982

Henry Jensen sits in the sun
in an open barn door, holds
his head in his hands, thinks
of the crosses on the graves
of young men killed in wars.
The day upsets Henry, he won't
celebrate by watching TV, or
take flowers to the cemetery
or read editorials with black bands
around them. All the killing
for nothing—he won't be mocked
by the word "patriotism," Henry
fought in France. He thinks of life
in young bodies with never a chance
to grow into its promise. Is life
sacred or has it no meaning?
He looks at his fields, always at work
with seeds faithful to rain and sun.
He thinks of the ground in Europe
soaked with blood, not his kind
of fertilizer. Deep in his spirit

a rage rises and he swears
he'd like to plow up the whole
goddamned world and plant white crosses
to grow into strong young men.

Mind-Boggled

His mind bent with the weight
of final moral judgments but he bore
his burden with assurance.
Though he spoke with conviction
contradictions troubled him
and a fiery sermon urging dissent
might be followed by a plea
for humility and obedience.
Not that he believed God carried water
on both shoulders but he craved
defense against censure and ridicule.
He struggled for balance but
celestial intimacies did not always
improve domestic occasions. The walls
of his mind kept tumbling down
before the trumpet call of the Gospels.

Moving Day

I have moved from one house
to another with my roots dangling.
Familiar furniture huddles
in new rooms, waits to be assigned
location. Public hands lay hold
in public places of private
mementos. Carpets try to accommodate

floors, beds, blankets, pictures,
books, a shaken piano testify
to the jostle of change. We stare,
wait for the will to unravel
confusion. I am uncertain in my
new garden plot if I outgrew the old
or felt the need to be transplanted.
But I know, or think I know, how a plant
feels pulled up by its roots.

No Argument

My gosh, she said, you two
stand in a steamy hot kitchen,
kettle boiling, jars sterilizing,
just to can your own tomatoes.
You set out the plants, weed them,
worry about rain and bugs.
Here you are canning the stuff
just to have some jars of your own
garden on the shelves for winter.
I can't figure it out, on a hot day
like this . . . you didn't even take
a vacation. Listen to me, you two,
I can jump in my car any winter day,
slip over to the supermarket
and buy six cans of tomatoes
if I want to. Doesn't that make
all this work seem kind of ridiculous?
"You are absolutely right," we said,
"now let's see . . . we must cool the jars
a bit before we screw the lids down tight."

Not to Give In

"I wouldn't take a horse
out in this kind of weather,"
I told my father, when he asked me
to jump on a horse and get the mail.
Rain falling, autumn chill braced
the air, road muddy, mailbox
a half mile away. I slogged
in rubber boots on determined feet
warmed by burning indignation.
I slipped and slid on the grassy edge
of the road, trees in the grove
waved at me with bare branches,
a flock of wild geese flew over,
I could hear their gabble
but they flew above low clouds.
I tucked the mail inside my bib
(overalls) and began to feel foolish.
After dinner on a rainy day
Father would have time to read the mail,
and who could ride Beauty better
than I? Father depended on me
to bring home the cows, run errands
to the neighbors, and here I tried
to make him ashamed for his request.
I slogged back, bent against
the southeast wind, determined now
to be magnanimous when he apologized.
But no one noticed I'd been away, took it
for granted I brought home the mail.
As I sulked at the dinner table, no one
saw the man in me who had not knuckled under
and made his own decision.

One Is Never Sure

The decision faced me with questions
as a stone tossed in the pond
of my solitude starts ripples of concern
of what do I owe to what I am doing
and how much to what I ought to do?
A shrill ring of the telephone
breaks the silence of my struggle
as she asks me to make up my mind
before it is too late for her
to change her plans. I had no idea
it was up to me to say the last word.
I did not mean to promise anything,
just made a suggestion she interprets
as a promise. Now torn by lack of memory
of what I really said in the heat
of the occasion, I can't seem to settle down
to my work. I tell you it is a risk
to find yourself involved when you
had no intention beyond the moment
of being taken seriously.
So here I sit, phone in hand,
dial tone in my ear—she hung up—
and clouds over the clear sky
of my morning. It seems we had
a lot of cloudy mornings lately,
though the sky clears off at night
when I get stars but need the sun.
Now with my morning shattered
by threatened storm I shall
play on the piano with one finger,
"Jesus wants me for a sunbeam,"
but I don't really know.

One Thing Leads to Another

A flock of geese and a basket
of grapes want common ground
but one thing leads to another.
She drained the juice from the grapes
and set the pan of empty skins
on the back porch. Warm weather
stirred the skins and days later
the back porch breathed a winery odor.
She wrinkled her nose and tossed
the fermented skins into the backyard.
The inquisitive geese without discussion
gobbled up the skins. Soon the entire flock
turned up their toes in drunken stupor.
The woman shouted to her husband,
she called, "Come quick, help me
pick them while their bodies are still warm.
I suppose they were poisoned by the grape skins."
They stripped off the feathers, stuffed them
in pillowcases. But as most drunkards do,
the geese woke from their debauch, staggered
around naked as Adam and Eve in the Garden.
"They look a mite chilly," he said.
"Oh, oh, oh," she cried, "the poor things,
whatever have we done? Do you think they feel
ashamed?" Her husband stared, then shook his head.
"I never heard of geese missionaries," he said.

The Provincial

The Frenchman asked,
"Where should I travel?
I live in Paris."
We are not so steeped

in the pride of home
that we ignore a glance at
"the glory that was Greece."
But we turn away from the green leaves
of life to seek the shrouds of death
in the cemeteries of old cultures.
Faith in my work keeps me
pleased with my own fields
where the earth is fresh and alive,
not soaked with blood of old
battles. What musty tomb
in a cathedral can give me the joy
of black earth rolling off the plow's
moldboard? I am rooted in the ground
I stand on. Let me be provincial,
I thrive where I grow, not in
tumbled palaces or stained statues.
I need my place here as a bird needs
air for flight.

Random Thoughts

Our plan of life together
shattered with the fragility
of a layer of ice skimmed
from the water trough, dropped
on frosty ground. Who could guess
we would be separated so soon?
Now you lie where roots prosper,
I remain to harvest the topsoil
of the year's crops. I do now what
a man does alone after he has shed
his tears, eaten his sorrow.
What I do for you I do mostly
for myself, keep the grass mowed

so that your bed looks clean and neat.
I lean on the mower handle and stare
at the horizon beyond which lies
who knows what country.
I gather my tools and drive home
while random thoughts keep me company.
When your last breath committed you
to silence, I burned with anger
at my helplessness, a humiliation
as shattering as when a plow point
strikes a buried stone.

Ruffle the Pages

An oak tree spread shade,
from a nearby field, a meadowlark
floated its song on a whisper
of wind. My thoughts drifted
like thistledown over the pot
of ashes we came to consecrate.
The mild summer air shimmered
beyond the oak tree's shade.
I ruffled the pages of memory
from the days I helped you
learn to walk to the time we
men worked the farm together.
There I read of the worry, anxiety,
debts we tried to pay. We owed
ourselves the wet, dry, good years
and paid with sweat and care.
The long rows of corn testified for us,
hired men, machines shared our burdens.
The house where Mother made a home
until our wives defeated her.
I read this in the name of security
for a day's food, night's rest, year's record.

Brother to thy sad graveside have I come
in wonder that so much effort
of our lives pays for this time of rest.

Sense of Order

On the farm we had no tunnels
but some days we went wrapped
in our own darkness. So I don't
know about light at the end
but I do know that a time comes
when you are transfixed by a special
moment, by a glimpse of your own
promise that tells you who you are.
It is a time that passes understanding.
It may come to you as you lie
out on the lawn after a hard day's work,
or at the end of summer as you listen
to the long corn rows stand
at attention with their full heavy ears,
or as you pass through the grove
enchanted by the towers of leaves.
You know the spirit within you
bears a kinship to all you have seen
and touched and labored for, and you feel
an enormous order of things assigned you
the part you must play.

A Show of Compassion

The man at her table frowned
when the waitress said, "No apple pie."
True, maybe she seemed too eager,

awkward, young, hands trembling
as she spilled coffee in the saucer
and he said, "Clumsy!" loud enough
for her to hear. But she did not
eat the apple pie.
Perhaps she was new, just hired,
needed the job, tried to learn.
A kind word, a show of compassion
from a customer and she could
tell her mother, "I like my work."

Take the Best Offer

Don't ask me which job to take,
try one and find out.
If it doesn't suit you
perhaps the other one will.
You're lucky to have two offers,
some folks scrounge around
half their lives and never find
work to fit their expectations.
I knew a man who spent two years
in search of a position he wasn't
overrated for. He ended in an
airplane factory making models
of what came off the drawing boards.
He wasn't too qualified to accept
that after a dozen universities
turned him down. Let me warn you
not to be choosy, when you're
up against the buzz saw with a wife,
two kids and a mortgage to support.
Don't be too highly classified
to accept an offer you can live with.
We all went through years when

the grass looked greener on the
other side of the fence.
But disappointment can turn
grass into weed if you count on
only the color.

There Is a Line Drawn

A buyer of discards,
he took off our hands
(at his price) a sick calf,
a cow with a broken leg,
a gaunt sow with no appetite,
sometimes a worn disc
or discarded harrow,
abandoned but useful.
He made the rounds
every few weeks and rid us
of our accumulations we'd no need for.
A working farm shrugs off
useless, ill, worn-out, old
and out-of-date items without a qualm.
This dealer in our castoffs
cleaned us up and put a few
dollars in our pockets.
Once we tried to sell him
a pile of parts and pieces,
iron braces and castings,
residue of broken machines.
He recoiled in righteous
anger, "I ain't no junk dealer."
And we learned of distinctions
we had never known before.

This Is How They Do It

"I own this farm," Henry Jensen
told the surveyors who tramped
across his fields to locate towers
for a transmission line, "and you
are trespassers, so get out."
In the argument that followed
their tripod fell down, one man
got the nose bleed and Henry found
a swelling bump on his forehead.
The next day the law invited him
to sit on the judgment seat. "Is it
my land or ain't it?" he asked a mite
loud in case the Judge was hard of hearing.
The Judge said, "They will pay
for an easement." Henry said, "I ain't
selling and my twelve gauge will back
my decision." The Judge answered,
"Condemnation procedures may be necessary."
Then a revelation came to Henry,
this is how they do it, this is how
they plaster cement for four-lane highways,
shopping centers, urban sprawl, over
the best farm land the Lord ever made.
This is how they do it, with money,
judges and the law. The bastards, may they
eat crow yet when the growing land is gone.

Wealth of News

A mile of main road and
a half a mile of crossroad
separated home from school

but a shorter path lay
across the fields. Barefoot,
in overalls and shirt I trudged
home through fields and
over fences. Gossamer threads
wavered out from wires,
I squinted at the tiny spider
glued to each thread.
A pheasant ran down the corn rows
of a neighbor's field, a rabbit
still as a statue waited for me
to pass through our meadow
beyond an abandoned meadowlark's
nest with its woven roof as a
bull snake wound its way among
long grasses. A gopher shrilled
at me but dropped in its burrow
when I threw a stone. I felt the sky
breathe a blue breath and our
big maple grove in its shadows
seemed to stir as it watched me pass.
I climbed the wall into the orchard
to wander among the loaded trees,
Grimes Golden, Jonathan, Russets,
Roman Stern, Fameuse, Plum Cider—
how could I taste so many?
I sat on our back steps with my
cookie and glass of milk and wondered
how I could tell all my news.

What They Said

Wait, they said, this is not the time.
The market is fluctuating badly
and the crops are not assured.

Wait, they said, love is a luxury
and marriage a responsibility.
What resources do you have
to support your decision?
They said, this is not the time.

When I was young and full of trouble
that is what they said, wait,
the international atmosphere is stormy,
there are signs of a break in relations.
This is not the time, they said.

But the flames of my youth
as my youth burned away
warmed my heart for the truth
that grows in here today.

So . . .
I married the girl, bought the farm, had the kids.
I have been both sad and happy but not sorry.

Where Did They Go?

Where did they go, the maple grove,
the rolling hills, the rows of corn,
the meadowlark's repeated tune?
This is the land where I was born
now in time's quicksand sunk too soon.

I see it now with memory's sight,
the dappled days of sun and rain,
the field's gate through a leafy lane,
where once I scoured the moldboard bright
but will not plow again.

Where We Live

We stole time to walk together
for the mail—no such thing
as spare time on a farm.
We sauntered between cornfields
and pretended they were parks,
the spring sun blazing in a blue bowl.

One half mile to the mailbox
and back in a season, at noon,
of pain and struggle for birth.
The mailbox carries our name
to show where we live, but holds
no news why a calf when born
staggers to its feet and begins
to suck its mother's teat, nor why
a duck sits on her eggs until
they hatch. The mailbox contains
news of the world, words from friends,
debts we have paid. We walk
together in the spring sunshine,
our empty hands speak for unfinished
chores and labor.

The miracle of life! The seed
we planted with care, with hope,
may testify. As we walk
soft explosions of desire burst
in field, in beast, in ourselves.

While Meadowlarks Sang

It began with the first eggs
I gathered, the first basket
of corn I carried, the first
day in the field, lessons
in the book of Work. I learned
them well. I read other books
and looked at the pictures
that instructed me in the habits
of time, how tomorrow loses
its promise when it becomes
yesterday. I saw the sundial
measure hours but not the sweat and
worry that filled them. I trudged
past women with May baskets,
past the leafy woods and flowering
meadows and plowed my furrows
while the meadowlarks sang.

Who Cares for History?

They tore down the old Saylor house,
the one historic mansion left in town
built by the first Saylor almost
two centuries ago. He grew rich from
furs from the Indians, a general store
for settlers, his motto said:
"If we don't have it, you don't need it."
When the last leaf fell, frail Miss Saylor,
fell from the family tree, they tore
down the house. We few remember
the exquisite walnut and cherry panels,
the wide stairway with its graceful curve,

the white marble Italian fireplaces.
A chrome and glass office building
will rise where it stood. Perhaps
the Mayor is right, you can't stop
progress. Probably our reproaches will
fade away and our children have
no emotion about it. No one will remember
the picture over the living room fireplace
of a stern elderly gentleman who watched
out the window at Indians
burning a log cabin.

A Wise Man Is No Fool

Back in the days of kiss-and-tell,
some old geezer had the nerve
to tell his wife, "I could not love
thee, dear, so much, loved I not
Honor More." Doesn't that kill you?
Imagine telling your wife you love her
better because you love this other chick.
Who was this "Honor More" anyway?
I'll say this, his wife was mighty
tolerant and forgiving, or else a fool.
Was More a neighbor, friend, relative,
how did he get by with it anyway?
Think of me some night, I roll over and say,
"Honey Bun, I wouldn't be so groovy about you
if I wasn't gone on that Tootsie Roll
down the street, you know, Sadie Menkovich."
Man, we wouldn't have enough blankets
to warm up the chill from that one.
Honor More must have had it in all the right places
and in all directions to get some Willie

to give out like that. What did he tell
his wife for, why not just leave it lay?
If he felt like a frolic, keep it under his hat.
Now, if thoughtful like, I'd say some night,
"Sweetie Pie, I couldn't be yours for
better or worse without those scrumptious
meals you cook and the cute way you horse
around in bed." Man, I got it made. Let
Honor More lick her own ice cream cone
or fly out the window on a broomstick—
she can't work our side of the street.

Without Your Good Morning

Perhaps I miss you more than I should,
it was my turn to go but here I hang
a bare branch on the family tree.
Life is not always kind.
We grew from the same roots
and faithful to our seeds
thrived on the ground we stood on.
Now with roots shriveled by time
you fall while I teeter
in precarious balance against
winter's blast. I wrestle my way
through another season
deprived of your support.
I cope with the age you should have had—
how still the silence without
your Good Morning to start my day.

Year after Year

By ones, twos and in groups
(with an occasional straggler)
the children flow toward school.
Their faces turned toward morning
show some clear-eyed, some sullen,
some faces seem to slog along as if
their owners were slaves of habit,
some shoulders hunched over the wheel
of a car hurry for the parking lot
as if they could overtake time.

After they are gone I wait. Rain or shine,
frost or storm—no postman he—
an elderly man jogs by the house
with a serious smile and limp wave.
I count on his greeting every morning.
It satisfies me to know someone in this world
finds the discipline of order worth the effort.
Each year the schoolchildren go by
with younger, different faces.

All my friends and relatives
are welcome to wish me a
Happy Passing and I will
respond to their salute with
my hope to "See you all later."

↝ Not a Birthday but a Deathday Party

And Some Seed Fell

You think because you own the ground
And had it plowed and bought the seed
That you are guaranteed a crop
To suit your purpose and your need.

The wasted slope beyond my fence
Was seeded by the wind and birds,
There thistles, dock and mullein weeds
Thrive as intentions thrive in words.

So cultivate your field at will,
You made a choice of what to grow,
And when the seed comes up you can
Walk each day up and down the row

And count what you will bring to bin.
But when the harvest time comes round,
You will learn which your heart affords
The fertile or the stony ground.

Comfort in Small Things

I saw them, a glanceful,
a flock of small brown birds
whirl to the top of an aspen tree,
filter down through the leaves,
dropping from branch to branch,
shaking the leaves slightly
as a rain shower would do,

the rustle of their descent
like a whisper of wind as they
worked down cleaning the leaves
of tiny insects for their breakfast.
I watched them drop through
the bottom branches and swoop
to the top of the next tree.
It seemed such a flutter of
haphazard down dropping to make
the whole tree tremble, to wake
the comfort I take in small things,
that I watched like a man who lets
his eavespout leak to see the water run,
or finds a flurry of chirping intentions
crowding him from a warm bed
on a chilly morning.

End of a Landmark

Power from a copper wire
pumped the water, the farm ignored
the windmill with its useless spinning
wheel. Tear it down, why keep
what's not useful? (A fact of life.)
We took a second look (often changes
the view): climb a seventy-five-foot
tower, lower the wheel and gears,
loosen bolts rusted tight, bring
down section by section the heavy
angle iron legs and guy wires.
Not for us, we thrive on destruction
if it suits us, let's drop the
whole shebang. We tied a hay rope
halfway up the tower, a tractor

on the other end. With a hacksaw
we cut two legs close to the ground
and pulled her over. Slowly the
other two legs bent, then out of
balance, heavy with its length,
it swooped down in an arc and hit
the ground, a bump, burst of dust,
clank of metal, that was all.
We stared cheated, all those plans and
preparation, and no grand finale for
history—we felt estranged from the
services for an old friend.

Fourth of July

Early in the morning
in a breath of fresh odors,
birds trying a few grace notes,
I stepped from the country of sleep
into the promise given by this day.
My country's birthday.
Let the eagle soar again over
crows and sparrows yammering
in public places.

America, America, my conscience blushes
for the pitchmen, shills, hucksters,
medicine men with red-white-and-blue
star-spangled sideshows flying
soiled streamers in your name.

Solid oak beams support my house,
my roadside blooms with native wild roses.

I'm a Christian but . . .

It gets pretty thick when
you're supposed to eat crow every morning
because some nitpicker wants to sell you
a deal about my brother's keeper for
a nice fat donation out of your pocket.
I say, let the bastards starve if they
won't work for a living, nobody helped us,
did they? Just because you pay
your taxes and keep your house
painted and lawn mowed, they think you've
got it made. But who knows what'll happen
to you tomorrow? You're supposed to dig
into the old sack for a few dollars here
and a few there because some guinea
on the other side of the world lost
his G-string in an earthquake.
Look at my grocery bill,
came in the mail today,
do you blame me for
hollering?

It Might Save Us

What they had in common
was common before they had it
like a box marked, "Pieces of string
too small to be saved," or a piece
of mail stamped "Occupant."
They made the most of what
little they had to make a show
of something they could
count on as blossoms on their

apple tree meant fruit however
gnarled and wormy in the fall.
What they lacked was an unspoken
language neither could translate
without the other's dictionary
and what they said did not fill
the empty sack of their needs.
Yet they lived together in a harmony
to shame more rambunctious neighbors
and maintained a lawn free from
creeping charley to make home
seem well tended. If they ever knew
how ordinary the tie that binds
bound them together, they wore
their hair shirts as illumination
and kept in touch day after day
with the instinct for preservation
which, god willing, may save us all.

The Malicious Spirit of Machines

Right in our own house,
stealthy, malevolent, obscured
by the appearance of innocence
a Mafia works for our downfall.
Days go by smoothly without a
threat or warning, then when we
least expect it the blow falls.
It is cold calculation, planned
to betray our dependence on things.
First, the dishwasher throws
suds in my wife's eyes, the
disposal chews up a silver spoon,
my electric razor ignores the switch.

Then the big guns start firing,
the furnace goes on strike, the
washing machine leaks, eats a sock,
the kitchen stove remains cool,
the car shudders twice then
plays dead. Always this happens
on weekends or holidays when there is
no one to hear our cries for help.

Need for a Quick Step

I noticed the cow in heat
as I drove the herd from the barn
out to pasture. The bull smelled her,
roared from his pen, scooped up straw,
and threw it over his back.
Let him snort, I thought, he can wait
till evening.
A wire on the barnyard gate
needed mending. I snubbed it tight
with a claw hammer and was just ready
to wrap it around the post when
my guardian angel spoke to me.
I turned and there he was,
right behind me, jaws frothy,
sweat shining on his shoulders,
a board from the broken door
spindled on one horn.
I took a quick step, slid through
the gate, locked it on the outside.
A surprise like that made me wonder
if our ancestors didn't have quick legs
to beat the dinosaurs to their caves.

No Answer

The sun rose up with a fuzzy eye,
didn't make up its bed of clouds.
Birds' racket shatters the air,
if you like dew, well, it glistens,
means wet feet on the garden path,
I slept well enough last night—
why do I feel so lousy this morning?

The car starts, faucets don't leak,
rained enough to keep the lawn happy,
flowers too, bending and swaying,
had scrambled eggs and mushrooms
for breakfast, my favorite dish.
But my mouth tastes awful—coffee too strong?
Why do I feel so lousy this morning?

Headlines no worse than yesterday's
accidents all over, everybody on strike,
nobody worth a damn won a baseball game.
That girl I met, full of joie de vivre,
called for an appointment, my blood
ought to jump instead of slog along,
quite a chick, I ought to be crowing instead—
Why do I feel so lousy this morning?

Not a Birthday but a Deathday Party

The indigent days beg me
to pay my obligations—
my debts to existence—
while I can still assure
myself of temperature by
the cricket's chirp, noon

by a tree's shadow, and wind
direction with a moist finger.
Payment by birthdays gives me
credit though no machine yet
known can compute their number.
I know it is the business of
the future to be dangerous
and the cakes whose candles
I blew out with a wish
prove my adventures. And since
celebrations inspire me
by their occasion I will
commemorate my last payment
to time with a deathday party.
All my friends and relatives
are welcome to wish me a
Happy Passing and I will
respond to their salute with
my hope to "See you all later."

Not for Sale

You thought a dollar sign imaged
her heart and decided to buy
the property. But sometimes a meadow
in bloom is not for sale and the garden
will not change hands—what title is there
to love or good earth?

She gave herself in trust
and you thought it was fee simple,
the promised land you hoped to settle.
She tried to tell you that love
can only be deserved but you
wanted to make a down payment
on a place you could never own.

Of Course It Matters

My neighbor stopped by this morning
to satisfy a need for company
and share a cup of coffee, his face
concerned as if he had eaten too
much crow. The plunge in cattle prices
had broken his back but the bank
flung him a loan to keep his debts
from drowning him. Thin weather,
he said, at our house, my two boys
in college will have to earn their
way and learn a lesson in finance.
He managed a smile as he leaned back
and said, the trees won't die nor
grass turn brown, we have no cancer
or jiggly minds, it's only money,
what does that matter?
I thought, but it does matter,
it tears the fabric of the neighborhood
when trouble comes, we know the fear
that feasts inside us like a crow
on dead rabbit. Misfortune looks
everywhere and cuts its pie in
many pieces to be passed around
most often when we have least appetite.

On Vacation

Your five days of driving
on your trek to the southland
wilts the flower of togetherness.
But now that you are there
I can imagine you wrapped
in suntan oil lolling on the beach.

If you raise your head you can see
the Cadillacs and Lincolns pass
in their search for fun. What fun
to peer at a menu with the same
steaks and chops you left at home
with enough fish to prove you are
near the ocean. After a nap you rise
to meet the folk next door, smile sweetly,
"How do you do, your first time here?"
Nah, they've been coming for years
as bored as dead fish eyes with
the conversation of a couple of ducks
quacking about the wonderful palms,
the moonlit nights, "Only, you know
we go to bed early." The sandy beaches,
days spent picking up shells, "You should
see our shell collection." And some morning
after coffee a faraway look in your eyes,
you'll say, "Let's go home," or if you
don't say it, you will think it
while you watch the Cadillacs
and Lincolns creep through traffic
toward Disneyland.

A Small Victory

Cold, the snow squeaked underfoot,
she filled the bird feeder, poor things,
cracked corn, peanuts, thistle and
hemp seeds brought a flutter of wings
all the short day. She stopped work
to enjoy her shy pensioners. When
a bold invader, a squirrel, leaped to
the ledge and hunched in a ball of fur
gobbled the feed, her eyes wept anger.

One more indignity to weigh down
her grievances, how she cleaned, cooked,
sewed, carried out the ashes, brought in
groceries, washed windows, made beds,
ran for the mail—no one put out
sunflower seeds for her or warmed her
spirit when chilled to the bone.
She thought, I'd like to burn down
the house just to see it disappear,
and then flamed with guilty blush.
She jerked open the door and threw a
cracked plate, wild toss with a true
aim knocked the squirrel ass-over-
appetite into the backyard. She set up
the ironing board and while she waited
for the iron to heat, in a cracked voice
sang a tune of victory she improvised.

The Supermarket's Secret Machine

Today my wife sent me to the
supermarket because she was busy
potting geraniums. That's how I
discovered the hidden scrambler
supermarkets have that makes a
shambles of your shopping list.
I have wondered (without comment)
at some of the packages that
appear on our kitchen table from
time to time. But now I understand.
It happened to me. Sometime,
somewhere after you enter the
store a secret exchange is made
between the shopping list you
thought you had and the one you

end with. The substitution takes
place with no discomfort to you
except a sudden lack of confidence
in your faculties. Like one of those
machines that scrambles codes,
you find that what you bought
does not jibe with what you were
sent for. My wife said it was written
plain, "toilet paper and detergent."
I came home with a box of fresh
mushrooms, a steak, and an avocado pear.

Threat of Violence

Icicles dripped in the
January thaw and prompted me
to buy a boar to seed down
my sows for a spring pig crop.
Bloodlines in the young boars
Henry Jensen raised suited me
and I went to see him. He
picked up a three-inch post as we
entered the barnyard. "I just
want to look at one," I said,
"not knock it on the head."
He grinned, "The bull is a mean
bastard, ripe for mischief."
Our old Shorthorn bull never
made much trouble, I'd heard
dairy bulls are different. This
Holstein saw us coming, man,
he looked big and ugly. Head up,
tail arched, he pawed the ground
and bellered. Then he came right
at us. I shrank in my clothes

but Henry marched to meet him.
He slammed that post across
the bull's nose, made the bull
stagger, back off, shake his horns.
I bought a boar but we did not
turn our backs. Now whenever a
threat of violence shakes our courage
I remember Henry and his bull.

To Shape Our Decisions

The question is
whether to choose
or do what comes first to hand.
(What difference did it make,
in the long run, which came first,
the chicken or the egg?)
But I am egged on (pardon)
by an uneasy conscience
to shovel out the ashes
from yesterday's fires.
If I chicken out (there I go again!)
piles of junk won't be moved
before winter sets its heel
on our days. Spring and summer
seemed endless, yet time creeps up,
strength runs down like an old clock,
blood slows its pulse.
Then let chores be light
and decisions easy.
It is not in ourselves, dear friends,
but in the pressures we feel
that point the road we take.

Title and First Line Index

First lines are in italics. Articles have
been retained for alphabetizing first
lines, but dropped in poem titles.